# Palgrave Studies in Political History

Series Editors
Henk te Velde
Leiden University
Leiden, The Netherlands

Maartje Janse
Leiden University
Leiden, The Netherlands

Hagen Schulz-Forberg
Aarhus University
Aarhus, Denmark

The contested nature of legitimacy lies at the heart of modern politics. A continuous tension can be found between the public, demanding to be properly represented, and their representatives, who have their own responsibilities along with their own rules and culture. Political history needs to address this contestation by looking at politics as a broad and yet entangled field rather than as something confined to institutions and politicians only. As political history thus widens into a more integrated study of politics in general, historians are investigating democracy, ideology, civil society, the welfare state, the diverse expressions of opposition, and many other key elements of modern political legitimacy from fresh perspectives. Parliamentary history has begun to study the way rhetoric, culture and media shape representation, while a new social history of politics is uncovering the strategies of popular meetings and political organizations to influence the political system.

Palgrave Studies in Political History analyzes the changing forms and functions of political institutions, movements and actors, as well as the normative orders within which they navigate. Its ambition is to publish monographs, edited volumes and Pivots exploring both political institutions and political life at large, and the interaction between the two. The premise of the series is that the two mutually define each other on local, national, transnational, and even global levels.

More information about this series at
http://www.palgrave.com/gp/series/15603

James Forde

# The Early Haitian State and the Question of Political Legitimacy

## American and British Representations of Haiti, 1804-1824

James Forde
Department of History
Griffith University
Brisbane, QLD, Australia

Palgrave Studies in Political History
ISBN 978-3-030-52607-8        ISBN 978-3-030-52608-5    (eBook)
https://doi.org/10.1007/978-3-030-52608-5

© The Editor(s) (if applicable) and The Author(s), under exclusive licence to Springer Nature Switzerland AG 2020
This work is subject to copyright. All rights are solely and exclusively licensed by the Publisher, whether the whole or part of the material is concerned, specifically the rights of translation, reprinting, reuse of illustrations, recitation, broadcasting, reproduction on microfilms or in any other physical way, and transmission or information storage and retrieval, electronic adaptation, computer software, or by similar or dissimilar methodology now known or hereafter developed.
The use of general descriptive names, registered names, trademarks, service marks, etc. in this publication does not imply, even in the absence of a specific statement, that such names are exempt from the relevant protective laws and regulations and therefore free for general use.
The publisher, the authors and the editors are safe to assume that the advice and information in this book are believed to be true and accurate at the date of publication. Neither the publisher nor the authors or the editors give a warranty, expressed or implied, with respect to the material contained herein or for any errors or omissions that may have been made. The publisher remains neutral with regard to jurisdictional claims in published maps and institutional affiliations.

Cover illustration: theendup/Alamy Stock Photo

This Palgrave Macmillan imprint is published by the registered company Springer Nature Switzerland AG.
The registered company address is: Gewerbestrasse 11, 6330 Cham, Switzerland

*To Fran and Fionn, whose love and patience I aim to repay so many times over.*

# ACKNOWLEDGEMENTS

The majority of research for this monograph was conducted while reading for my doctorate at Griffith University. Dr Mike Davis was a wonderful supervisor, who supported and challenged me in appropriately equal measure and has graciously continued to advise and guide when requested. A great deal of gratitude must also be extended to Dr Peter Denney and Dr Philip Kaisary, whose insights were crucial to the direction that this study took, and who inspired me to explore ideas I would never have considered without their guidance. I also thank Dr Jim Watt at the University of York, who directed me towards this area of study. Griffith University provided me with funds to undertake this project and to conduct research trips in the UK and the United States, for which I am grateful.

Supportive friends—too many to mention by name—in Australia, the UK and the United States enabled me to see this project through to the end. Without their generous hospitality, a great deal of this research simply would not have happened. Their enthusiasm to hear about the progress of the project not only inspired me but also provided me with the challenge of regularly trying to articulate the meaning and value of the work to those outside of the field—a humbling but invaluable exercise.

My parents, Tony and Edie, have never wavered in their support for the paths I have chosen, and for this I will be forever grateful. My wife Frances has been a constant source of inspiration, honesty and

viii ACKNOWLEDGEMENTS

encouragement—providing doses of each at exactly the right times and in accurate quantities. Finally, to Fionn, who knew the least of all about this book, but who has contributed so much—thank you for the smile that has never left my face since the day you were born.

# CONTENTS

| | | |
|---|---|---|
| 1 | Introduction | 1 |
| 2 | "The Bonaparte of the New World": American and British Reactions to the Emergence of Emperor Dessalines | 25 |
| 3 | President Christophe and Commercial Legitimacy | 71 |
| 4 | King Christophe and the Question of Monarchical Legitimacy | 93 |
| 5 | The Death of a New World Monarch in Transatlantic Republican Thought | 129 |
| 6 | The Promise and the Threat of Boyer and Haitian Republicanism | 155 |
| 7 | Conclusion | 189 |
| | Bibliography | 197 |
| | Index | 213 |

CHAPTER 1

# Introduction

In the early nineteenth century, reports of the culmination of the Haitian Revolution shook the Atlantic world to its core. Between 1791 and 1804, the colonial powers of France, Spain and England all tried and failed to subjugate the revolutionary black ex-slaves and freemen.[1] The loss of France's most prized colony in the Caribbean—the so-called "pearl of the Antilles"—and the victory of the revolutionary slaves over the imperial might of Europe amounted to an "unthinkable" event for the powers of the West.[2] On 1 January 1804, the first leader of independent Haiti, Jean-Jacques Dessalines, addressed the citizens of Saint-Domingue and confirmed the new nation's separation from colonial France. In the process, Dessalines proclaimed the abolition of slavery forever from the island and renamed the country, "Haiti".[3]

In the four decades that followed Haiti's Declaration of Independence, a number of leaders—all of whom had fought in the Revolution—would adopt a variety of forms of government in their attempts to cement a foothold for the fledgling Haitian state in the political world of the Atlantic. Following Dessalines's death in 1806, Haiti was divided by internal conflict. As a result, Henry Christophe assumed control of the north, and Alexandre Pétion did likewise in the south. Jean-Pierre Boyer succeeded Pétion after his death in 1818 and, following the death of Christophe in 1820, Boyer once more unified the north and south of the country, where he remained as leader until 1843. Despite their vastly different approaches to political leadership and their distinct visions for the future of the nation,

© The Author(s) 2020

J. Forde, *The Early Haitian State and the Question of Political Legitimacy*, Palgrave Studies in Political History, https://doi.org/10.1007/978-3-030-52608-5_1

all of Haiti's early leaders faced the same dilemma: how could the Western hemisphere's first independent black state thrive—or even survive—on the Atlantic stage? In particular, the fact that Britain, France and the rest of Europe's global powers refused to recognise officially Haiti's sovereignty as an independent nation until the mid-1820s—and American recognition would not come until 1862—was a damaging blow to the prosperity of the Haitian state and one from which it never fully recovered. For Haiti's early leaders, the successful revolution against Europe's colonial powers was only the beginning of a long battle for independence and recognition. As Michel-Rolph Trouillot has observed, Haiti was the "first testing ground of neo-colonialism" and it therefore experienced the "somber implications of that policy for the third world very early".[4]

Haiti's first leaders faced an abundance of challenges in their attempts to secure Haiti's economic future, to solidify its independence, and to elicit official recognition from the powers of the West.[5] Limits were imposed upon Haiti by countries such as America and Britain in its crucial, formative years, and these undoubtedly were critical to Haitian attempts to enhance its opportunities for progress. But this is not to suggest that Haiti's early leaders were denied significant political agency. Rather, throughout their time in office, these heads of state were constantly faced with a number of choices to make—choices that were "crucial for subsequent history".[6] These choices, along with the hopes and concerns of Haiti's first politicians, were laid bare in the various proclamations and constitutions produced in these early years—documents that were disseminated and reported upon widely throughout various forms of print media in America and Britain.[7] These early Haitian leaders adopted a variety of strategies—some proactive, some reactive—in their attempts to assert Haiti's independence to the wider political world and to publicly call on Western leaders to recognise its sovereignty. Such calls would, unfortunately, go unheeded for the first two decades of its existence.

This book is an exploration of how observers in America and Britain reflected upon the early years of Haitian independence, and how they represented Haiti's early leaders in a variety of politically-charged narratives. In particular, the modes of government and the multiple titles adopted by Haiti's early leaders were used as central points of reference in American and British discourses that centred on the concept of political legitimacy. These debates were often an inward reflection of the legitimacy and superiority—or otherwise—of America's and Britain's own forms of government. These transatlantic depictions demand to be read alongside each other as American reflections on legitimacy often looked towards Britain, and vice versa. America in this time was attempting to re-position itself from that of an ex-colonial entity to a sovereign power in its own right, but Americans debated the extent to which they wanted to distance themselves from the former mother country. Britain, on the other hand, was looking to reassert its authority in light of the rise of Napoleon and the emerging powers of the New World, led by America. Conservatives, liberals and radicals in both nations looked to each other at varying times with regret, disdain and envy. But these observers also increasingly fixed their gaze on Haiti's attempts to establish strong and sustainable modes of political leadership. By analysing the different ways that the early Haitian state was perceived in America and Britain—and by figures with widely different agendas—one can better understand the dreams and anxieties of American and British political commentators in this period, and where and why these overlapped or diverged.

As this book will demonstrate, the early Haitian state and its leaders had a profound impact on political narratives in print culture on both sides of the Atlantic. The impact of these representations on governmental policy or on collective political or social thought is, of course, almost impossible to measure with any degree of certainty. But the value in these representations lies in analysing why these depictions were constructed, who used these, and how they were formed. Whether or not they were successful, these portrayals were at times designed to support or call into question American and British policies and attitudes towards the early Haitian state. A number of representations were undoubtedly designed to support policies of non-recognition and were eager to see the black state fail—thereby supporting Trouillot's suggestion that Haitian independence was just as much of an unthinkable event as the revolution that preceded it for the Western world in the nineteenth century.[8] At times, however, American and British writers looked to impact the recognition question by overtly suggesting that the hand of political friendship should be offered to Haiti's early leaders. But these depictions were also often designed to impact debates on the legitimacy and effectiveness of Atlantic world forms of governance—including America's and Britain's. In both critiques and celebrations of Haiti's independence, the early Haitian state subsequently became a central entity in transatlantic debates on how political leadership should operate in the Atlantic world in the early nineteenth century.

The enormous impact of the Haitian Revolution on American and British debates of slavery and its abolition has been well established. This impact continued in the immediate aftermath of the Revolution as newspapers, pamphlets and literary texts continued to portray the shocking violence perpetrated by French colonial forces and Haitian revolutionaries, as well as the destructive nature of the Revolution for the colonists and the colony as a whole.[9] The political messages underpinning these narratives were largely "bifurcated" as pro- and anti-slavery supporters on both sides of the Atlantic looked back on the events in Saint-Domingue as vital instruments for their respective campaigns.[10] Anti-slavery supporters such as James Stephen and Thomas Clarkson saw the success of the black revolutionaries as proof that slaves in the colonies not only desired emancipation but also had the necessary capabilities to achieve it on their own terms.[11] At such a crucial time in anti-slavery debates in Britain and America, abolitionists asserted the idea that if their respective governments did not act swiftly, a second Saint Domingue would inevitably occur in the British colonies or in the southern slave states of America.[12] Pro-slavery supporters mirrored this strategy of the abolitionists by playing on a similar fear and asserting that this revolutionary spirit could spread beyond the newly formed Haitian state—something Ashli White has termed the "contagion of rebellion".[13] Pro-slavery memories of the Revolution also focused on the apparent meddling of French abolitionists who were claimed to have stirred up ideas of revolution among the hitherto contented black populations of Saint-Domingue as a way to indict the increasingly vocal and influential abolitionist movements. In this way, the Haitian Revolution had a pivotal role to play for both supporters and opponents of slavery in the nineteenth century.

Scholarly studies on the impact of the Revolution and Haitian independence often argue that Atlantic receptions to the Revolution were largely race-based reactions to a revolution of slaves and the presence of the Western hemisphere's first independent black state. David Nicholls, for example, has argued that Haiti became a "symbol of anti-colonialism and racial equality" and as a result European powers were "apprehensive about the existence of a free black state" in the early nineteenth century.[14] Furthermore, Trouillot's argument regarding the unthinkability of the Revolution is based on the contention that European and American observers at the time believed that "enslaved Africans and their descendants could not envision their freedom".[15] A central part of Trouillot's argument is that European and American observers of the Revolution and Haitian independence viewed these events through a prism of "ready-made categories"—categories that were largely formed by eighteenth- and nineteenth-century ideas of race. More recently, Marlene Daut's work has expanded upon Trouillot's argument by exploring in much more detail these categories and by underpinning the significance of perceptions of race in Atlantic reactions to Haitian independence. Daut's exhaustive study of literary representations of the Revolution and Haiti in Western discourses until the mid-nineteenth century demonstrates that the events surrounding Haitian independence were "incessantly narrated in a particularly 'racialized' way".[16]

While the role of race was undoubtedly pivotal in American and British reactions to the emerging Haitian state and its leaders in the early nineteenth century, they were also shaped and formed by a number of other social and political concerns. If, as Daut argues, "'racial' thinking" was central to how Western observers understood Haiti, then what other modes of thought influenced nineteenth-century reactions to the Haitian state?[17] In particular, if nineteenth-century perceptions of race were so central to depictions of Haiti's revolutionary figures, which other ideas also influenced American and British thought towards Haiti's early leaders?

The representations of Haiti explored in this study sometimes reflect an anxiety towards the presence of an independent black state. However, American and British depictions of Haiti were at times reflective of other, alternative domestic political anxieties—tensions that often had little to do with Haiti itself. Pre-existing perceptions of political legitimacy and leadership in America and Britain were at times strengthened, and at other times called into question, by the actions of Haiti's early leaders. This in turn demonstrates that the impact of Haiti's independence was not only felt in transatlantic debates of slavery, colonialism and race. This is, of course, not to contest the arguments put forward by Daut and Trouillot regarding the central role of race in Western reactions to the Revolution and Haitian independence. Rather, this book contributes to this body of work by outlining the wide variety of ways in which Haiti's independence provoked responses in both America and Britain in the early nineteenth century. As such, it seeks to further underline the idea that Haitian independence had a profound impact on the shaping of discourses far beyond its immediate geographical location, and that the breadth of these discourses is still to be fully understood.

A number of crucial studies have begun to demonstrate the broader significance of Haiti's fight for independence, and these works have highlighted the impact of the Revolution for America and Britain in a wide variety of social, political and economic ways.[18] More specifically, scholars have shown the enduring legacy of the Revolution and Haitian independence for African-Americans throughout the nineteenth century.[19] Other work has underlined the impact that representations of Haiti had on American and British diplomatic relationships with the fledgling Haitian state.[20] Such studies are reflective of the multiple prisms through which some observers were willing to view Haiti in the early years of its independence—prisms that were ultimately self-serving in their motivations. This work has started to expose the extent to which the emergence of an independent Haiti impacted upon European and American political discourses—discourses that were not always confined to discussions of race, slavery or colonialism. As such, we have started to understand more fully the significance of not only the Haitian Revolution but also Haitian independence as a seismic moment in Atlantic history—a significance that was recognised and reflected upon by a wide array of political commentators at the time.

Studies on the central role of Haiti in Atlantic world politics in the nineteenth century have increasingly looked towards 1804 as a starting point rather than an end point in their attempts to underline the impact of Haiti's independence. Despite these crucial studies, we are only beginning to fully understand the extent to which Haitian independence impacted political discourses and ideas in the nineteenth century. Laurent Dubois has called for the need to "question, deconstruct, and rewrite narratives of Haiti's history in ways that simultaneously illuminate the past and the future", particularly by focusing on the development of the Haitian state throughout the nineteenth century.[21] Dubois has further argued that greater scholarly attention towards Haiti in the nineteenth century would be a "vital step in the broader struggle to debunk teleological certainties and recast the suffocating stories about Haiti's past that too often imprison the present".[22] In this way, this study aims to contribute to a greater understanding of the impact of Haiti for the wider Atlantic world in the nineteenth century.

Central to this book is the suggestion that the broader contexts of American and British politics are often overlooked in analyses of depictions of the early Haitian state—and in particular of Haiti's early leaders. This study therefore focuses on receptions to the governments of three of Haiti's first heads of state: Jean-Jacques Dessalines, Henry Christophe and Jean-Pierre Boyer. From 1804 to 1843, these three leaders—all stalwarts of Haiti's revolution against France—introduced different modes of government in their attempts to secure economic prosperity for the new state and diplomatic recognition on the world stage. As such, American and British observers witnessed Haitian heads of state variously adopt the titles of president, emperor and king at different junctures as each leader projected his own vision of Haiti's future. This book examines reactions to these early leaders in the first twenty years of Haiti's independence: from Dessalines's establishment of the first Haitian government in 1804 and his creation of the Empire of Haiti in 1805; to the 1807 succession of Christophe and his establishment of the first Haitian monarchy in 1811; through to the death of the Haitian king and the emergence of President Boyer and the Haitian Republic in the early 1820s.

While recent studies have begun to consider the complexities of Haiti's early leaders more carefully, Toussaint Louverture—the famed and fated leader of the Revolution—continues to dominate scholarly discussions. This is undoubtedly because Toussaint featured much more prominently in contemporary depictions on both sides of the Atlantic. An unintentional consequence of this focus on Toussaint, however, is that the attention that Haiti's early leaders also received from Atlantic observers has yet to be fully appreciated. This book therefore deliberately focuses on three of Haiti's early leaders in order to argue that these leaders prompted much more nuanced and, at times, provocative transatlantic reactions than is often realised.

A significant omission to this study of early leaders is the figure of Alexandre Pétion. Pétion served as the president of the southern republic of Haiti from 1807 to 1818 at a time when Haiti was divided by internal conflict, with Christophe serving as leader of the northern part of the island. The absence of Pétion in this book is not intended to suggest that he is not a figure worthy of study. On the contrary, while he is perhaps the most neglected of Haiti's early leaders in academic studies—particularly those led by American and British scholars—Pétion's impact and legacy on the development of independent Haiti was significant. In contemporary American and British discussions of Haiti and its early leaders in the early nineteenth century, however, Pétion was largely a peripheral figure. Exactly why this was the case is difficult to deduce with certainty. Perhaps Pétion did not manage to promote his government and plans for the Haitian state to an international audience as well as his revolutionary counterparts. Perhaps the economic prosperity and potential of northern Haiti was more alluring to American and British commentators. Or, perhaps more simply, the figures of Dessalines, Christophe and Boyer excited American and British imaginations in ways that Pétion did not. Dessalines's tenure consisted of passionate anti-colonial declarations, violent acts of retribution, and culminated in a grisly end. Christophe founded the first and only Haitian monarchy—the first of its kind in the New World. And Boyer would unite northern and southern Haiti after a public revolt against the Haitian king, who, like his predecessor, also met a gruesome fate. After an initial conflict with Christophe, Pétion—in the eyes of external observers at least—seemed to go about the business of establishing southern Haiti as a viable Atlantic world nation with a quietness that possibly excluded him from the narratives explored in this study. Whatever the reasons, Dessalines, Christophe and Boyer certainly captured the attentions, and to some, the hearts, of a wide range of American and British writers, editors, illustrators and playwrights. As such, this book focuses on these three leaders to try to ascertain what excited these imaginations, and how the actions of these leaders spoke in favour of or against the political agendas of American and British commentators.

Boyer would rule as president until 1843, but this study focuses on the period from 1804 to 1824—the years in which the powers of Europe and America were united in their refusal to recognise officially the sovereignty of the Haitian state. This united front diminished when France recognised Haiti's independence in 1825, but only after the Haitian state agreed to pay the French government compensation for their perceived losses since relinquishing their prized colony. From 1825, American and British narratives about Haiti were largely impacted by France's recognition, as well as its significant demands towards the Haitian state. In particular, the issue of recognition after 1825 would be framed in American and British print media within the context of France's "deal" with its ex-colony, and how this would impact America and Britain. But this book focuses on the period leading up to this point in order to outline the different voices that at times aligned with, and at other times spoke against, America's and Britain's non-recognition of Haiti's early governments—voices that were not influenced by French recognition and the question of whether this would threaten America's or Britain's own interests.

The turbulent nature of the political world of the Atlantic in this period of time had a significant impact on the way in which Haiti and its leaders were perceived in America and Britain. In particular, Haiti's first governments emerged at a time when challenges to traditional forms of political rule swept through Europe and the Americas from the early 1800s until the mid-1820s. And the threat or promise that these challenges posed to American and British interests coincided with Haiti's attempts to establish the legitimacy of its own government in the eyes of the polities of the Atlantic world. The different modes of governance adopted by Haiti's early leaders were at times derided and at other times celebrated by a variety of political commentators, and these perceptions were often reflective of a broader reaction to changes in governance and political leadership throughout the Atlantic world in the early nineteenth century. American and British depictions often situated the adoption of these different modes of leadership within narratives that sought to attack or celebrate the virtues of such a mode of governance—narratives that in turn looked to strengthen their own notion of political identity.

One of the fundamental issues of political debate in America and Britain during the early nineteenth century centred on political legitimacy and, in particular, the perceived virtues of different forms of government and political ideologies. As Immanuel Wallerstein has demonstrated, when discussing the very concept of legitimacy, at the heart of this discourse lies the issue of sovereignty.[23] Mlada Bukovansky has traced the "transformation of the terms of political legitimacy" to the American and French revolutions, arguing that perceptions of legitimacy "lay at the heart" of these revolutions.[24] In the aftermath of the revolutions in America and France— and in the face of revolutionary action throughout Europe and Latin America in the 1810s and 1820s—American and British political observers in the early 1800s constantly evaluated and re-evaluated the foundations of political sovereignty and the terms of legitimate governance. In particular, Wallerstein has argued that the French Revolution "reoriented the concept of sovereignty, from the monarch or the legislature to the people" and that, as a result, "the politics of inclusion and exclusion became a center-piece of national politics".[25] At a time when American and British commentators were still coming to terms with the consequences of this reorientation, the Haitian state was at times included—and at other times excluded—from assertions of the legitimacy and sovereignty of post-revolutionary states more generally.

Perhaps most pertinently for discussions of the Haitian state in the early nineteenth century, as Wallerstein elaborates, "in the modern-world system, the legitimacy of sovereignty requires reciprocal recognition".[26] A number of studies have underlined the motivations behind—and damaging consequences of—the lack of official recognition of the sovereignty of the early Haitian state from around the world.[27] Britain would not recognise officially Haiti's sovereignty until after Boyer agreed in 1825 to pay the crippling reparations to France. Britain's refusal to recognise the

Haitian state stemmed largely from a fear that to do so would effectively legitimise the notion of slave revolution—a potentially dangerous statement for Britain's Caribbean colonies, which would not abolish slavery until 1838. Haitian hopes for British recognition were also severely dented by a secret agreement between Britain and France at the 1815 Congress of Vienna. As part of these peacetime negotiations, Britain agreed to stand aside from French dealings with its former colony—including if France decided to attempt to reclaim the island—in return for official French acceptance of Britain's right to trade with the Haitian state.[28]

America would not recognise officially the Haitian state until 1862. Despite the lucrative opportunities for advancing American trade with Haiti through official channels, for successive American governments "the history of how [Haiti] had come to power offered a potentially inflammatory example" to the free and enslaved black populations of the United States.[29] This anxiety also extended to a fear among some Americans of the presence of black diplomats in American corridors of power. Such ideas continued to influence attitudes towards Haiti until the mid-nineteenth century, particularly among the politicians of America's southern states. With the secession of the southern states in 1861, Abraham Lincoln was persuaded to finally recognise the sovereignty of the Haitian state, almost sixty years after it had declared its independence.[30]

As some have argued, "[p]olitical legitimacy…requires external recognition", and the representations of the Haitian state discussed in this book demonstrate a willingness among some American and British thinkers to assert Haiti's political legitimacy, despite the absence of official recognition from their own governments.[31] The very issue of the sovereignty of Haiti's early governments became central to a number of narratives that reflected upon the legitimacy of America's and Britain's own political leaders. If, as Bukovansky argues, political legitimacy is "conceptualized and contested through the medium of political culture", then this book examines the different political cultures that formed depictions of the Haitian state—formations that, in moments of convenience, sought to deny or assert the sovereignty of the Haitian state.[32]

Affirmations of the superiority or inferiority of American and British modes of governance were also often used in both nationalist and antinationalist narratives on both sides of the Atlantic in the early nineteenth century. Both loyalists and radical thinkers used nationalist rhetoric as a key component in their discussions of political legitimacy. And, as the work of Linda Colley and Sam Haynes has shown, such assertions of patriotism and considerations of national identity were often reactionary constructions to the governments and political leaders of foreign others. For Colley, a key factor in the emergence of British national identity in the eighteenth century was a desire among Britons to be viewed as separate and superior to the French—a belief that continued into the nineteenth century.[33] Similarly, Sam Haynes has noted how America's own national identity became more prominent and defined in the early nineteenth century, largely as part of a desire to be separated culturally and ideologically from America's ex-colonial power.[34] A number of scholars have further emphasised that the end of the War of 1812 was a defining moment in early American history as it marked a final and more definitive break away from the political and cultural influence of Britain.[35] Benedict Anderson's observations that nations are, in essence, "imagined communities" have been well noted and are further supported by Wallerstein's argument that nations are "myths in the sense that they are all social creations".[36]

With this in mind, the way in which Haiti was depicted in the early nineteenth century in America and Britain gives an insight not only into how some observers imagined the early Haitian state, but also how they imagined their own nation and system of governance. As Laura Benton has highlighted, "sovereignty is more myth than reality, more a story that polities tell about their own power than a definite quality they possess".[37] Importantly, the ways in which Haiti was represented say as much about how a number of actors perceived their own country and government as they do about how they perceived Haiti itself. These reactions to Haitian independence provide a greater understanding of how both American and British observers constructed depictions of political others in their affirmations and questioning of their own national identity in the early nineteenth century.

In order to highlight effectively the motivations behind these depictions of the early Haitian state, the American and British historical contexts in which these representations and commentaries emerged are key. At the same time that the newly independent Haitian state was seeking to establish its sovereignty in the eyes of Western politicians, the early American republic was looking to further assert the legitimacy of its own government both to the powers of the Atlantic and to its own citizens. In particular, since America's own revolution the notion of popular sovereignty or the "consent of the governed" remained an essential component of American discourses concerned with political legitimacy—something that persisted well into the nineteenth century. Since the American

Revolution, Americans had "claimed a right to judge the actions of government, and to violently overthrow it if it pervasively acted without the consent of the governed in ways that threatened life, liberty and the pursuit of happiness".[38] Edmund Morgan has further argued that the perceived sovereignty of the American people was largely a "fiction" that persisted into the nineteenth century—a political construct that enables "the few to govern the many".[39] Sandra Moats' work has advanced Morgan's argument by examining how America's early leaders looked to promote the notion of popular sovereignty to the people through symbols and rituals—especially in contradistinction to the "monarchical pomp and ceremony" that largely defined European governments in the early nineteenth century.[40] Thomas Jefferson's political rhetoric played a vital role in asserting the significance of the consent of the people in truly legitimate forms of government—an assertion that continued as presidents such as James Monroe similarly and publicly tried to further distance the American republic from the pretensions and symbols of monarchical rule.[41] In this way, the notion that popular sovereignty constituted a more legitimate form of sovereignty than dynastic monarchy was a key component of American political thought in the early nineteenth century.

In the early 1800s debates abounded as to the precise policies and ideologies that should be promoted in order to secure economic and social prosperity for the early American republic.[42] Jefferson's second electoral victory in 1804 served to solidify the ideology of the Democratic-Republicans as the president looked to once and for all cement a republican identity in America—one that turned its back on the traditional political structures and hierarchies of Britain and the Old World dynasties.[43] The idea that the people were central to the American political system was promoted by Democratic-Republicans, and Jefferson in particular saw it as central to the political identity of the early American republic. This was contested, particularly by Federalist Americans who associated democracy with the dangers of Jacobinism and who warned that affording too much agency to the people would see America descend into the political chaos and violence of revolutionary France.[44] Federalists and Anglophiles wailed at the perceived destruction of traditional political hierarchies and lamented the increasing power of the people in democratic policies.[45] However, despite this opposition, the power and influence of the Federalist party eroded significantly in the 1810s. The Jeffersonian ideology that emphasised the role of the people in governmental affairs largely dominated American politics in the early 1800s—something that was seen to be a vital distinction between the legitimacy of the American republic and the nation states of Old World Europe, and which was perceived to confirm America's status as the "strongest government on earth".[46]

After Jefferson's final term came to an end in 1809, the subsequent presidencies of James Madison and James Monroe both sought to find ways to secure America's economic future and to further strengthen the ideologies of the Democratic-Republican party.[47] By doing so, these successive administrations sought to solidify the legitimacy of America's republicanism to its own citizens. Despite the electoral successes of the party, the lack of partisan resistance in American politics in the late 1810s meant that by 1820 some Americans had started to question the increasing power of their federal government and projected fears and anxieties of the formation of an unopposed tyrannical government on American soil—one that seemingly only answered to itself.[48] Domestic crises in this time, including the economic distresses of the late 1810s, only served to fuel American thought that the government had started to fail the people it should serve.[49] In this climate, Americans once again debated the legitimacy of its republican government and the policies it should adopt both in order to succeed and to effectively serve its citizens.

One of the key concerns for America's political leaders in the early nineteenth century was the best method for the republic to further legitimise its place in an Atlantic world still largely dominated by the regimes and politics of Old World Europe.[50] In the early 1800s, both Democrats and Federalists largely agreed on the necessity of America carving its own unique place in Atlantic world politics and they in general "welcomed the collapse of the Old World colonial order" as a "validation" of their own revolution and the formation of a republican government.[51] But unlike Anglophile Federalists, Democratic-Republicans viewed America's ex-colonial power as an enemy, and one that not only threatened the commercial interests of the early republic but also the very notion of republicanism around the globe.[52] The attachment to Britain that remained in Federalist minds largely faded when America would once more go to war with its former colonizer in 1812. America's perceived victory over Britain in 1815 has been described as a watershed moment in American history—one that began to finally solidify American confidence in its place in Atlantic world politics.[53] Although anxieties towards the government would emerge more prominently with the economic difficulties of the late 1810s, Americans largely remained united in their derision for the Old

World forms of governance that continued to dominate Atlantic politics in the early 1820s.[54] By the beginning of the 1820s, American politicians believed with more conviction that conflicts between countries—and particularly those of the Old World and the New World—were largely ideological and based on which system of government would best succeed on the Atlantic stage.[55] Politicians and citizens alike therefore collectively asserted that the American republic was the leading light in discussions of legitimate political sovereignty in the early nineteenth century—a light that cast a long shadow on Old World, dynastic claims to legitimacy.

In this way, the early nineteenth century was a period of fervent political action and debate in America, and the perceived successes or short-comings of Haiti's early administrations were scrutinised and manipulated to suit a range of political commentaries—narratives that in turn sought to assert what constituted legitimate governance for a New World republic. Within these narratives observers often turned to Haiti and its leaders as evidence of the virtues or pitfalls of the various modes of governance that the early Haitian state adopted. The legitimacy of Haiti's various governments, therefore, often served to underline or call into question the legitimacy of America's own infant republic.

Debates surrounding the foundations of legitimate forms of political rule were equally crucial to British discourses in the early nineteenth century. British political anxieties at the beginning of the nineteenth century centred on the emergence of Napoleon Bonaparte and his plans for the French republic. Britain's continuing war with France from 1803 to 1815 increased anti-French sentiment as loyalist narratives underlined the threat—both ideological and tangible—that Napoleonic France posed to Britain. In this wartime period, British political voices were largely united in their denunciations of the French leader. Central to these derisions was the perceived illegitimacy of Napoleon's status as head of the French republic. The illegitimacy of Napoleon was further highlighted by his self-nominated emperorship—a title that British loyalists very publicly mocked. Stuart Semmel has argued that it was in response to Napoleon that the very notion of legitimacy emerged as a central frame of reference and debate in British political discourses.[56] Within this context, the figure of Napoleon remained a focal point in British commentaries on political legitimacy and leadership throughout the first two decades of the nineteenth century.

But the impact of perceptions of events in France on British debates surrounding governance, legitimacy and national identity of course preceded the rise of Napoleon. In response to the perceived horrors of the French Revolution, the virtues of Britain's constitutional monarchy were once more pronounced.[57] As a result, in the latter half of his reign, George III soon enjoyed the kind of popularity of which most other British monarchs could have only dreamed.[58] Christopher Bayly has further argued that the withdrawal from public life of George III allowed the British government to "enlarge the importance of royalty as the symbolic centre of a nation at war and to elaborate the idea of an Imperial Crown".[59] Even British radicals and reformers in general did not necessarily promote anti-monarchical rhetoric in the early 1800s—rather, reformers simply "desired a monarch who was accessible and responsible to his subjects".[60] The institution of the British monarchy, therefore, was an important consideration in British discussions of legitimate sovereignty and affirmations of the superiority of Britain's political system.

Both loyalists and reformers in the nineteenth century generally portrayed Britain's constitutional monarchy not only as a system of legitimate governance, but one that was to be revered and protected.[61] Where these sides of the political spectrum differed, however, was in whether the virtues of such a system of government were still present in the early nineteenth century, or whether this had already disappeared.[62] By the mid-1810s, British radical voices had become more prominent in the face of increasingly harsh governmental policies which were aimed at suppressing dissident political voices. The Peterloo Massacre of 1819 signified a defining, divisive moment in British politics and was an event which further strengthened a shift towards republican ideals within British radical circles by the late 1810s.[63] With the death of the popular George III—and the coronation of the derided George IV—the merits of Britain's form of political leadership were hotly, and in some cases vociferously, contested. The popularity of the British monarchy was severely dented by the succession of George IV, whose time as Regent had proved for many observers that he lacked any sense of paternal care for his subjects. His apparent complicity in the events of Peterloo, and the subsequent crackdown on non-loyalist voices and publications, further strengthened radical thought by the 1820s that the British government and monarchy equated to a single form of tyrannical oppression for the British people—something that, for some prominent radicals at least, pointed to the merits of republicanism over Britain's once great, but now flawed, constitutional monarchy.[64]

16   J. FORDE

At a time of such political conflict and uncertainty on both sides of the Atlantic, this book is a study of how Haiti's early governments and leaders impacted political thought in literature, images, newspapers and periodicals in America and Britain in the early nineteenth century. A key factor in this study is Benedict Anderson's assertion that the emergence of a global print culture was central to the formation of nationalist ideas and imagined communities in the eighteenth and nineteenth centuries.[65] With this in mind, the depictions of Haiti explored in this study afford a greater understanding of how American and British print culture contributed to debates and constructions of national identities in the early nineteenth century. The work of Jeffrey Pasley has perhaps best outlined the central role that newspapers played in American politics from the eighteenth to the nineteenth century. In particular, Pasley highlights the words of Reverend Samuel Miller, a prominent political writer in America who wrote in 1803 that newspapers had become "the vehicles of discussion in which the principles of government, the interests of nations…are all arraigned, tried, and decided". As such, Miller concluded, newspapers were "immense moral and political engines closely connected with the welfare of the state, and deeply involving both its peace and prosperity".[66] Kevin Gilmartin has similarly highlighted how literature, newspapers and pamphlets were central in the circulation of both radical and counterrevolutionary ideas in Britain by the end of the eighteenth century.[67] Gilmartin has underlined the regularity with which "disruptive political energies" emerged through literary mediums in the early nineteenth century.[68] This book engages with a range of literary forms to help establish the multiple ways in which the early Haitian state was imagined, and the motivations that laid behind such depictions.

The chapters in this book, therefore, examine how different forms of governance and moments of political change in Haiti were represented by a range of different of observers and political thinkers in America and Britain. The book begins by focusing on transatlantic reactions to Haitian independence and, more specifically, to the figure of Haiti's first head of state—Jean-Jacques Dessalines. This section explores reactions to Dessalines from 1804 to 1806 in newspapers, periodicals and literary texts—reactions which were largely framed within narratives asserting the illegitimacy of post-revolutionary, self-created sovereigns. Although Dessalines received pockets of support from American and British depictions, his presence as a political leader was largely derided. Rather than simply being a race-based reaction to the presence of a black leader of the

Western hemisphere's first independent black state, however, the depictions explored in this opening chapter suggest that derisions of Dessalines served to strengthen American and British denunciations of the perceived illegitimacy of another self-created leader of a post-revolutionary state—Napoleon Bonaparte. American republicans and British loyalists often constructed representations of Dessalines to draw parallels between the ideologies of these self-proclaimed emperors of post-revolutionary entities. In this way, the figure of Dessalines ultimately served to underline the illegitimacy of Napoleon's political leadership and to reinforce the idea that either America or Britain represented the only true form of respectable, stable and legitimate governance.

Henry Christophe succeeded as leader of the north of Haiti following Dessalines's death in 1806. Christophe's presidential tenure ran from 1807 until his decision to establish a monarchy in 1811, and these first four years of his time as leader of the north are often overlooked in scholarly discussions. But, as Chap. 2 attests, Christophe's time as president is essential to understanding how titles and modes of government impacted American and British reactions to Haiti, particularly in comparison to both Dessalines's time as emperor and Christophe's own turn to a dynastic form of Old World governance. Christophe's presidential status was warmly received by American and British commentators who were eager to secure commercial alliances with the Haitian state. The presidential title worked in Christophe's favour as it allowed American supporters to claim that he was not interested in mimicking Old World forms of governance (unlike Dessalines) and could therefore be trusted. For British supporters, Haiti's change in government from Emperor Dessalines was an important detachment ideologically from Napoleon's own emperor status—one that allowed for more positive portrayals of the Haitian state as a whole.

Chapter 3 explores how Christophe's Kingdom of Haiti was received in America and Britain, and how the King of Haiti was subsequently depicted in newspapers, periodicals, and literature until his death in 1820. Christophe's coronation and his presence on the Atlantic stage throughout the 1810s as the self-proclaimed "first crowned king of the New World" came at a time when American republicans more vociferously derided the dynastic regimes of the Old World. In particular, after the end of the War of 1812, Americans looked to finally separate the ideologies of American republicanism from Europe's hereditary monarchies. In such narratives the Haitian monarch was equally derided for his adoption of an allegedly regressive, archaic mode of governance. However, some

Americans—mostly those who wished to trade with the Haitian state—in fact defended Christophe's monarchy and formed arguments in favour of its legitimacy, despite and often in contradiction to a continuing discourse of derision towards European monarchies. British reactions to the Haitian monarchy were largely favourable. After the end of Napoleon's rule over most of Europe in 1815, British loyalist discourses celebrated the stability and superiority of monarchical forms of governance. Although these narratives stopped short of fully legitimising the self-created New World king, Christophe's successes in implementing successful educational and agricultural programs were used as proof of the virtues of monarchical rule in loyalist celebrations. In this way, on both sides of the Atlantic, Haiti's first and only monarch significantly impacted debates around the legitimacy or otherwise of monarchical rule in the Atlantic world.

The fourth chapter explores how Christophe's death in 1820 was reported and how these representations contributed to anti-monarchical narratives in both America and Britain in the early 1820s. Americans increasingly cemented the division between America's progressive republican ideologies and the oppression of Old World regimes. The death of Haiti's monarch, therefore, became a central entity within American narratives that derided the tyranny and oppression of Old World monarchies. The revolution against Christophe by his own citizens and troops that preceded his death was similarly lauded by British radicals who had become increasingly republican in their writings since the late 1810s. The uprising against the Haitian monarch was situated within narratives of growing discontent of the British government and the newly-crowned George IV as well as discourses that celebrated the republican revolutions sweeping Europe in 1820. As these representations demonstrate, the death of King Christophe represented a unique opportunity for British radicals to overtly celebrate the death of a monarch at a time of increasing laws against sedition imposed on them by the British government.

The final chapter of the book focuses on American and British reactions to the emergence of Boyer and his unification of the north and south of Haiti to one form of republican government. Despite the domestic crises of the late 1810s, Americans were largely united in their belief that their republican form of government was one that deserved to be lauded and universally admired. In this context, President Boyer became, for some, a symbol of the universal desire among people to be governed by strong, republican leaders. Boyer's unification of Haiti under one single form of republican rule after Christophe's death was similarly praised by British radicals who legitimised Haiti's new form of government and depicted it as evidence of the virtues of republicanism. Although these narratives often sought to legitimise the notion of republicanism itself, a number of commentators used Haiti's republican turn as a central argument to recognise formally the Haitian state. In this way, Haiti's adoption of republican principles united republicans and radicals on both sides of the Atlantic in their celebration of the Haitian republic—celebrations that once again had debates surrounding political legitimacy and sovereignty at their core.

This book analyses a range of depictions of the early Haitian state from a number of distinct moments in its history—moments that were perceived in positive and negative lights at different times and by different people. By focusing on these reactions to political change and transition in Haiti—and how these moments elicited both derision and support from various quarters—it is possible to better understand the political ideologies and tensions that were central to American and British imaginings of Haiti in the early nineteenth century. Although the presence of the Atlantic world's first black republic was undoubtedly confronting for the white political elites of America and Britain, the depictions of Haiti outlined in this study ultimately suggest that in order to understand fully the complexity and nuanced nature of reactions to the early Haitian state, they demand to be considered in the context of more domestic political anxieties and conflicts for America and Britain in the early nineteenth century. By analysing these alternative lenses through which Haiti was viewed, we can better understand the significant impact that the Haitian state had on American and British political discourses in the early nineteenth century— an impact that transcended racial, social and political boundaries.

## NOTES

1. There is now an abundance of literature on the key events of the Revolution and its major motivations and consequences. Some of the most insightful accounts are: David Patrick Geggus and Norman Fiering, eds., *The World of the Haitian Revolution* (Indianapolis: Indiana University Press, 2009); Jeremy D. Popkin, *Facing Racial Revolution: Eyewitness Accounts of the Haitian Insurrection* (Chicago: University of Chicago Press, 2007); Laurent Dubois, *Avengers of the New World: The Story of the Haitian Revolution* (Cambridge: Harvard University Press, 2004); Carolyn E. Fick, *The Making of Haiti: The Saint Domingue Revolution from Below* (Knoxville: The University of Tennessee Press, 1990); C. L. R. James, *The*

*Black Jacobins: Toussaint L'ouverture and the San Domingo Revolution* (1938, reprint, New York: Vintage, 1989).

2. Michel-Rolph Trouillot, *Silencing the Past: Power and the Production of History* (Boston: Beacon Press, 1995), 73.

3. In fact Dessalines named the new nation "Hayti"—a spelling that would remain until well into the late nineteenth century. It is worth noting that American and British writers used the names "Hayti", "Saint-Domingue" and "St. Domingo" as virtual synonyms for the Haitian state in the early to mid-nineteenth century.

4. Michel-Rolph Trouillot, *Haiti: State against Nation* (New York: NYU Press, 1990), 57.

5. Laurent Dubois, *Haiti: The Aftershocks of History* (New York: Metropolitan Books, 2012); Julia Gaffield, *Haitian Connections in the Atlantic World: Recognition after Revolution* (Chapel Hill: University of North Carolina Press, 2015); David Nicholls, *From Dessalines to Duvalier: Race, Colour and National Independence in Haiti* (Cambridge: Cambridge University Press, 1979). Although this book engages heavily with modern Anglocentric scholarship, it is important to note the significant work of nineteenth century Haitian historians in understanding the strategies of these leaders. For two such seminal works, see Beaubrun Ardouin, *Etudes Sur l'Histoire d'Haïti Suivies De La Vie Du Général J.M. Borgella* (Port au Prince: F. Dalencour, 1958); Thomas Madiou, *Histoire d'Haïti*, vol 3 (Port au Prince: J. Courtois, 1847).

6. Trouillot, *State against Nation*, 59.

7. Deborah Jenson, *Beyond the Slave Narrative: Politics, Sex, and Manuscripts in the Haitian Revolution* (Liverpool: Liverpool University Press, 2012); Sybille Fischer, *Modernity Disavowed: Haiti and the Cultures of Slavery in the Age of Revolution* (Durham: Duke University Press, 2004), 227–271.

8. Trouillot, *Silencing the Past*, 73.

9. For a general overview of the impact of the Revolution on abolitionist debates see Robin Blackburn, *The Overthrow of Colonial Slavery, 1776–1848* (London: Verso, 1988), 216–265; "Haiti, Slavery and the Age of the Democratic Revolution," *The William and Mary Quarterly*, 63, no. 4 (2006): 643–674.

10. Matthew Clavin, "Race, Revolution, and the Sublime: The Gothicization of the Haitian Revolution in the New Republic and Atlantic World," *Early American Studies: An Interdisciplinary Journal*, 5, no. 1 (2007): 1–29. For a further discussion of the way these debates "bifurcated" see also Raphael Hoermann, "'A Very Hell of Horrors'? The Haitian Revolution and the Early Transatlantic Haitian Gothic," *Slavery & Abolition*, 37, no. 1 (2016): 183–205.

11. James Stephen, *The Opportunity; or Reasons for an Immediate Alliance with St. Domingo* (London: C. Whittingham, 1804); Thomas Clarkson, *The History of the Rise, Progress, and Accomplishment of the Abolition of the African Slave-Trade by the British Parliament* (London: R. Taylor and Co., 1808). For a detailed analysis of the effect of the success of the Revolution on the British abolitionist movement see David Geggus, "British Opinion and the Emergence of Haiti, 1791–1805," in *Slavery and British Society, 1776–1846*, ed. James Walvin (London: Macmillan Education UK, 1982), 123–149; "Haiti and the Abolitionists: Opinion, Propaganda and International Politics in Britain and France, 1804–1838," in *Abolition and Its Aftermath: The Historical Context, 1790–1916*, ed. David Richardson (London: Frank Cass and Company Ltd., 1985), 113–140.

12. For an overview of the impact of the Revolution on slavery debates in America see: James Alexander Dun, *Dangerous Neighbors: Making the Haitian Revolution in Early America* (Philadelphia: University of Pennsylvania Press, 2016); Ashli White, *Encountering Revolution: Haiti and the Making of the Early Republic* (Baltimore: The Johns Hopkins University Press, 2010); Alfred N. Hunt, *Haiti's Influence on Antebellum America: Slumbering Volcano in the Caribbean* (Baton Rouge: Louisiana State University Press, 1988).

13. White, *Encountering Revolution*, 125.

14. Nicholls, *Dessalines to Duvalier*, 4.

15. Trouillot, *Silencing the Past*, 73.

16. Marlene Daut, *Tropics of Haiti: Race and the Literary History of the Haitian Revolution in the Atlantic World, 1789–1865* (Liverpool University Press, 2015), 3.

17. Ibid., 26.

18. Elizabeth Maddock Dillon and Michael J. Drexler, eds., *The Haitian Revolution and the Early United States: Histories, Textualities, Geographies* (Philadelphia: University of Pennsylvania Press, 2016); Julia Gaffield, ed. *The Haitian Declaration of Independence: Creation, Context, and Legacy* (Charlottesville: University of Virginia Press, 2016); Doris L. Garraway, ed. *Tree of Liberty: Cultural Legacies of the Haitian Revolution in the Atlantic World* (Charlottesville: University of Virginia Press, 2008); David Geggus, ed. *The Impact of the Haitian Revolution in the Atlantic World* (Columbia: University of South Carolina Press, 2001).

19. Sara Fanning, *Caribbean Crossing: African Americans and the Haitian Emigration Movement* (New York: New York University Press, 2015); Matthew Clavin, *Toussaint Louverture and the American Civil War: The Promise and Peril of a Second Haitian Revolution* (Philadelphia: University of Pennsylvania Press, 2010); Maurice Jackson and Jacqueline Bacon, eds.,

*African Americans and the Haitian Revolution: Selected Essays and Historical Documents* (New York: Routledge, 2010).

20. Gaffield, *Haitian Connections*; Tim Matthewson, *A Proslavery Foreign Policy: Haitian-American Relations During the Early Republic* (Westport, Connecticut: Praeger, 2003).

21. Laurent Dubois, "Thinking Haiti's Nineteenth Century," *Small Axe*, 18, no. 2 (2014), 72.

22. Ibid., 79.

23. Immanuel Wallerstein, *World-Systems Analysis: An Introduction* (Durham: Duke University Press, 2004), 44.

24. Mlada Bukovansky, *Legitimacy and Power Politics: The American and French Revolutions in International Political Culture* (Princeton: Princeton University Press, 2002), 1.

25. Wallerstein, *World-Systems Analysis*, 51–52.

26. Ibid., 44.

27. Gaffield, *Haitian Connections*, 41–57; Fanning, *Caribbean Crossing*; Laurent Dubois, *Haiti*, 138–154.

28. Dubois, *Haiti*, 71–76.

29. Ibid., 139.

30. Ibid., 152–154.

31. Bukovansky, *Legitimacy and Power Politics*, 2.

32. Ibid., 1.

33. Linda Colley, *Britons: Forging the Nation, 1707–1837* (1992; reprint, London: Pimlico, 2003).

34. Sam W. Haynes, *Unfinished Revolution: The Early American Republic in a British World* (Charlottesville: University of Virginia Press, 2010).

35. David Waldstreicher, *In the Midst of Perpetual Fetes: The Making of American Nationalism, 1776–1820* (Chapel Hill: University of North Carolina Press, 1997), 296; Gordon S. Wood, *Empire of Liberty: A History of the Early Republic, 1789–1815* (New York: Oxford University Press, 2009), 168.

36. Benedict Anderson, *Imagined Communities: Reflections on the Origin and Spread of Nationalism* (London: Verso, 1983); Wallerstein, *World-Systems Analysis*, 54.

37. Lauren Benton, *A Search for Sovereignty: Law and Geography in European Empires, 1400–1900* (Cambridge: Cambridge University Press, 2009), 279.

38. Andrew Shankman, "Conflict for a Continent: Land, Labor, and the State in the First American Republic," in *The World of the Revolutionary American Republic: Land, Labor, and the Conflict for a Continent*, ed. Andrew Shankman (New York: Routledge, 2014), 4.

1 INTRODUCTION   23

39. Edmund S. Morgan, *Inventing the People: The Rise of Popular Sovereignty in England and America* (New York: W. W. Norton & Company, 1989), 14.

40. Sandra Moats, *Celebrating the Republic: Presidential Ceremony and Popular Sovereignty, from Washington to Monroe* (DeKalb: Northern Illinois University Press, 2010), 4.

41. Wood, *Empire of Liberty*, 199; Moats, *Celebrating the Republic*, 84–108.

42. Wood, *Empire of Liberty*, 301.

43. Sean Wilentz, *The Rise of American Democracy: Jefferson to Lincoln* (New York: W. W. Norton & Company, 2005), 106.

44. For an analysis of these kinds of narratives see Rachel Hope Cleves, *The Reign of Terror in America: Visions of Violence from Anti-Jacobinism to Antislavery* (Cambridge: Cambridge University Press, 2009).

45. Linda K. Kerber, *Federalists in Dissent: Imagery and Ideology in Jeffersonian America* (Ithaca: Cornell University Press, 1980), 177.

46. Thomas Jefferson, "First Inaugural Address" (4 March 1801) in Conrad Cherry, ed. *God's New Israel: Religious Interpretations of American Destiny* (Chapel Hill: University of North Carolina Press, 1998), 106–110.

47. Arthur Scherr, "James Monroe's Political Thought: The People the Sovereigns," in *A Companion to James Madison and James Monroe*, ed. Stuart Leibiger (Oxford: Wiley-Blackwell, 2013); Wilentz, *American Democracy*, 142–177.

48. Andrew R. L. Cayton, "Continental Politics: Liberalism, Nationalism, and the Appeal of Texas in the 1820s," in *Beyond the Founders: New Approaches to the Political History of the Early American Republic*, ed. Jeffrey L. Pasley, Andrew W. Robertson, and David Waldstreicher (Chapel Hill: University of North Carolina Press, 2004), 305.

49. James E. Lewis, *The American Union and the Problem of Neighbourhood: The United States and the Collapse of the Spanish Empire, 1783–1829* (Chapel Hill: University of North Carolina Press, 1998), 128.

50. Jay Sexton, *The Monroe Doctrine: Empire and Nation in Nineteenth-Century America* (New York: Hill and Wang, 2011), 10.

51. Ibid., 38.

52. Russell L. Hanson, *The Democratic Imagination in America: Conversations with Our Past* (Princeton: Princeton University Press, 1985), 105.

53. J. M. Opal, "Natural Rights and National Greatness: Economic Ideology and Social Policy in the American States, 1780s–1820s," in *The World of the Revolutionary American Republic: Land, Labor, and the Conflict for a Continent*, ed. Andrew Shankman (New York: Routledge, 2014), 306; Wood, *Empire of Liberty*, 191.

54. Eliga H. Gould, *Among the Powers of the Earth: The American Revolution and the Making of a New World Empire* (Cambridge: Harvard University Press, 2012), 213.
55. Lewis, *Problem of Neighbourhood*, 160.
56. For an overview of British perceptions of Napoleon and the French republic in the nineteenth century see: John Richard Moores, *Representations of France in English Satirical Prints, 1740–1832* (Basingstoke: Palgrave Macmillan, 2015); Stuart Semmel, *Napoleon and the British* (New Haven: Yale University Press, 2004).
57. Marilyn Morris, *The British Monarchy and the French Revolution* (New Haven: Yale University Press, 1998).
58. Linda Colley, "The Apotheosis of George III: Loyalty, Royalty and the British Nation 1760–1820," *Past & Present*, no. 102 (1984): 94–129.
59. Christopher Alan Bayly, *Imperial Meridian: The British Empire and the World 1780–1830* (New York: Longman, 1989), 110.
60. Morris, *British Monarchy*, 174. It is important to note, however, that some radical figures in the early nineteenth century in fact espoused anti-monarchical and regicidal visions: Steve Poole, *The Politics of Regicide in England, 1760–1850: Troublesome Subjects* (Manchester: Manchester University Press, 2000).
61. James Vernon, *Politics and the People: A Study in English Political Culture, c. 1815–1867* (Cambridge: Cambridge University Press, 1993), 295–330; James Epstein, *Radical Expression: Political Language, Ritual, and Symbol in England, 1790–1850* (Oxford: Oxford University Press, 1994), 3–28.
62. Vernon, *Politics and the People*, 298.
63. Malcolm Chase, *1820: Disorder and Stability in the United Kingdom* (Oxford: Oxford University Press, 2013), 52; Epstein, *Radical Expression*, 100–146.
64. Poole, *Politics of Regicide*, 154.
65. Anderson, *Imagined Communities*, 49.
66. Samuel Miller, *A Brief Retrospect of the Eighteenth Century, Vol. II* (New York, 1803), 251. Cited in Jeffrey L. Pasley, *The Tyranny of Printers: Newspaper Politics in the Early American Republic* (Charlottesville: University of Virginia Press, 2001), 196.
67. Kevin Gilmartin, *Writing against Revolution: Literary Conservatism in Britain, 1790–1832* (Cambridge: Cambridge University Press, 2007); *Print Politics: The Press and Radical Opposition in Early Nineteenth-Century England* (Cambridge: Cambridge University Press, 1996).
68. Gilmartin, *Literary Conservatism*, 2.

CHAPTER 2

# "The Bonaparte of the New World": American and British Reactions to the Emergence of Emperor Dessalines

In a matter of weeks following Haiti's official declaration of independence at the beginning of 1804, Jean-Jacques Dessalines ordered Haitian troops to undertake a campaign of mass genocide against the remaining white French inhabitants of Haiti—a directive that would come to define his reign in American and British discourses in the nineteenth century and beyond. Reports of the massacres spread quickly and widely among news sources in America and Britain and, as Julia Gaffield has highlighted, the impact of the massacres was such that they "altered the trajectory of the discussion about Haiti in the Atlantic world".[1] Early reactions to Haiti's first post-independence leader in both America and Britain were thus largely framed within accounts of the massacres, and Dessalines's "work of death" served as proof in these reports of his "fierce...savage...brutish" nature.[2] Dessalines produced a number of proclamations in this time that were intended in part to justify the killings but also to underline Haiti's intention to fulfil its radical post-revolutionary vision.[3] However, these proclamations were perceived by some as "the rhapsody of a man, in whose breast nature appears to have implanted some generous and lofty sentiments, all of which are borne down, and almost extinguished by a torrent of fanaticism, vindictiveness, and cruelty".[4] Therefore, although the massacres were intended primarily as retribution for France's perceived crimes in the colony, Dessalines had unwittingly dealt a devastating blow to the potential for American and British public support for the new Haitian republic.

© The Author(s) 2020

J. Forde, *The Early Haitian State and the Question of Political Legitimacy*, Palgrave Studies in Political History, https://doi.org/10.1007/978-3-030-52608-5_2

25

Not long after American and British audiences learned of the massacres, they also heard of Dessalines's decision to adopt the title of Emperor of Haiti. Dessalines had served until this point as Governor-General-For-Life, but by 6 October 1804 his new imperial title had been confirmed in a lavish ceremony in Haiti, reports of which soon made their way into British and American newspapers. This change of title was a way for Dessalines to cement his status as leader of Haiti and to further consolidate his power. The decision to adopt this imperial title was made only months after Napoleon Bonaparte—until then the First Consul of France—had decided to name himself Emperor of the French. Dessalines's motivations behind adopting the title of emperor included a desire to be seen as a political equal to Napoleon and the belief that declaring an imperial government in turn declared Haiti's independence to the rest of the world.[5] This strategy nevertheless failed to secure official diplomatic recognition of Haiti's sovereignty from America or Britain, and both countries—despite pressure from within private political and mercantile circles to do otherwise—refused to sanction official trade agreements with the new Haitian state.[6]

Reactions in both America and Britain to Haiti's first head of state were largely negative as commentators struggled or refused to comprehend the notion of a black political leader leading an independent post-slavery state. But perceptions of Haiti's first post-independence leader in the early nineteenth century were neither simply based on memories of the massacres, nor were they exclusively a racist reaction to the prospect of a sovereign black political leader. Undoubtedly, a number of narratives of the Revolution and Haitian independence relied on discourses of "black savagery" in order to frame Dessalines as an "incomprehensible demon".[7] While race was an essential driver in a number of Atlantic narratives concerned with Dessalines, to frame American and British receptions to him as solely race-based reactions to a black political leader is too limiting to fully comprehend the significance of Dessalines's presence on the Atlantic political stage. The image of Dessalines was formed and re-formed by American and British commentators to assert a number of socio-political arguments during his reign—arguments that often had more to do with transatlantic reactions to the changing political landscape of the Atlantic world as a whole than any serious considerations of Haiti itself.

In the early months of Haiti's independence—before Dessalines's imperial nomination—several writers and journalists displayed a willingness to overlook the massacres of the French and defended Dessalines's and Haiti's claims to sovereignty. Although these defences were often motivated by a desire to see America or Britain establish formal trade agreements with the new Haitian state, they nonetheless call into question the idea that transatlantic observers were collectively and vehemently against Haiti's presence on the Atlantic stage as a sovereign political entity.

Dessalines's decision to adopt the title of emperor, however, appears to have been an even more damaging blow to any potential for support from America and Britain than his orders to kill the French citizens of the island. The majority of these reports served to denounce and dismiss the first black sovereign of the Atlantic world. But Dessalines's decision to adopt an imperial title often took precedence over his race or memories of the massacres of the French colonists. In the broader political climate of the early nineteenth century—one that provoked recurring questions over the basis of political legitimacy on both sides of the Atlantic—depictions of Dessalines were a key contributor to denunciations of Napoleon and France as writers sought to draw parallels between the ideologies and claims of legitimacy of these self-proclaimed emperors of post-revolutionary states. In her study of Dessalines, Deborah Jenson observes that historians from the mid-nineteenth century onwards would go on to "recontextualise" Dessalines as a "proto-Napoleonic imperial figurehead".[8] To expand upon this point, this chapter will demonstrate how this recontextualization occurred while Dessalines was alive, in both America and Britain. In this way, transatlantic depictions of Dessalines were as much to do with discussions of governance and political legitimacy as they were about race—discussions which in turn served to reinforce the idea that America or Britain represented the only true form of respectable, stable and legitimate governance. Ultimately, if Haiti's declaration of independence had "raised profound questions about revolutionary legitimacy", then the presence of a self-proclaimed black emperor continued to raise similar questions in America and Britain.[9]

## AMERICAN PERCEPTIONS OF THE NEW WORLD'S FIRST BLACK EMPEROR

In America, Haiti's newly declared independence led to a projection of anxieties over the presence of a black republic so close to America's southern slave-owning states. Plantation owners worried that the successful revolution of slaves against the might of Napoleonic France would provide inspiration for slaves throughout the Americas, and that this revolutionary spirit would be transported to the southern states of America. As a number of historians have demonstrated, at a time when American newspapers and politicians expressed such concern over the presence of the newly independent black state, open expressions of support for the ex-slave leader responsible for the deaths of thousands of white colonists were almost impossible to assert, and a variety of American newspapers in fact seemed to thrive on such stories as they sought to outline the supposedly savage and brutish nature of the black revolutionaries.[10] In this tense and fearful climate, news of the massacres of the French inhabitants of the newly independent Haiti essentially eradicated the prospect of American governmental support for Haiti's claims to sovereignty and political recognition and, as such, generally ended sympathetic portrayals of Haiti's leader.[11]

The massacres also played into the hands of supporters of Jefferson's trade embargo with the Haitian state. In the face of calls from some American merchants to lift this legislation, supporters of the embargo argued that to do so would be to support a "Negro republic". Such assertions drew a line that connected advocating Haitian trade relations with legitimising the violent actions of the black revolutionaries. To further emphasise their point, embargo supporters also suggested that government-sanctioned trade with Haiti would potentially provoke war with France—something that had narrowly been avoided only a few years earlier and continued to be a fear among the citizens of the still young and fragile American republic. For these reasons, as one historian has summarised, the embargo essentially resulted in "suffocating Haitian independence".[12]

Despite the negativity surrounding Dessalines at this time, after the massacres there were some—albeit rare—reports which claimed that the Haitian leader was being unfairly depicted in the American press, and such depictions spoke directly to the interests of those who in fact wanted to trade to occur between America and Haiti. In her study of the connections between trade and diplomacy regarding America's relationship with Haiti in the early nineteenth century, Julia Gaffield has argued that despite Jefferson's refusal to officially recognise Haiti as a sovereign political state, a number of American merchants treated Haiti as though it were an independent state.[13] Gaffield further notes that American merchants in Haiti had genuinely positive experiences in Haiti and held Dessalines in relatively high regard, something they emphasised in correspondence to contacts back in America.[14] In this context, newspaper reports which sought to absolve Dessalines from responsibility of the massacres, or that attempted to align Haitian independence with America's own revolution, would have served the interests of Americans who hoped for favourable trade agreements to be negotiated between the American and Haitian governments.

Some newspapers therefore tried to counter negative portrayals of Haiti's leaders in an attempt to legitimise Haiti as a viable and trustworthy commercial partner. In an article informing its readers of the massacres, *The Connecticut Herald* reported in April 1804 that Dessalines was in fact a man "of great moderation" and "his conduct has been regulated by good faith". The newspaper even went so far as to claim that he was "not unlike the unfortunate Toussaint"—a significant point of departure even from apologists of Dessalines that tended to concede that he was incomparable to the venerated Toussaint Louverture. The *Herald* tried to distance Dessalines from the massacres of the colonists by claiming that "the authority of Dessalines cannot prevent their frequent assassination". While the report sympathised with the colonists, it also made clear that they were simply being subjected to the same kind of brutality that they themselves had perpetrated during the Revolution.[15] Other newspapers also tried to diminish Dessalines's agency in the massacres by claiming that his arrival in towns such as Aux Cayes meant that "tranquility was restored". Such reports claimed that under the leadership of Dessalines no further massacres took place and that there would be a restoration of "order and good government".[16] By emphasising order and tranquillity under Dessalines's leadership, such reports were thus able to promote Haiti as a viable and legitimate commercial partner.

The concept of "good government" was a key indicator of support for the Haitian state and Dessalines's status as a viable political leader. After its initial indication of support Dessalines, the *Connecticut Herald* would go a step further only a few weeks later when it printed a letter supposedly from a Haitian resident to his friend in Baltimore. The letter asked readers to recollect the atrocities committed by Leclerc, Rochambeau and the French troops during the Revolution. It graphically described scenes of torture against black men and the inhumane killing of black women, which in effect served as a thinly veiled defence of the Haitian massacres against the French. But, more strikingly, the letter also underlined the political legitimacy of the new Haitian state by referring to the "people of St. Domingo, [who] enter with majesty, the rank of nations". The report alluded to the revolutionary pasts of both Britain and America and appealed for understanding from the English "who have changed your government" and most importantly from Americans "who have ceased to be Englishmen".[17] Reports such as this demonstrate how some observers saw the question of Haiti's legitimacy as a political state as key to trying to stem the tide of negative perceptions of the new nation. By drawing a parallel between Haiti's revolution and that of America's, the legitimacy of the post-revolutionary state could be asserted emphatically.

Not all positive depictions of Dessalines and the early Haitian state were necessarily fuelled by pro-trade motivations, however. As Philip Kaisary and Julia Gaffield have shown, some American observers without any clear commercial motivations also sought to defend Dessalines's legitimacy as a strong and viable political leader. This claim is based on the unearthing of a short play performed by two seniors at Dartmouth College, New Hampshire in August 1804 that was titled: "A Dialogue on the Revolution in St. Domingo Between Toussaint and Dessalines". As suggested in its title, the play was an imagined conversation between the deceased Toussaint and the leader of the new Haitian state. As Kaisary and Gaffield highlight, the play was remarkable for how it countered the common representations of the "brute" Dessalines. Despite the negative stories of Dessalines that were prevalent in America by the time the play was performed, the Dartmouth students portrayed the Haitian leader as "every bit the intellectual equal" of Toussaint. When the figure of Dessalines spoke in the play he did so with power and fluency and his thoughts demonstrated "a worldliness and knowledge that traverses multiple canons and cultures".[18] According to Kaisary and Gaffield, the play was unique for the way in which it called for a reconsideration of Dessalines as a man of ethics and a viable statesman, while more generally "challenging assumptions about Haiti's universal stigmatization in the early nineteenth century".[19]

Evidence of portrayals such as this—along with newspaper reports that sought to defend or excuse Dessalines—complicate the often-held view that "there was a united front of revulsion of a black nation" at this time.[20] But assertions of the legitimacy of the Haitian leader would become even more contentious after news that Dessalines had adopted an imperial title reached American newspapers by the end of 1804. American audiences were consequently presented with not only an independent black leader of a post-revolutionary, post-colonial state but with the first black emperor in the history of the Western world. As historians have argued, Dessalines likely adopted the title to place himself and the nation as political equals with France.[21] As well as consolidating his own power, it was a bold, considered attempt to legitimise Haiti's political independence and to therefore place Haiti on a more stable footing to negotiate economic stability for the fledgling state. News of Dessalines's decision to adopt the imperial title reached American audiences only a few months after readers had learned of Napoleon's imperial nomination in France. Although a number of American publications would thus attempt to discredit the Haitian leader as a "mimic emperor", Dessalines was in fact more of a "critic emperor".[22] Dessalines's adoption of the title was a display of empowerment against Haiti's ex-colonial rulers by demonstrating that as an independent political entity, they too could adopt such imperial titles and restructure their own government.

Whatever Dessalines's intentions, the presence of a black emperor was initially met with excessive derision in American publications. A number of reports relied on racist ideology by attesting to the "absurdity" of a black imperial sovereign and by inviting readers to see it in a comical and farcical light. As one writer claimed: "When I first heard of the black chief of St. Domingo bestowing on himself the title of emperor of Hayti, I could not help smiling".[23] This same report depicted the coronation as an attempt to flatter Napoleon and France, insisting that the title was evidence of the desire of blacks everywhere to emulate their white superiors. As a result, Dessalines was effectively dismissed as "a specimen of that miserable and childish spirit of imitation, which some think characteristic of the negro race".[24]

Although reports such as these looked to mock the newly crowned emperor, Dessalines still found pockets of support within the American press. Such support suggests that for a number of Americans, the desire for trading opportunities often trumped any ideological stance based on politics or race. Pro-mercantile commentators, in particular, sought to play down the significance of Dessalines's title by asserting that the Haitian government, like the American government, was not hereditary.[25] The question of Dessalines's legitimacy as an imperial sovereign was also addressed in reports that asserted his status as the "legitimate Emperor of Hayti" and claimed his "title is equally as good as that of one of his brethren in Europe".[26] Some commentators even went so far as to claim that Dessalines and Haiti had a greater right to these titles as "their superiority to all black nations" was greater than France's "pre-eminence above other European nations".[27]

Other reports were framed within assertions of the supposed virtues of republicanism by depicting Dessalines as a kind of reluctant emperor and one who was far removed from the self-fulfilling ambitions normally associated with imperial nominations. Yet again, such reports were designed to legitimise Haiti's political sovereignty and to further the cause of merchants who wished to see America establish an official commercial relationship with Haiti. Newspapers claimed that rather than adopt the title himself, with "that modesty which we suppose is inherent in great minds, he long held out" and that eventually "he yielded to the wishes of the people".[28] Other newspapers speculated that Dessalines's coronation had been met with "probably more general acclamation" than had occurred in Paris for Napoleon's coronation.[29] While these kinds of reports accepted that the new title consolidated his powers, they also distanced Dessalines from suggestions that Haitian leadership was hereditary, instead claiming that Dessalines would nominate his successor. But perhaps more significantly, these same reports claimed that this successor would be "one who shed his blood for the interest of his country", thereby pre-empting any criticism or accusations of nepotism to which the Haitian leader might be subjected.[30] Reports such as these ultimately sought to show that Dessalines was listening to and acting on his people's wishes, thus playing to the American notion of the people's role in sovereignty, and the assertion by some that citizens should have an active say in governmental affairs.[31] In essence, even though Dessalines had adopted the title of emperor, he did so by adhering to the collective will of the people. The legitimacy and viability of Haiti's sovereignty, therefore, was one that could still be defended.

Pro-trade supporters that defended or dismissed the significance of Dessalines's imperial title were demonstrating an awareness of the more general debates surrounding political legitimacy and appropriate forms of government in America in the early 1800s—debates in to which they did not wish to see the Haitian emperor drawn. As Jenson observes, American newspapers noted that Dessalines's coronation came within an "imperial year" and at a time when negative feeling towards the dynasties of Europe was on the rise. For a decade Europe had been plagued by war, and the brief moment of peace offered by the Treaty of Amiens in 1803 had ended one year later. For many American observers, the imperial ambitions of European emperors and monarchs were the root cause of these conflicts and their devastating consequences for European citizens. In turn, the criticism aimed at European rulers served to further strengthen America's political identity—advocated by Jefferson—as the "best government on earth" and its unique republican status in the face of both traditional and newly created European dynasties.[32] For many Americans in the early nineteenth century, popular sovereignty was viewed as the "apotheosis of modern governance." America's national identity, therefore, was increasingly dependent on the uniqueness of its republican form of governance.[33]

The scorn with which Old World forms of governance were viewed in America in the early 1800s can be seen in the newspaper reports that derided them. In this period of time, American newspapers were concerned that Europe would be "overrun with Emperors and Empires" and that a "predilection for high-sounding titles" was becoming the norm among the Old World states. The adoption of these imperial titles was seen as a "precedent established by Buonaparte [sic]", and Federalists and Democratic-Republicans seemed united in their denunciations of Europe's post-revolutionary states and the adoption of such titles.[34] Federalists lamented the destruction of traditional hierarchies and claimed that Jefferson was leading America down a similarly destructive path if he continued to ignore traditional modes and procedures of governance.[35] One newspaper even mischievously claimed that in such an imperial year, "Thomas I of Fredonia might be next".[36] Democratic-Republicans, on the other hand, scorned Federalists for their perceived support of traditional dynastic forms of government and claimed that the Federalist "monarchical program" was "counter to the libertarian impulses of America's republican ideology".[37]

News of Dessalines's coronation reached American shores within this climate, and Republican-leaning publications focused on Dessalines's decision to base the new Haitian republic on a model of Old World dynastic governance to further underline Republican attacks on Federalists' apparent attachment to traditional forms of political power. These reports often attested to the apparent absurdity of a black New World statesman mimicking archaic forms of political leadership, and they simultaneously denied Dessalines his new title—at once attacking and delegitimising his imperial name. Republican publications such as New York's *The Bee* refused to call Dessalines by his newly adopted title, instead asserting that "the black general" had "performed the farce of being crowned emperor of Hayti".[38] Other newspapers also played on the supposedly farcical nature of the coronation of a "negro chief".[39] Reports such as these were clearly racially-charged, but one of their primary aims was to rebuke the notion of this new black republic mimicking Old World forms of governance, just as (so they claimed) the Federalists would like to do.

34   J. FORDE

Despite their different agendas, both sides of the American political spectrum in fact looked to Europe's emperors with derision and asserted America's unique—and superior—mode of governance. It is within this context that negative receptions to Dessalines in America must be considered as the Haitian leader soon found himself rebuked from both of America's political parties. Whereas denunciatory depictions of the Haitian leader had at first focused on the massacres of whites or more generally on his apparently savage and ferocious nature, Dessalines soon became situated within American derisions of the legitimacy and sovereignty of Europe's new post-revolutionary states. In this climate, pro-trade supporters feared that if American observers found it difficult to offer support to a black leader, then support for one who had adopted a form of governance almost universally detested throughout America—and one that went against the principles of both major political parties—would be almost impossible. Such fears were soon realised. News of Dessalines's coronation was confirmation for some newspapers that this "predilection" for imperial titles had extended to the West Indies, leading to the conclusion that "the disorder of Emperor-making seems to be contagious".[40] More specifically, a number of newspapers sought to frame Dessalines in denunciations of the actions of Napoleon and the other "tyrants" of Europe. As newspapers in this time asserted that "true republicans, are generally no great admirers of kings and emperors" then depictions of Emperor Dessalines became a source not only of derision for black political leadership but also as a contributor to the more general scorn for Old World forms of governance.[41]

American reports—regardless of their political leanings—often aligned Dessalines with these newly made emperors of the Old World and sought to include him in denunciatory narratives aimed at the very concept of these new dynasties. For this reason, articles in America often referred to Dessalines by his imperial title until the end of his reign. While some headlines claimed a black emperor to be a shocking "spectacle", other publications—such as Samuel Relf's Federalist-leaning *Philadelphia Gazette*—more generally made exclamations pointing to "Another Emperor" or the "New Emperors".[42] In this sense there was a general acceptance of Dessalines's imperial title within the American press. However, this acceptance was not intended to translate to more respect for the Haitian leader. Rather, for newspapers with Republican sympathies, such as Francis Childs's *Daily Advertiser* (New York), the coronation in Haiti was portrayed as symptomatic and representative of a "rage for titles" being witnessed in France and other parts of Europe.[43] Wording such as this that portrayed Haiti's change to an imperial form of governance as following a trend ultimately sought to dismiss its legitimacy and in turn the legitimacy of Europe's other self-constructed dynasties. As such, in attempting to gain public support from within America, the meaning invested in titles of governance was a damaging factor for Dessalines—something that was reflected in the reactions he received from Republicans and Federalists alike.

These kinds of reports wanted to ensure that the Haitian emperor and the new emperors of Europe were aligned in their political ideologies, and the idea of a kind of ideological fraternity among these sovereigns was key to such depictions. One article that appeared in a number of American newspapers, but which was originally from the widely read *Poulson's Daily American Advertiser*, was an imagined proclamation from the Haitian leader. By the time of Dessalines's coronation, American newspapers were well accustomed to the numerous proclamations and decrees that Dessalines had authored—proclamations that were circulated widely among American news sources. As Jenson has demonstrated, these proclamations were designed to create a "Haitian political identity and agency that would resonate on the world stage".[44] Even though these decrees clearly called on Haitian citizens to forever renounce France, the *Advertiser's* "proclamation" claimed to be addressed to "Brother Napoleon" from his "best brother", Dessalines. This proclamation also made reference to Dessalines's "Cousin Talleyrand" and his "Nephew of Spain".[45] Reports in other publications wondered whether Napoleon's fondness of "uniting his relations in marriage to great families" would result in the marital union of one of his relatives with one of Dessalines's daughters.[46]

The editor and publisher of the *Advertiser*—Zachariah Poulson Jr—was an affirmed abolitionist, but clearly Dessalines held greater value as a way to attack Old World politics than to support the first Atlantic World nation to renounce slavery forever. Instead, the idea that these Old and New World—white and black—empires were related was constructed as a way for early American commentators such as Poulson to call into question the legitimacy of these new imperial forms of government. In essence, Haiti, France and the other new dynasties of Europe were equal in their illegitimacy, and each served to undermine the other's call for sovereign and respectful recognition. In this way, such reports denied Dessalines's claims for a unique political identity for the new Haitian state by positioning him—and in turn the Haitian state as a whole—as a member of the increasingly despotic family of nations of the Old World.

The idea that Dessalines himself looked up to Napoleon as a political older sibling—and the value that this held for American observers as a means by which the emperors of Haiti and France could be attacked—is best exemplified by a mock poem that appeared in Joseph Dennie's widely-read periodical, *The Portfolio*. Born in Boston to a wealthy merchant family in 1768, Dennie contributed to a number of Federalist-friendly journals before establishing *The Portfolio* at the turn of the nineteenth century. Dennie was a supporter of the Federalists and a fierce opponent of Jefferson's brand of politics. Described by one historian as a "reluctant exile" from Britain, Dennie saw Jeffersonian democracy as a viable threat to the destruction of traditional hierarchies that he saw as essential to the security and prosperity of nations everywhere—most significantly for early America.[47] *The Portfolio* was thus used to get this message across with a mixture of newspaper reports and original literature.

In an edition published in March 1805, Dennie included a poem said to have been found on a French ship seized in the West Indies titled, "An Heroic Epistle from JAQUES I, Emperor of Hayti, To NAPOLEON I, Emperor of the French". Much like the imagined proclamation that appeared in the *Poulson Advertiser*, the epistle sought to frame the Haitian leader in an alternative light to the anti-French and anti-colonial rhetoric of Dessalines's own proclamations. As in the *Poulson Advertiser*, Dessalines sent "greeting to our brother/For one great Emperor should greet another", and the poem drew parallels between the two emperors, who were said to be "Alike in fortune, alike in fame". The poem framed Napoleon and Dessalines together in their past actions as Dessalines "observed" that "No ancient, or no modern name can shine/In acts of blood, compar'd with yours and mine".[48]

The suggestion that Dessalines's cruelty was in imitation of the example set by his supposed idol was used by other reports at the time which claimed that "[t]he Emperor of Hayti exercises the most despotic government, like his great prototype in France".[49] In doing so, reports such as these were able to suggest that any past atrocities committed in Haiti—and indeed the tyranny that continued—were less to do with Dessalines himself and more a consequence of the reckless and inhumane example set by Napoleon. In the *Heroic Epistle*, the anonymous author drew these comparisons to highlight that Napoleon had in fact exceeded his "brother" emperor in acts of tyranny in a damning indictment of the French ruler.

Napoleon was shown to far outdo his Haitian counterpart in dishonour for the betrayal of those who once claimed to fight for the French leader, including the by-now infamous Toussaint and Jean-Charles Pichegru—celebrated figures whose only crime was that they had "dared to dispute your right to reign".[50] Unlike Napoleon, Dessalines declared: "Revenge is sweet; but e'en to gain my ends/I can't betray my patrons, kill my friends". The poem alluded to Dessalines's massacres and supposed atrocities during the Revolution, but it appeared to offer a defence by claiming that these were the logical actions of one who had been subjected to slavery. Although the poem was far from a celebration of Dessalines, the clear suggestion was that the Haitian emperor's crimes paled in significance compared to those of Napoleon.

The poem was an opportunity for Dennie to show—through the examples of Dessalines and Napoleon—the danger of post-revolutionary empires and the capitulation of traditional hierarchies that they represented. For Dennie, this destruction of traditional order was seen to lead to the kind of corruption of power that could occur when figures such as Dessalines and Napoleon ruled nations. Although the poem alluded to the French emperor having committed the greater atrocities to date, it ended with a suggestion that Napoleon's thirst for expansion would be abetted by his Haitian imperial sibling. Dessalines was shown to encourage the French ruler to "be greater still/Make all things stoop to your imperial will". Jeffersonian policy was criticised as the poem claimed it was Britain—not America—that "bars us from unbounded power", leading Dessalines to call on Napoleon to "Sink the proud isle! Or your imperial crown/Will totter on your head, and tumble down". It should be no surprise that Dennie, a self-proclaimed Anglophile, would look to Britain as the potential saviour from the perceived combined threat of Dessalines and Napoleon. But more than this, Britain represented a form of stable governance based on traditional hierarchy—something that united Federalists and drove Dennie's writing.[51]

In this respect, Dennie's denunciation of Dessalines was not entirely based on the threat that a black political leader posed. Rather, it was used to propagate Federalist arguments in favour of a republican form of governance that rested on the concept of traditional hierarchy. Dessalines's despotism—along with Napoleon's—served as a stark warning of what could happen if non-traditional leaders were allowed into governmental power. The writing of Dennie demonstrates a counter-revolutionary response to Haiti's newly found independence and suggests that denials of

38   J. FORDE

Haiti's political legitimacy were sometimes founded on American Federalist calls for the support of traditional forms of political leadership.

As some historians have noted, Federalists such as Dennie insisted that "Americans interpret the French Revolution as a cautionary tale" because democracy "was never static; constant vigilance was required to keep popular government stable".[52] Others, most notably Rachel Cleves, have furthered this argument by demonstrating how the Federalist rhetoric of anti-Jacobinism—formed in America during the French Revolution—continued to play a central role in American discourses throughout the early nineteenth century which were used by American conservatives to "suppress democratic challenges" to traditional hierarchies and to perpetuate a fear of democratic violence.[53] Dennie's portrayal of the power-hungry, despotic Dessalines meant that Haitian independence was appropriated as a similar warning for American audiences and reinforced the need for traditional forms of leadership within the American government, otherwise America would risk degenerating into the chaos of post-revolutionary states such as Haiti. In this way Dessalines became central to discussions not only of the legitimacy of black political sovereignty but of the illegitimacy of post-revolutionary governments (with the exception of America) more generally.

The way that American observers approached Dessalines's self-proclaimed emperorship can also be perceived as a means to silence the political agency of Haiti's revolutionary leader. But the "forgetting" of Dessalines's political origins as a revolutionary leader, in favour of stressing his imperial designs, was clearly a tactic that was also employed by contemporary commentators. The emphasis on Emperor Dessalines—and an ideological alignment with Napoleon—was deployed by American commentators at the time to transform his political significance as an anti-colonial, independence-fighting revolutionary, to that of an autocratic, power-hungry, vain, aspiring monarch. Even the *Poulson Advertiser*'s fake proclamation subverted the anti-colonial—and specifically anti-French—message of Dessalines's early proclamations by re-imagining Dessalines as an imperial mimic, and one who desperately wanted friendly communications with Napoleon and France. Thus, Dessalines's political significance was reduced by his alleged desire to be elevated to the same status as the backward and non-progressive European dynasties.

This narrative of Dessalines, in turn, presented a more uncomplicated solution to the paradox he presented to American observers. Haiti's revolutionaries—like America's—had defeated their colonial masters to establish their own independence, and Dessalines represented another revolutionary, anti-colonial figurehead in the Americas. But if early America's political identity was largely reliant on its status as the first post-colonial republic in the Western hemisphere, Haiti's republican status challenged the notion of this uniqueness. By aligning the tyrannical Emperor Dessalines with Napoleon and the other new European dynasties—and by calling into question the legitimacy of these new empires—American commentators were able to assert more forcefully the superiority of America's form of liberal governance. If Americans in the early 1800s began to question if there was "a difference between aristocracy and leadership" then Emperor Dessalines—along with his brother emperors in Europe—enabled American commentators to show to the American public this distinction more clearly and, crucially, one that allowed America to assert its exceptional approach to political leadership.[54] The formation of the Haitian empire meant that Dessalines could be more easily dismissed as another example of the corrupting nature of power and the lust for self-ambition that seemed to be so evident in countries other than America, but that, crucially, was a destructive path that America could find itself going if due vigilance was not adopted. The Haitian leader therefore became further proof for American commentators of the incompatibility of republican ideologies and imperial titles. By emphasising Dessalines's emperor status and forgetting his revolutionary, republican past, American commentators could continue to more easily perpetuate the idea that America was the only truly free and democratic republic in a world of despotic dynastic forms of government.

This denunciation of Dessalines was something that both major political parties in America could support. If Federalists in the early nineteenth century maintained a belief that "ordinary" people had no right to contribute to the governance of a nation and instead relied on more traditional forms of power and leadership, then Dessalines—the black, ex-slave—represented the ultimate rejection of traditional governance and the disastrous consequences this could have on a nation. But at the same time, if Democratic-Republicans opposed "traditional monarchies...with their bloated executives and standing armies" and had effectively sustained an attack on the concept of "monocracy", Dessalines's imperial nomination asked for him to be positioned alongside these dynastic leaders.[55] The ideological paradox that Dessalines's title created—that of an ex-slave, anti-colonial, post-revolutionary imperial sovereign—ultimately worked against him from both sides of the American political spectrum. In this way, assertions of Dessalines's imperial title served to both diminish his and Haiti's significance as a political voice in the Americas, while also reasserting American perceptions of superiority and their unique form of republicanism in an Atlantic world caught up in a "rage for titles" and autocratic rule.

American perceptions of Haiti's first head of state were similarly formed by discourses of political legitimacy. In particular, Dessalines's coronation as emperor united American observers in their denunciations of a black revolutionary who sought to implement the policies and ceremonies of Old World dynasties. The significance of Dessalines's emperor title was thus asserted in American narratives that debated the best way forward for the American republic and the ways in which its own government should function. Denunciations of the emperor served to further the cause of both sides of the American political divide. Federalists used depictions of the apparent chaos found in Haiti to emphasise the social and political calamities that can befall a nation when traditional social and political hierarchies are allowed to be completely eradicated. Democratic-Republicans used Dessalines as evidence of the farcical nature of Old World dynasties and the ease with which they could be replicated—something that helped to expose the baselessness of hereditary claims to true political legitimacy. In this way, Dessalines's presence as a political agent was as central to American derision of self-created dynasties everywhere as it was to racist denunciations of black political sovereignty.

## BRITISH REACTIONS TO THE EMPEROR OF HAITI

In Britain, as in America, early reactions to the new Haitian state and Dessalines were soon heavily influenced by reports of the 1804 massacres. A number of these depictions contributed to continuing anti-Jacobin rhetoric in loyalist British publications by reminding readers of the September Massacres of 1792 in France. These reports were an attempt not only to provoke a fear of black Jacobinism but to remind British audiences of the threat of Jacobinism more generally. Newspapers reported on the scale of the Haitian genocide as they claimed that immediately after Dessalines's orders were known "between five or six hundred persons fell under the bloody hatchet of the Haytians" in one town alone. A common claim in these reports was that cannibalism was a central feature during the massacres, something that had also been a prevalent feature of anti-Jacobin narratives that sought to demonise the French revolutionaries and to "reveal the violence that resulted from each Jacobin evil".[56]

Allusions to cannibalism during the 1804 massacres in Haiti contributed to an anti-Jacobin rhetoric that had gained new momentum following Britain's renewal of war with France in 1803. Second-hand accounts of Haiti were circulated that described how "cannibals vied with each other...for the honour of striking the first blow" as white colonists were routinely decapitated in broad daylight.[57] The inhumane nature of the killings was made explicit as reports claimed that "the warm stream of blood which ran...quenched the thirst of their murderers who went on their knees to receive it" and that women and children had been massacred in "one common ruin...the infant sucking at the breast and the unoffending mother from whom it derived its nourishment".[58] Claims such as these that pointed to the suffering of women and children were a particularly common theme as reports espoused indignation that mothers were forced to watch "the shocking spectacle of [their] murdered daughters, weltering in their blood".[59] These gothic images of the suffering endured in Haiti paralleled loyalist depictions of the apparent atrocities committed by French revolutionaries that had been in regular circulation in Britain since the beginning of the French Revolution. The Haitian massacres were thus situated in a more general and continuing counter-revolutionary discourse in Britain in the early nineteenth century—one that served to further underline for loyalist writers the destruction and degradation of morality that can occur in revolutionary moments. From the very beginning of Haitian independence, therefore, the infant state was susceptible to British criticisms of post-revolutionary political entities more generally.

As a result of this alignment with French Jacobinism, a significant proportion of British observers—particularly pro-slavery figures—criticised calls for respectful dealings with the newly independent black state. When news of Dessalines's massacres arrived, this "further alienated British opinion".[60] If stories of black violence and savagery during the Haitian Revolution were countered with examples of French atrocities, Haitian supporters this time had little to offer in response. The killing of thousands of white Europeans in the Caribbean—so close to Britain's own colonies and citizens—made overt support for Dessalines almost impossible to declare publicly, and the lack of positive depictions of Dessalines from within Britain certainly seems to support this claim. Although anti-French sentiment was at a peak in Britain at this time, any notion of support or praise for the deaths of white colonists at the hands of black revolutionaries was evidently too radical for even the staunchest anti-French enthusiast.

More significantly, British abolitionists, who had hitherto been luke-warm at best towards Dessalines, now almost completely turned their backs on him despite the key role the Revolution had played in their debates only a couple of years previously. As a nation, Haiti still elicited support among some British abolitionists. Prominent figures such as William Wilberforce expressed annoyance that anti-Haiti reports failed to see the brutality Dessalines himself had suffered and were anxious of the damage that these depictions of Dessalines could cause to their campaign.[61] James Stephen's 1804 publication *The Opportunity* echoed Wilberforce by claiming that Dessalines's reputation had been deliberately tarnished by supporters of the slave trade, while also calling on the British government to assist Haiti in securing its independence.[62] Stephen even alluded briefly in footnotes to the "moderation" and "humanity" of Dessalines during the Revolution.[63] Stephen's text failed to offer anything more substantial in terms of support for Haiti's first post-independence leader, however. In fact, Stephen likened Dessalines to the warring Roman king Hostilius and framed him as a "most unworthy successor of the humane Toussaint".[64]

It is apparent that in the wake of the massacres, British abolitionists were reluctant, or felt unable, to stem the tide of negative press towards the Haitian leader, and this resulted in a damaging blow to British perceptions of Haiti so early on in Dessalines's reign. In almost all of these reports, the architect of the massacres against the French was ignored or silenced. Instead, abolitionist supporters focused on remembering the allegedly more moderate and humane Toussaint, referring more abstractedly to the obstacles faced by the Haitians and the progress they had made in such challenging circumstances.[65] In doing so, British supporters of abolitionism sought to supplant Haiti's violent present with memories of its heroism and its capacity to advance—both apparently exemplified by the universally admired Toussaint.

David Geggus has noted how—with the exception of the writing that appeared after Toussaint's death—Haiti received surprisingly little attention from British literary figures in the early years of its independence.[66] Certainly in literary texts, support for Dessalines was almost completely absent. Unlike the venerated Toussaint, who had inspired biographies and poetry, Dessalines's divisiveness meant that he was almost completely ignored in British literature. However, a notable exception to this silence that is often overlooked is a brief but telling passage found towards the end of Marcus Rainsford's *An Historical Account of the Black Empire of Hayti* (1805).

Little is known about Rainsford other than that he was a British military officer who served in the Caribbean at the end of the eighteenth century. Rainsford claims to have been in Saint-Domingue towards the end of 1799, but recent research suggests he had in fact left by that time and was more likely to have been on the island in the previous year.[67] Nonetheless, Rainsford went on to publish two early accounts of his experiences on the island before revising and elaborating on these texts in his third version—the much-lengthier *Historical Account*. This account in particular became the subject of much attention in Britain and would eventually be translated into two other languages. Rainsford's account and the engravings included in it are still often used as an important historiographical source for the Haitian Revolution.

Rainsford's book gained such popularity at the time largely because of its position as an authoritative voice on the events of the Revolution, and because there was an audience hungry for details on how the Atlantic World's first independent black state came to be. But the account also focused on Haiti's attempts to establish its sovereignty and the wider question of what makes true, legitimate leadership. In particular, Rainsford was scathing of the actions of Charles Leclerc and his successor, Donatien-Marie-Joseph de Vimeur, vicomte de Rochambeau—generals who were both tasked by Napoleon to bring a swift end to the Revolution. In line with most British accounts of the Revolution at the time, Rainsford depicted the two leaders as being strategically inadequate and utterly inhumane in the sanctioned tortures and killings of black revolutionaries that occurred under their leadership. For Rainsford, the generals' lack of understanding of New World politics, combined with their brutal tactics, had doomed French efforts to quell the Revolution long before Haiti's independence was declared. This was, therefore, a warning to all colonial powers of the need to ensure that sufficiently prepared leaders were in charge of colonies, particularly in the unpredictable climate of the New World.[68]

Although Rainsford's anti-French sentiment permeated his text, his critical gaze was also directed closer to home. The conduct of British governors in the "lawless frontier" of the British Caribbean had become a particularly pertinent issue in Britain by the publication of the *Historical Account* in 1805, and Rainsford's writing demands to be read within this context. Most significantly, Thomas Picton—Britain's former governor of Trinidad—had been formally accused of torture and the unlawful killing of slaves and free citizens without due process.[69] Although Rainsford never referred to Picton directly in his own text, it is hard to believe that reports of the conduct of a British governor in a British colony could have escaped the attention of an "acute political analyst" such as Rainsford.[70] Similarly, it is unlikely that these reports would have failed to elicit a response from a figure who had served for years in the British Caribbean. Given Rainsford's military background, any reluctance on his part to overtly criticise a hitherto celebrated general of the British army such as Picton is understandable. Nevertheless, his book instead more subtly drew parallels between the charges levelled at Picton and the actions of Leclerc and Rochambeau during the Revolution. In doing so, Rainsford portrayed the French disaster in Saint-Domingue as a reason for monitoring the actions of Britain's own colonial governors more closely and as a warning of the potentially catastrophic consequences of leaders such as Picton.

Despite the book's focus on critiquing the leadership of these colonial generals and governors, Rainsford's writing also suggested a genuine admiration for the achievements of the Revolution, and for the possibility of true political reform that the new nation-state apparently represented. In his 1802 *Memoirs*, Rainsford had already alleged that he had witnessed a "perfect system of equality...for the first time" among the Haitian revolutionaries. This was presented in more detail as he outlined a dinner he had apparently attended at a hotel where military personnel of all ranks "sat at the table indiscriminately". Most significantly of all, the famed Toussaint "did not take the head of the table, from the idea...that no man should be invested with superiority but in the field".[71] Three years later, in his *Historical Account*, Rainsford would stress this idea of social inclusion and equality in the new nation-state even further as he wrote approvingly of Toussaint as "one of those characters who invite the principle of an elective monarchy, but which are too rarely found to advise its universal adoption".[72] In addition to this, Toussaint "found little difficulty in the formation of a temporary constitution, of which justice and equality...should be the basis". Although this could have been alluding patriotically to British notions of liberty, Rainsford stressed that—unlike in Britain—Toussaint's notion of equality was based on "right only, not property".[73] For Rainsford, Toussaint's leadership had had the potential to form a more democratic and inclusive society than that of even Britain.

Rainsford wrote glowingly of Toussaint's leadership, but this praise also extended to Dessalines. In the concluding pages of his text, Rainsford reflected on Dessalines's role in the Revolution and the formation of the Haitian state in a more positive light than was the norm in Britain at the time. Key to this positivity were the qualities of leadership that Dessalines had exhibited, particularly in contrast to Napoleon's failed generals and Trinidad's disgraced governor. Unlike Leclerc, whom Rainsford remembered as being "so weak a governor" that it was inevitable he would be unable to suppress the black troops during the Revolution, the "brave Dessalines" was remembered as an astute and determined military officer who had "resolved vigorously to push the war to a termination".[74] Rainsford was scathing of the self-serving interests of colonial leaders such as Picton and Leclerc, and he warned of the consequences of this approach to governance. In Leclerc (and in a not-so-subtle nod to Picton), Rainsford saw a colonial governor who "considered only his own aggrandizement", and whose actions were served to satisfy personal ambitions as opposed to acting in the best interests of the colony and its inhabitants.[75] In stark contrast, Rainsford portrayed Dessalines as the kind of selfless leader who would be for the benefit of his nation's citizens. Rainsford wrote in glowing terms of Dessalines's attempts to have worked for the betterment of the island and to "combine the people more closely"—clearly hinting at a unity among the island's black inhabitants that was impossible to find in the divisiveness that leaders such as Leclerc, Rochambeau, and Picton brought with them, even among the colonial white populations of the Americas.[76]

Rainsford's praise for Dessalines was brief and far from all encompassing. However, the snippets offered were a point of departure from the monster depicted in British reports at the time—a depiction that Rainsford would observe as severely impeding any chance of success for the fledgling black state. Exactly how successful Rainsford wanted Haiti to be as an independent state is unclear from his writing, but his portrayal of Dessalines—at a time of extremely negative reports on the Haitian leader in Britain—suggests that he harboured hopes of a continuation of the "experiment" of a black republic in the New World, and that he wanted to see it thrive as an independent state "unmolested by European powers". Rainsford concluded his text by asserting that "no deliberative body should prescribe for the *internal polity* of a country at a distance, such as precludes an intimate and constant knowledge of its concerns".[77] He clearly saw in Haiti a new kind of political nation, one which was not shackled by the ideas and limitations of "ancient states", and one that was operating under new, unique conditions. Central to this admiration was the "pristine simplicity" of Dessalines's government that Rainsford claimed was comparable with the "simplicity of the earliest institutions".[78] This perceived simplicity of its government was viewed as a refreshing alternative to the corrupt and class-restrictive nature of Old World governments and, by portraying its leader in a more positive light, Rainsford attempted to offer a more positive outlook for the Haitian state—one that looked excitedly to its potential as a political agent in a changing Atlantic world.

Although defences such as Rainsford's were few and far between in British publications throughout Dessalines's reign and beyond his death, another notable appraisal of Dessalines is John Aikin's obituary of the Haitian leader, written in 1807. Aikin was a physician and author, and his writing spanned multiple themes and issues, from memoirs of medical practitioners to children's books.[79] Aikin's strong political beliefs—such as his commitment to Rational Dissent and support for civil liberty across the world—were a cornerstone of his writing.[80] Aikin worked for a period of time as editor for the periodical *The Athenaeum* and, after Dessalines's death, Aikin looked to defend the memory of Haiti's first leader in the first volume of the 1807 edition. In it, Aikin asserted that Dessalines deserved to be aligned "with those characters [of] the extraordinary and eventful revolutions of modern times". Within this glowing obituary, Aikin legitimised Dessalines's form of political leadership, and he claimed that the former Haitian head of state had displayed exactly the kinds of qualities for independent nations—and their people—to thrive. In turn, Aikin's obituary allowed him to further underline his own beliefs and observations on what constituted effective and sustainable modes of governing.

To begin with, the obituary remembered the "patriotic chief" who had delivered his country from "the most horrid tyranny" and who had subsequently looked to provide for its "future security, independence and happiness". Particularly praiseworthy was the decision to name the new nation-state "Hayti" as a signpost to their indigenous origins, and Dessalines's proclamation that Haiti would never again succumb to colonial rule. Comments such as these should not necessarily be read as anti-colonial in nature. Rather, they aligned with Aikin's belief in the necessity of independence for true patriotism to thrive (and, in turn, in the importance of patriotism to the prosperity of a nation).[81] In one of his more well-read publications—*The Spirit of the Constitution*—Aikin sought to defend criticisms of Dissenters in Britain by highlighting their support for freedom and patriotism. In Aikin's obituary, Dessalines's patriotism not only helped Haiti to secure its independence, but it was also a key component of Dessalines's character as an assiduous political leader who planned for the "internal regulation and government" of the new nation.[82]

Aikin was an ardent supporter of true constitutional monarchy—as outlined in *The Spirit of the Constitution*—and he argued that Dessalines's decision to adopt an imperial form of governance "raised" the state of the whole country. For Aikin, it was the adoption of this mode of governing that afforded Dessalines the opportunity to better cement Haiti's independence, while also placing the Haitian leader as the provider for his country. In this position, Aikin also seemed to feel that Dessalines was best placed to ensure that civil liberty was at the centre of Haiti's political foundations, and the Haitian emperor was portrayed as one who decided which laws to enact based on how appropriate they would be for the wellbeing of his countrymen. Ultimately, according to Aikin, a patriotic leader with a real duty of care for his people would be best served by a constitutional monarchy, and vice versa.

Aikin asserted the "popularity" of Dessalines among Haitians and highlighted the "inconsistency and contradiction" of accounts that had detailed Dessalines's apparent crimes since his death. The obituary denounced the actions of those who turned against their leader and argued that "conspiracy" was a more apt noun for the event than the often-cited "revolution"; thereby distancing Dessalines from accusations of tyranny, and instead placing the blame on the jealousy and ambitions of his contemporaries. Part of the defence of the Haitian leader against these accusations was that Dessalines's popularity had possibly been too great as this "excites envy, and envy hatred". For Aikin, Dessalines's apparent successes in securing independence for his countrymen, and in setting the new nation on a path of prosperity, were part of his downfall. Aikin had written elsewhere of the dangers of complacency in times of liberty and prosperity, as these were allegedly the moments when vices are produced and the destruction of countries can occur.[83] Aikin had framed these arguments in relation to Britain at the end of the eighteenth century and as part of his argument that Dissenters were "patriotic guardians of British virtue and liberty against the dangerous effects of Luxury".[84] But the issue clearly continued to be central to this thoughts that countries and leaders can be at their most vulnerable in times of liberty and prosperity. If Dessalines had any real flaws in the eyes of Aikin, therefore, it was that he had not sufficiently safeguarded himself from the consequences of his own success.

48    J. FORDE

Most remarkably of all, Aikin's obituary ended by outlining the "lenient and humane" Dessalines. The 1804 massacres were not mentioned, with Aikin instead preferring to remind his readers of the atrocities committed by French leaders such as Leclerc and Rochambeau in the final years of the Revolution. As with Rainsford's text, the focus placed on reminding British readers of the inhumane acts of the French was almost certainly designed to contribute to the anti-French sentiment of the author and his readership. But to dismiss this article as existing solely for the purpose of anti-French propaganda would be too limiting and would overlook the praise directed at the ex-Haitian leader. Aikin asked his readers to remember that during the Revolution Dessalines had conducted himself with "great skill and intrepidity".[85] By ignoring the 1804 killings, Aikin was able to paint the portrait of a leader who had displayed "common forbearance" under circumstances that, for lesser men, would "steel the heart and…render it callous to every tender and sympathetic emotion".[86] The manner of Dessalines' death may have helped to feed Aikin's apparent pessimism of the prospect for political and social reform outside of Britain.[87] But in the years that he was leader, Aikin clearly felt that Dessalines had displayed the qualities necessary to maintain Haiti's independence and to lead the new nation-state to prosperity and security.

Aikin's obituary was notable not only for the way in which it sought to defend the character of Dessalines but also his legitimacy as a political agent—a figure that had not only fought valiantly in the Revolution but one who had also done what he could to secure Haiti's political footing as a sovereign nation. Although such defences as these were undoubtedly rare in British newspapers while he was alive, there is evidence that some publications were similarly willing to assert the legitimacy of Haiti's first leader. One newspaper report in July 1804 claimed that Dessalines had assumed for Haiti "the style and dignity of an independent and equal state, and [he] issues his orders with all the solemnity of a regular and established government"—a very different picture to the disorder and chaos of Haiti presented in so many other reports of the time.[88] The same report also asserted the "superiority" of Dessalines's education, when compared with that of some of the other leaders of the Revolution—again, an unlikely counter to the depictions of Dessalines as an uncivilised and murderous brute. Other reports referred to a decree made by Dessalines that he would pay repatriation costs of forty dollars for every native Haitian that had migrated to America during the Revolution, describing it as an act originating from the "genuine and blended principles of policy and humanity".[89] Reports such as these sought to counter reports of Dessalines as irrationally violent and uncontrollable, and instead tried to paint a picture of a dignified political leader.

Attempts to counter the negative depictions of Dessalines in Britain with the portrayal of an educated, civilised and prudent political leader would have certainly helped the cause of those in Britain who wished to see trade agreements between Britain and the Haitian state formally ratified. As historians have pointed out, behind closed doors British politicians initially advocated the need to secure favourable trade agreements with Haiti and to guarantee its independence—largely as a strategy to weaken the economic strength of both France and America.[90] And even after news of the massacres emerged, the killings were sidelined in British political discourses as hopes of securing trade agreements with the fledgling republic remained alive.[91] In private correspondence, at least, some British colonial officials and politicians seemed willing to ignore the massacres in their attempts to secure commercial prosperity for Britain in the Caribbean.[92] Therefore, newspaper reports that asserted the legitimacy of Haiti's government and Dessalines's leadership were in turn asserting the legitimacy of the Haitian state as a potentially lucrative trading partner.

Another reason why some British newspapers may have asserted the successes of Haitian independence, was that such reports would have served as a potentially useful contribution to the anti-French narratives that were dominating the British press at the beginning of the nineteenth century. As Linda Colley's work has highlighted, the Francophobia of British loyalists was explicit from the eighteenth century, but this was solidified even further with the resumption of war between Britain and France in 1803.[93] In this context, reports of Dessalines's hatred of France—and reminders of Haiti's continuing independence from their former colonial power—served to strengthen and universalise the anti-French perspectives of British loyalists. The *Derby Mercury* remarked on an early proclamation from Haiti and noted that its "principal features are eternal hatred to Frenchmen and the French name".[94] Other reports emphasised that Dessalines and his generals "have all sworn to resist forever the authority of France, and to die rather than live under its dominion". But these depictions also attempted to remove a perceived threat of Haiti—a threat that was felt throughout the Caribbean as colonists feared an exportation of the Revolution—by insisting that Dessalines's anticolonial stance was reserved exclusively for the French. As if to quell fears of the spread of the Haitian Revolution, the proclamation was seen as proof that "all ideas of conquest and aggrandisement" were absent from the Haitian government's plans. Some reports even attempted to anglicise the Haitian leader as "John James Dessalines" in their efforts to promote the Haitian leader as a prominent anti-French and potentially pro-British ally.[95]

As in America, news of Dessalines's change of title reached Britain in the later months of 1804. And, as with publications across the Atlantic, Dessalines's coronation appears to have finally eradicated any remnants of support for the Haitian leader within British newspapers. It is important to note that some of Dessalines's supporters did attempt to defend the new Haitian emperor's imperial title. Writing against the idea that Dessalines was some kind of self-appointed oligarch, Marcus Rainsford stressed that he had been "unanimously appointed" by the people of Haiti. Rainsford defended Dessalines's choice of title by claiming that "the Imperial dignity was the reward for the courage and experience of the Chief".[96] Similarly, Aikin's obituary addressed the issue of the imperial title by claiming that this was "invested" in him, rather than a title that he had chosen himself.[97] Rainsford enthused over Dessalines's coronation by claiming that it painted a "grand and impressive picture".[98] However, although there is evidence of some newspapers defending Dessalines's title by similarly asserting that it had been thrust upon him by the will of the people and that the title was a reasonable way to assert Haiti's independence from France, in general such defences were uncommon.[99]

Instead, depictions of the new emperor's coronation sometimes played on stereotypically racist ideology as the event was described as a moment of barbarity and ridicule. Reports taken from American newspapers were circulated among British publications and attested to the "spectacle" of the "creation of an Emperor". Such reports claimed that the Emperor of Haiti was as "ugly, as ill-shaped and as disgusting a little black fellow as I ever beheld on any of the plantations of Virginia or South Carolina". Depictions such as these not only sought to delegitimise the "jet black" Dessalines as a political ruler, they also served to deride completely the whole notion of a black imperial court. Dessalines's aides, including Christophe, were described as "swaggering fellows" who had little "mental faculties" and were not "overburdened with sense". Instead, these reports claimed, "painted Europeans" worked in the background to advise and guide the new Haitian empire. These narratives also reinforced racist discourses by claiming that the Haitian public who attended the ceremony were completely naked and "flew like madmen" when called to attend the ceremony by gunfire. This "mob" of Haitians was depicted as celebrating the coronation in a state of noisy, naked frenzy that served to underline the notion of their black "savagery" and lack of civilised refinement.[100]

Despite these racialised discourses, however, a number of British depictions of Dessalines's coronation largely omitted such overtly racist rhetoric from their writing. Instead, it seems that a significant number of publications were more concerned with the fact that a New World emperor had emerged at the same time that the much-maligned Napoleon had adopted the imperial title. The timing of Dessalines's decision to adopt the same title as Napoleon was emphasised in British newspapers which suggested that the Haitian leader, despite his anti-French pretensions, had changed his title of rule in imitation of the newly-crowned French emperor. Newspapers reported on the "farce" of the Haitian coronation "as seen in France" and at times referred to Dessalines as "Jaques I" in order to align the Haitian emperor with his French idol, the newly crowned "Napoleon I".[101]

Reports such as these ignored, or perhaps were unaware, that Dessalines's coronation had in fact occurred in October 1804—some two months before Napoleon's coronation in France (although Dessalines's proclaimed intention to adopt the title had come some months after Napoleon's imperial nomination in May 1804). Regardless, newspapers such as the *Northampton Mercury* published reports via American sources that went so far as to suggest that Dessalines was planning to create a cardinal from his own family to sanctify his coronation. According to this report Pope Pius VII was "too fatigued" to make Dessalines's coronation—an allusion to the fact that Pius had made the journey to attend and sanctify Napoleon's coronation. Pope Pius VII's attendance at Napoleon's coronation was derided by British satirists, who depicted the pope as someone who was coerced into attending out of fear of the despotic Napoleon.[102] Therefore, the idea that Dessalines would simply create a cardinal in order to replicate this part of the coronation ceremony—and to further legitimise his title—was invented by the *Mercury* to underline the absurdity of Dessalines's mimicry and to call into question the legitimacy of this process of the self-coronation of post-revolutionary imperial rulers.

By depicting Dessalines's title as an attempt to mimic that of Napoleon's, British loyalist commentators were able to recontextualise Dessalines not as an anti-French figurehead in the Caribbean, but as one who in fact looked to imitate French forms of political leadership in the ultimate display of flattery. In fact, even prior to his self-nomination, some reports had

52   J. FORDE

already sought to align Dessalines with his European "brother" by suggesting that Dessalines's "greatest ambition is to ape the supposed policy of Bonaparte". As a result, he soon earned the title "The Bonaparte of the New World".[103]

This recontextualisation also extended to Dessalines's self-constructed status as the anti-colonial avenger of the Americas. Instead, reports in publications such as the *Caledonian Mercury* portrayed Dessalines as an imperial leader with similar colonial ambitions as Napoleon. Such reports often drew parallels between the two leaders' perceived "objects of ambition", claiming that while "one has gained the complete and indisputable ascendancy over the Continent of Europe; the other pants for the same ascendancy over the West Indies".[104] When news reached the British press that Dessalines had decided to nominate himself as emperor and to declare the Haitian state an empire—only months after Napoleon had done the same—the *Caledonian Mercury* came to the conclusion that Dessalines sought to be "as absolute as his brother Emperor, Bonaparte, is in France".[105] For Whig-leaning publications such as the *Mercury*, which supported constitutional over absolutist monarchies, Dessalines was thus used to underline the relentless and dangerous ambition of self-created absolutist emperors such as those apparently now found in France.

Portraying Dessalines as a mimic Napoleon served to undermine the political agency of Haiti's first head of state, but the question of which emperor came first was a central concern in some British reports. As Deborah Jenson has demonstrated, although news of Dessalines's nomination did not reach the American press until early October of 1804—a number of months after Napoleon had been nominated the title of emperor—Haitian documents backdated the Haitian nomination as occurring in January or February of the same year in order to defend the Haitian emperor from charges of mimicry.[106] Whether newspapers bought this attempt to backdate the nomination is unclear. Nevertheless, Dessalines was officially crowned in October 1804—two months before Napoleon's coronation would finally take place. British newspapers such as the *Aberdeen Journal* seized on this timing and delighted in suggesting that Dessalines might "take precedence" of Napoleon in the "Sovereigns of the World".[107] Similar reports wondered, quite logically, whether Dessalines had "precipitated his coronation" so that "in the catalogue of Emperors in the world" Dessalines would rank higher than the French emperor.[108] These depictions argued that Napoleon's emperor status was not confirmed until his coronation, and that Dessalines was therefore an "older Emperor than the Corsican".[109] Such assertions contributed to British anti-Napoleon narratives by calling into question which emperor was in fact the one to be accused of mimicry.

In this way depictions of Dessalines became entangled in British narratives of political and imperial legitimacy—narratives that were constructed to deride self-appointed dynasties and that in turn served to underline the superiority of Britain's traditional hereditary monarchy. However, while newspapers such as the *Aberdeen Journal* enthusiastically reported that Dessalines had overtaken Napoleon in the race to become emperor, other loyalist observers were not as positive in their interpretation of events. Newspapers such as the *Morning Post* saw both coronations as an affront to the tradition and legitimacy of imperial forms of government. The *Morning Post*'s editor at the time—Nicholas Byrne—has been described as being sycophantic towards the Prince Regent during his long tenure.[110] As such, the self-appointed monarchs of Haiti and France were severely rebuked for dragging down the dignity of titles held by figures such as the British king. In the *Post*'s report, Dessalines "seems no more aware than Emperor Nap, that he is bringing the Imperial dignity to a Jakes".[111] The play on words and association between the first name of Haiti's emperor—Jaques—and a jakes (a colloquial term for a toilet) was clearly intended as a rebuke of the Haitian emperor. But more significantly for newspapers such as this, both self-coronations served to tarnish the very concept of true imperial titles—as exemplified in Britain—and should therefore be derided.

Historians have noted that British loyalists undermined Napoleon's legitimacy by reminding British audiences that the French emperor had not been born into the role.[112] With the nomination of a black emperor at the same time as the emergence of Europe's new imperial sovereigns, some British writers saw a unique opportunity to use discussions of Dessalines that would serve British interests to a much greater extent than just supporting racist ideology. By aligning the nomination of a black, ex-slave emperor with that of the "Corsican upstart", British loyalists could more easily highlight the supposedly absurd and illegitimate nature of the imperial claims of the newly crowned French emperor.[113] Likewise, in the process British observers were able to equally dismiss any notion of legitimacy in Dessalines's title. In this way, both Napoleon's and Dessalines's forms of government were presented as equal in their illegitimacy and therefore each served to undermine the other's claim of sovereign rule.

54   J. FORDE

Two texts published at the beginning of 1806 particularly sought to emphasise similarities between Napoleon and Dessalines in their attempts to denounce both the French and Haitian empires, while simultaneously asserting Britain's superior form of traditional and legitimate governance. Founded in 1797, *The Spirit of the Public Journals* was an annual collection of essays, newspaper articles and other texts from numerous sources that were edited and published by Stephen Jones until 1814. Although details of Jones's political leanings are hard to ascertain, it appears that Jones was a freemason.[114] Jones's editing of the *Journal* at times reflected the tendency of masonic lodges in the late-eighteenth and early-nineteenth centuries to be "prominent and sometimes dominant in provincial royal celebrations", and his selection of reports to include in this annual collection certainly appeared to adhere to the loyalist sentiments of the mason's celebrations of the British monarchy by depicting the rise of self-proclaimed European dynasties with utter contempt.[115]

The publisher of the *Spirit* was James Ridgway, a veteran radical who was said to be "at the center of radical booksellers' publishing efforts in Newgate" in the 1790s.[116] Ridgway was sentenced to four years in Newgate prison in 1793 for publishing works by Thomas Paine. Despite being an early and very vocal supporter of the French Revolution, by the beginning of the nineteenth century Ridgway had become a "respectable Piccadilly publisher-bookseller".[117] While the *Spirit*'s reporting of the Haitian leader lacked any empathy for his revolutionary successes, it nonetheless sought to denounce the self-proclaimed emperor of the post-revolutionary state. As such, a publisher with a record for radical tendencies would have likely supported writing that sought to mock political leaders who adopted Old World forms of monarchical leadership.

The 1806 edition (being a collection of reports from 1805) contained a depiction of Dessalines's coronation as originally printed in Byrne's *Morning Post*. That this report was published and then re-published by two editors who wanted to be seen to be defending the legitimacy and uniqueness of Britain's monarchy is unsurprising. The report claimed to be a first-hand account of the Haitian coronation and consisted of the kind of racially motivated language found in other reports of the time that served to both mock the newly appointed Haitian emperor and to deny the Haitian state any legitimacy or importance. In the account, Dessalines was parodied as an exotic African chief who attempted, but failed, to mimic the Western imperial mode. The "Supreme Obeahman" was depicted as sitting "upon a pile of empty hogsheads" with a "wooden sceptre" as he surrounded himself with "his three favourite Empresses" who were "squatted at the foot of the Imperial throne".

Although this kind of rhetoric undoubtedly both caricatured Dessalines's blackness and denied his agency as a respectable leader of a sovereign nation, the article also emphasised more generally the pomp and ceremony attached with such ceremonies. This was largely achieved by mocking the notion of titles and dignitaries handed out by self-proclaimed emperors; in this case to the "Imperial Pipe-bearer", the "Imperial Mule-driver" and the "Chief Pot-boiler".[118] The distribution of titles of kingship and nobility to anyone in favour of the Emperor—regardless of the value of their claims to such a title—was also a common point of attack on Napoleon by British satirists. Printers such as James Gillray portrayed the French emperor as creating imperial titles at will throughout Europe without any regard to traditional claims of such nobility. Gillray's 1806 print *Tiddy-doll, the great French-gingerbread-baker; drawing out a new batch of kings*, exemplifies both the scorn for these newly created titles and the ease with which British loyalists believed that they were being created.[119] With reports of Dessalines similarly distributing imperial titles among his court, therefore, it is possible to see how British commentators adopted the same kind of approaches to denounce Dessalines's legitimacy as they did in their attacks on the French emperor.

The depiction of Dessalines's coronation in the 1806 edition of the *Spirit* should not be read as a standalone reaction to the prospect of a black emperor. Rather, Jones's editing meant that the coronation would be framed as part of a greater critique of post-revolutionary empires. The author of this depiction included in his observations a request that it be printed alongside reports of Napoleon's coronation as "a comparison will display the magnificence of each more distinctly and manifestly". However, he also asked that this be done "without injury to the account of the rival Coronation". Undoubtedly the author was being mischievously sarcastic here, and Jones also saw the value of aligning reports of the two emperors together. Immediately prior to the account of Dessalines's coronation, Jones presented his readers with numerous pieces dedicated to Napoleon, including an article from the *General Evening Post* titled "The Death of the First Consul, and the Birth of the Emperor".[120] In it, the "First Consul" had died in 1804 as a result of an "Imperial purple fever" and the newly-born Emperor is told admiringly that "'There is no crime you have not basely perpetrated, nor a virtue that you have not wilfully violated, insulted and scorned. These are undeniable claims to revolutionary authority, and a genuine merit to obtain a revolutionary sceptre'".[121]

Poems such as this sought to expose the hypocrisy and tyranny of the new imperial form of governance in post-revolutionary France. Other articles and poems were included that all served to scorn Napoleon's new title, but two poems in particular were placed immediately before the account of Dessalines to most aptly highlight Jones's belief that the self-coronation of post-revolutionary emperors should be a point for universal derision. The first poem, "A Fragment"—originally published in the *Morning Post*—proclaimed: "My God, what havoc doth Ambition make amongst thy works!" and continued to decry those "who on the right hand of Ambition stood/In the mock majesty of kingly robes". The second, titled "Indignation, an Ode to the Continental Powers", then asked for action among the European powers to put an end to Napoleon's rise: "How long, ye torpid nations, will you gaze/In mute dismay, in motionless amaze/While yonder tyrant upstart uncontroll'd/Wanton with pride, with pow'r securely bold/Insults you day by day, and laughs to scorn/ Your whining independence?—Fie for shame!".[122] Thus, if read alone, the account of Dessalines's coronation could be interpreted as merely one more example of a British depiction hindered by the racist ideology of the time. But read together with these attacks on Napoleon, as Jones's editorship no doubt intended, it is clear that for some observers Dessalines's coronation fitted into a more universal narrative against the rise of post-revolutionary illegitimate rulers that challenged the concept of traditional hierarchies and governance.

Jones's final editorial trick in this attack on Napoleon was not only to align the French and Haitian emperors together but to also position them both unfavourably against a mock-mayor of Britain. Beginning in the eighteenth century in the English hamlet of Garrat, a series of mock elections were held. They often elected labourers and other laymen to the position of "mayor" of the hamlet at the same time as Britain's general elections. The elections became notorious in southern England and were widely reported in the press.[123] The inclusion of a report of the "Coronation at Garrat" immediately after accounts of Dessalines and Napoleon's coronation enabled Jones to further ridicule the nature of both leaders' accessions and to question the legitimacy of their self-proclaimed titles. In this report, the mayor of Garrat, "Sir" Harry Dimsdale, had decided to take the emperor title "to the great disappointment of the citizen rabble". But, in a show of humility absent in British depictions of the French coronation, Dimsdale decided to delay his nomination so that he did not "like a certain Corsican upstart ...represent the vanity of his own ambition" and would only assume the title once he was "better assured of the sentiments of those who were to have become subjects of his Imperial sway".[124]

As Stuart Semmel has demonstrated, this piece was undoubtedly designed as an attack on Napoleon. But in aligning the coronations of Napoleon and Dessalines—and contrasting them with Dimsdale—Jones was able to universalise the self-serving nature of self-appointed emperors. To further this idea, Jones included a poem titled "An Imperial Ode" that more explicitly aligned the three sovereigns.[125] Unsurprisingly, the poem portrayed Dimsdale as the preferred choice of emperor. The "mock majesty" of Napoleon was likened to Dessalines, "Who rears a throne on Domingo's wrecks/Proclaiming freedom to his brother blacks/By fastening yokes about their necks/And tying burdens upon their backs". British loyalist tracts liked to portray Napoleon as the tyrannical dictator and, as a result, the French population as a whole were recast as slaves to an oligarchic master—a return to the ways in which anti-French narratives depicted the French in pre-revolutionary times.[126] Such a tactic was similarly deployed in writing such as this on Dessalines. By claiming that the Haitian emperor had once more subjected the Haitians to a state of slavery, the poem was able to align Dessalines's despotism with Napoleon's, while simultaneously reducing the revolutionary citizens of Haiti once more to that of oppressed subjects and thereby diminishing their political agency as revolutionary agents.

The author called to mind the violent pasts of both Dessalines and Napoleon, while in contrast the British emperor's "robe is not so richly dy'd in human blood" and so, ultimately, "Harry's reign, perhaps, will be the longest/And Harry's subjects the most happy". This celebration of an emperor nominated in a British hamlet proposed to denounce completely both Dessalines's and Napoleon's claims for legitimacy by claiming that a British muffin-seller had as much authority to such claims of imperial titles. These pieces—and Jones's careful editorship—invited British readers to view the falseness and illegitimacy of Napoleon's newly-nominated French empire by viewing his emperorship through the lens of the uncivilised and savage empire of Haiti and that of the imagined Emperor Dimsdale.[127]

This alignment and dual denunciation of the French and Haitian emperors subsequently contributed to emerging discussions of British national identity at the beginning of the nineteenth century. Historians have argued that the end of the eighteenth century to the beginning of the nineteenth was a crucial time in British attempts to make sense of a collective national identity.[128] As Colley has argued, from the beginning of the eighteenth century the British defined themselves "in reaction to the Other beyond their shores".[129] In this way, by drawing comparisons between the French and Haitian emperors, British loyalists were able to emphasise Napoleon's otherness by likening him to an even more polarising and different Other—a black, ex-slave, post-revolutionary emperor. The imperial coronations of both figures enabled some British conservative observers to classify Napoleon and Dessalines as examples of tyrannical leaders born of revolution—and, significantly, as leaders far removed from the supposedly stable form of governance maintained by Britain's support of traditional hierarchies. Napoleon's foreignness was a commonly used factor in British depictions that underlined his illegitimacy as Emperor of France.[130] Therefore, by aligning Napoleon alongside the first black emperor of the New World—but opposite the imagined British Emperor of Garrat—British loyalists were able to further cement Napoleon's otherness while asserting the superiority and legitimacy of Britain's own hereditary form of rule.

Jones was not the only literary figure to see a unique opportunity in drawing parallels between Napoleon's emperorship and that of Dessalines's. *The Female Revolutionary Plutarch*, published in 1806, was dedicated to the memory of Marie Antoinette, the "lamented victim of the inhospitable rage and ferocious character of revolutionary Frenchmen".[131] This text positioned its loyalist sentiments to "legitimate sovereigns" that were called upon by the author to avenge Antoinette's death at the hand of the French revolutionaries. The book was a follow-up to the 1804 anti-Napoleon tract *The Revolutionary Plutarch* and both texts are commonly credited to Lewis Goldsmith.

Goldsmith's history is ambiguous and at times dependent on his own outlandish claims. What appears to be clear, however, is that although an initial supporter of France's republican cause at the end of the eighteenth century, Goldsmith's attitude towards Napoleonic France had significantly soured by the beginning of the nineteenth century, despite the fact that he continued to live in Paris. Indeed, it is often thought that around the time that these texts were published, Goldsmith was living in Paris against his will as French government officials suspected him of being treacherous to the republic and thus denied him permission to leave the country.[132]

2 "THE BONAPARTE OF THE NEW WORLD": AMERICAN AND BRITISH...    59

Goldsmith would eventually be successful in his petitioning to leave Paris, and his writing is certainly reflective of someone who was disillusioned with the political leadership demonstrated by Napoleon. Although it would be difficult to claim that Goldsmith was a British loyalist at this time (although by the 1810s he wrote for a number of loyalist publications), both *Plutarch* texts serve to undermine the validity of Napoleon's claim to be a legitimate leader of an enlightened post-revolutionary state, and they are written with a genuine disdain for the French leader that would have undoubtedly pleased British conservatives of the early 1800s.

In the *Female Revolutionary Plutarch*, central to Goldsmith's writing was a portrayal of Napoleon's wife, Josephine, as a barely-disguised attack on the French emperor. In fact, Josephine was portrayed rather admiringly for such an anti-French text. Goldsmith claimed that she was able to see through the ridiculous pomp associated with her husband's new title and that she worried about the consequences of the "lustre of those golden chains" associated with imperial titles. Likewise, according to the writer, it was Josephine—not Napoleon—who could see through the false adulation aimed at his emperorship.[133] The effects of the French Revolution were attacked as they had made "a Corsican vagabond their sovereign". It was claimed: "Since an emperor, he is become more intolerable and cruel. His tyranny has increased with his rank". Central to the section on Josephine Bonaparte were the imagined letters from Josephine that criticised her husband's decision to take the imperial nomination and hoped that he could rise above the allure of such titles.[134] But these same "letters" emphasised that Napoleon had reneged on the original republican principles upon which the French republic had been founded.

*The Female Plutarch*, as with *The Spirit of the Public Journals*, drew readers' attentions to the coronation in Haiti in order to further question Napoleon's claims for legitimacy. Again, the supposed focus of this section of the text—immediately after the writing on Josephine Bonaparte—was of Dessalines's wife, Marie-Claire Heureuse Félicité. But, again, the real focus of the piece was the empress's husband. Whether Goldsmith was aware of the name of Dessalines's wife or not is difficult to say as there is little evidence of newspapers that referred to her by name in Britain, but the text seemed unconcerned as it presented her as "Josephine Dessalines" to emphasise the similarities between the two empresses as well as to evoke the notion of imitation between the Haitian and French empires.

Dessalines was presented as Napoleon's "African brother emperor", and the similarities between them were outlined to call into question the basis for Napoleon's claims to sovereign rule. As well as their titles, both were allegedly not "native" to their country—a first indicator of their illegitimacy. Both were guilty of crimes, particularly "genocide", and both were susceptible to the deception of those closest to them. The two emperors apparently married "cast-off Creole mistress[es]" and were susceptible to "avarice and ambition", something which allegedly compelled them to acts of barbarity and savagery. Both leaders manipulated their judicial systems for personal gain and, perhaps most damning of all, both betrayed the men responsible for their rise to power. Unsurprisingly, the text made explicit a desire that both "usurpers" would be "swallowed up in the same tomb"—tellingly, placing the two emperors side by side in death as well as in life.[135]

This depiction of the Haitian empire was a radical point of departure from British loyalist accounts that drew parallels between Napoleon's and Dessalines's approaches to political leadership. Although loyalist depictions often denounced Dessalines's leadership and attacked Napoleon at the same time, they did so by claiming Dessalines to be a poor imitation of Napoleon, and therefore placing him as an inferior to the maligned French leader. What was striking, then, was Goldsmith's assertion that Dessalines's court was perhaps a better alternative to Napoleon's. Just how much Dessalines wanted to imitate his French counterpart was questioned and this was shown by Dessalines's apparent refusal to take Napoleon's name. Indeed, "Napoleon" was instead allegedly reserved for Dessalines's favourite dog.[136]

Despite their similarities, Dessalines was in fact portrayed as "the less ambitious, the less barbarous [and] the less guilty".[137] According to the text, this was in part because Dessalines was surrounded by foreign diplomats in Haiti who were "more honest, more industrious, and more spirited" than those that surrounded Napoleon in France. According to Goldsmith, the diplomats of Dessalines's court did not adhere to blind admiration and unwavering adulation like their French counterparts. Instead, if Dessalines or his court participated in fraud or reneged on agreements, the diplomats "enter and publish immediate protests". Also, unlike in Napoleon's France, "foreign agents are not dragged like slaves in their suit"—a reference to when Napoleon and his wife allegedly participated in public events simply so "the imperial couple may shine by the crowd and the merits of others".[138]

A final example of the superiority of the Haitian empire over the French was the "humane, good-natured and unaffected" Haitian empress. Unlike

## 2 "THE BONAPARTE OF THE NEW WORLD": AMERICAN AND BRITISH... 61

Josephine Bonaparte, Madame Dessalines did not gamble, she gave no reason for her husband to suspect her of infidelity or disloyalty, and her "humanity" was proven in the stories that she had saved numerous whites from the massacres carried out on her husband's orders.[139] The praise of Empress Dessalines was not, of course, unconditional. The text alluded vaguely to her apparent "errors", but these were not detailed in any way. The author defended her by claiming that such flaws "are those of her contemporaries" and that, in contrast, "her good and respectable qualities belong to herself alone". The Haitian empress was summarised as a "luminary among barbarians". Whether the barbarians referred to here alluded to other Haitians or other empresses was left—presumably intentionally—ambiguous. But, most significantly, she was "beloved as a good and kind sovereign" by the Haitians—a claim that could not be made on behalf of Josephine of France.[140]

The writing found in both *The Female Plutarch* and *The Spirit of the Public Journals* is indicative of the alternative, and often contradictory, ways with which loyalist British writers approached the nomination of Emperor Dessalines and the Haitian empire. *The Spirit* relied on reports of Dessalines's coronation that were representative of early-nineteenth-century racist narratives, particularly in relation to the prospect of an independent, black figurehead. Dessalines's blackness was undoubtedly a main focal point for a number of reports—especially of his coronation—that aimed to either ridicule the Haitian state or to mock Napoleon by drawing similarities between him and a black ex-slave. But to view British receptions to Dessalines and the infant Haitian state as a pre-dominantly race-based reaction to the fear of a black independent state is to ignore the way in which other reports of Haiti were framed within events closer to home. British reactions to the emerging presence of a French empire and a growing body of literature aimed at denouncing Napoleon and the political ideology of imperial France meant that in Britain, at least, positive depictions of a Haitian emperor and of post-revolutionary Haiti would have complicated an easier, singular narrative aimed at denouncing post-revolutionary France.

Denials of Dessalines's legitimacy as a ruler of such a state did not necessarily represent British attitudes towards the Haitian state itself, although in some cases they would have undoubtedly played a part. Rather, these denials were part of a larger discourse aimed at both denouncing post-revolutionary states in general (and France, in particular), as well as to call into question the claims of legitimacy of these rulers. In turn, these

62    J. FORDE

representations sought to assert a British identity based on the otherness of these apparently unstable, volatile self-created empires. In contrast, Britain offered legitimate, permanent and stable governance. Representations of Dessalines and Haiti were thus manipulated as tools in a concerted attempt to completely discredit the emerging threat of Napoleonic France and to assert the need and value of more traditional hereditary structures.

## CONCLUSION

Dessalines's relatively short reign as Emperor of Haiti came to a violent end on 17 October 1806. Troops dissatisfied at his increasingly autocratic form of leadership rebelled against their leader and his body was bayoneted and cut to pieces. Only a local woman saved his remains from being desecrated further and insisted on a proper burial. Laurent Dubois has observed that the nature of Dessalines's demise was "a tragic testament to the way that Haiti's glorious independence collapsed into violence".[141] In general, American and British newspapers seemed happy to maintain the narrative that Dessalines's cruelty and tyranny led to his brutal downfall. Early depictions of his death focused on Haiti once again freeing itself from tyranny and finding "tranquillity" with the removal of the emperor.[142] Newspapers published propaganda notices written by his political rival, Alexandre Pétion, and his advisers that celebrated Dessalines's death and the "campaign against tyranny". These reports insisted that the extent of Dessalines's autocracy was such that it unified the whole of Haiti as blacks and mulattoes, soldiers and labourers, all took up arms and wished for an end to his reign. The violent death of the Haitian emperor was proof for some observers of the need for moderate and inclusive government as ultimately "tyrants have many flatterers, but no friends".[143] Dessalines's death and the public reaction against his form of rule served to strengthen the idea in American and British reports that violent, self-fulfilling modes of government bred instability and revolutionary sentiment. Where observers on both sides of the Atlantic had hitherto used Dessalines's rise to power to denounce the concept of post-revolutionary emperors, his death confirmed the folly of these self-created dynasties and reaffirmed the apparently superior and stable modes of government found in America and Britain.

## NOTES

1. Julia Gaffield, *Haitian Connections in the Atlantic World: Recognition after Revolution* (Chapel Hill: University of North Carolina Press, 2015), 84.
2. *Morning Post*, 23 July 1804; *Caledonian Mercury*, 13 October 1804.
3. Laurent Dubois, *Haiti: The Aftershocks of History* (New York: Metropolitan Books, 2012), 43.
4. *Morning Post*, 23 July 1804.
5. Deborah Jenson, *Beyond the Slave Narrative: Politics, Sex, and Manuscripts in the Haitian Revolution* (Liverpoool: Liverpool University Press, 2012), 142.
6. It is important to note that despite this lack of official recognition, American and British merchants continued to conduct business from Haiti. For an overview of the unwillingness of the American and British governments to sanction official trade treaties—and mercantile opposition to this—see Tim Matthewson, *A Proslavery Foreign Policy: Haitian-American Relations During the Early Republic* (Westport, Connecticut: Praeger, 2003), 119–137; Gaffield, *Haitian Connections*, 124–281.
7. Marlene Daut, *Tropics of Haiti: Race and the Literary History of the Haitian Revolution in the Atlantic World, 1789–1865* (Liverpool University Press, 2015), 84–85.
8. Jenson, *Beyond the Slave Narrative*, 142–144.
9. Gaffield, *Haitian Connections*, 2.
10. James Alexander Dun, *Dangerous Neighbors: Making the Haitian Revolution in Early America* (Philadelphia: University of Pennsylvania Press, 2016), 217–223; Ashli White, *Encountering Revolution: Haiti and the Making of the Early Republic* (Baltimore: The Johns Hopkins University Press, 2010), 179.
11. Deborah Jenson, "Dessalines's American Proclamations of the Haitian Independence," *Journal of Haitian Studies* 15, no. 1/2 (2009), 93.
12. Linda K. Kerber, *Federalists in Dissent: Imagery and Ideology in Jeffersonian America* (Ithaca: Cornell University Press, 1980), 48–49.
13. Julia Gaffield, "'Outrages on the Laws of Nations': American Merchants and Diplomacy after the Haitian Declaration of Independence," in Julia Gaffield, ed. *The Haitian Declaration of Independence: Creation, Context, and Legacy* (Charlottesville: University of Virginia Press, 2016), 162.
14. Ibid., 161–165.
15. *Connecticut Herald*, 17 April 1804.
16. This report was widely published. See, for example, *Middlesex Gazette*, 16 March 1804; *Virginia Argus*, 24 March 1804; *The Hive*, 27 March 1804.
17. *Connecticut Herald*, 1 May 1804.

18. Julia Gaffield and Philip Kaisary, "'From Freedom's Sun Some Glimmering Rays Are Shed That Cheer the Gloomy Realms': Dessalines at Dartmouth, 1804," *Slavery & Abolition* 38, no. 1 (2017), 157.
19. Ibid., 164.
20. Jenson, *Beyond the Slave Narrative*, 125.
21. Sybille Fischer, *Modernity Disavowed: Haiti and the Cultures of Slavery in the Age of Revolution* (Durham: Duke University Press, 2004), 213.
22. Jenson, *Beyond the Slave Narrative*, 106.
23. *Literary Magazine and American Register, for 1804, from April to December*, vol. 2 (1804), 655.
24. Ibid.
25. *The Balance and Columbian Repository*, 23 July 1804.
26. *Columbian Centinel*, 24 November 1804.
27. *Literary Magazine and American Register, for 1804, from April to December*, vol. 2 (1804), 656.
28. *The Balance and Columbian Repository*, 16 October 1804.
29. *Mirror of the Times and General Advertiser*, 13 October 1804.
30. *The Spectator*, 13 October 1804.
31. Edmund Morgan argued persuasively that popular sovereignty in America was a "fiction" created to exert better governmental control in the post-revolutionary climate: Edmund S. Morgan, *Inventing the People: The Rise of Popular Sovereignty in England and America* (New York: W. W. Norton & Company, 1989), 286–287.
32. Gordon S. Wood, *Empire of Liberty: A History of the Early Republic, 1789–1815* (New York: Oxford University Press, 2009), 286.
33. Peter S. Onuf, "The Empire of Liberty: Land of the Free and Home of the Slave," in *The World of the Revolutionary American Republic: Land, Labor, and the Conflict for a Continent*, ed. Andrew Shankman (New York: Routledge, 2014), 195.
34. *True Republican*, 31 October 1804.
35. Sean Wilentz, *The Rise of American Democracy: Jefferson to Lincoln* (New York: W. W. Norton & Company, 2005), 107.
36. *The Annals of the Times*, 26 November 1804.
37. Wood, *Empire of Liberty*, 276.
38. *The Bee (Hudson, NY)*, 6 November 1804.
39. *Daily Advertiser*, 16 November 1804.
40. *Connecticut Herald*, 18 December 1804.
41. *The Farmer's Cabinet*, 15 July 1806.
42. *Haverhill Observer*, 4 September 1804; *Philadelphia Gazette*, 8 October 1804.
43. *Daily Advertiser*, 16 November 1804.
44. Jenson, "Dessalines's American Proclamations," 76.

## 2 "THE BONAPARTE OF THE NEW WORLD": AMERICAN AND BRITISH... 65

45. *The Telegraph and Daily Advertiser*, 6 August 1804.
46. *New England Palladium*, 29 July 1806.
47. Catherine O'Donnell Kaplan, *Men of Letters in the Early Republic: Cultivating Forums of Citizenship* (Chapel Hill: University of North Carolina Press, 2008), 149.
48. *The Portfolio*, 2 March 1805.
49. *New York Commercial Advertiser*, 18 October 1806.
50. Pichegru was a French military commander who was found guilty of a conspiracy to overthrow Napoleon near the end of 1803. He died while in prison, reportedly by committing suicide: Steven Englund, *Napoleon: A Political Life* (New York: Simon and Schuster, 2010), 225–234.
51. Kaplan, *Men of Letters*, 141–151.
52. Ibid., 199.
53. Rachel Hope Cleves, ""Jacobins in This Country": The United States, Great Britain, and Trans-Atlantic Anti-Jacobinism," *Early American Studies: An Interdisciplinary Journal* 8, no. 2 (2010), 414.
54. Morgan, *Inventing the People*, 287.
55. Wood, *Empire of Liberty*, 276; Wilentz, *American Democracy*, 107.
56. Cleves, ""Jacobins in this Country"," 434.
57. *Caledonian Mercury*, 6 September 1804.
58. *Cobbett's Weekly Political Register*, 28 July 1804; *Chester Chronicle*, 27 July 1804.
59. *Hull Packet*, 11 September 1804.
60. Geggus, "British Opinion," 149.
61. Ibid., 144.
62. Stephen, *The Opportunity*, 125–126, as cited in White, *Encountering Revolution*, 180; Geggus, "Haiti and the Abolitionists," 115.
63. Stephen, *The Opportunity*, 120–121.
64. Ibid., 47; 126.
65. In addition to the 1804 publication of Stephen's *The Opportunity*, a number of writers sympathetic to the abolitionist cause published texts that eulogised Toussaint. See Marcus Wood, *Slavery, Empathy, and Pornography* (New York: Oxford University Press, 2002), 229–235.
66. David Geggus, "British Opinion and the Emergence of Haiti, 1791–1805," in *Slavery and British Society, 1776–1846*, ed. James Walvin (London: Macmillan Education UK, 1982), 145.
67. Paul Youngquist and Gregory Pierrot, "Introduction," in *An Historical Account of the Black Empire of Hayti*, ed. Paul Youngquist and Gregory Pierrot (Durham: Duke University Press, 2013), xxxiv.
68. James Forde, "Saint-Domingue 'Remembered': Marcus Rainsford and Leonora Sansay's Lessons for Atlantic World Governance," *Limina* 22, no. 2 (2017).

66   J. FORDE

69. James Epstein, "Politics of Colonial Sensation: The Trial of Thomas Picton and the Cause of Louisa Calderon," *The American Historical Review* 112, no. 3 (2007), 716.
70. Gregory Pierrot, ""Our Hero": Toussaint Louverture in British Representations," *Criticism* 50, no. 4 (2008), 589.
71. Marcus Rainsford, *A Memoir of Transactions That Took Place in St. Domingo, in the Spring of 1799* (London: R. B. Scott, 1802), 8–9.
72. Marcus Rainsford, *An Historical Account of the Black Empire of Hayti: Comprehending a View of the Principal Transactions in the Revolution of Saint Domingo; with Its Ancient and Modern State* (Ivy-Lane: James Cundee, 1805), 210.
73. Ibid., 253
74. Ibid., 135, 313–315, 336.
75. Ibid., 312.
76. Ibid., 355.
77. Ibid., 360–364.
78. Ibid., 348, 356.
79. Marilyn L. Brooks, "Aikin, John (1747–1822)," *Oxford Dictionary of National Biography*, online edition (Oxford University Press, 2004), http://www.oxforddnb.com.libraryproxy.griffith.edu.au/view/article/230.
80. Stephen Daniels and Paul Eliot, "'Outline maps of knowledge': John Aikin's Geographical Imagination," in *Religious Dissent and the Aikin-Barbauld Circle, 1740–1860*, ed. Felicity James and Ian Inkster (Cambridge University Press: 2011), 94–125.
81. Kathryn Ready, "'And make thine own Apollo doubly thine': John Aikin as literary physician and the intersection of medicine, morailty and politics," in James and Inkster, *Religious Dissent*, 79–81.
82. John Aikin, "Obituary of Distinguished Persons: Jean Jaques Dessalines," *The Athenaeum: A Magazine of Literary and Miscellaneous Information* (London: 1807), 190.
83. Ready, "John Aikin," 83.
84. Kathryn Ready, "Dissenting Patriots: Anna Barbauld, John Aikin, and the Discourse of Eighteenth-Century Republicanism in Rational Dissent," *History of European Ideas*, 38, no. 1 (2012), 528–529.
85. Aikin, "Jean-Jacques Dessalines," 189.
86. Ibid., 191.
87. Ready, "John Aikin," 83.
88. *Trewman's Flying Post*, 12 July 1804.
89. *Derby Mercury*, 10 May 1804.
90. David Geggus, "Haiti and the Abolitionists: Opinion, Propaganda and International Politics in Britain and France, 1804–1838," in *Abolition*

2 "THE BONAPARTE OF THE NEW WORLD": AMERICAN AND BRITISH...    67

*and Its Aftermath: The Historical Context, 1790–1916*, ed. David Richardson (London: Frank Cass and Company Ltd, 1985), 114.

91. Philippe R. Girard, "Jean-Jacques Dessalines and the Atlantic System: A Reappraisal," *The William and Mary Quarterly* 69, no. 3 (2012), 549; Gaffield, *Haitian Connections*, 83–85.

92. Gaffield, *Haitian Connections*, 153–181.

93. Linda Colley, *Britons: Forging the Nation, 1707–1837* (1992; reprint, London: Pimlico, 2003), 303–313.

94. *Derby Mercury*, 10 May 1804.

95. *Caledonian Mercury*, 24 May 1804.

96. Rainsford, *Historical Account*, 359.

97. Aikin, "Jean Jaques Dessalines," 191.

98. Rainsford, *Historical Account*, 356.

99. See for example *Hampshire Telegraph and Sussex Chronicle*, 26 November 1804.

100. This report was circulated among a number of newspapers. See for example: *Caledonian Mercury*, 7 January 1805; *Aberdeen Journal* 16 January 1805.

101. *Northampton Mercury*, 24 November 1804; *Aberdeen Journal*, 16 January 1805

102. Roberta J. M. Olson, "Representations of Pope Pius VII: The First Risorgimento Hero," *The Art Bulletin* 68, no. 1 (1986), 81.

103. *Chester Chronicle*, 19 October 1804.

104. *Caledonian Mercury*, 9 July 1804.

105. *Caledonian Mercury*, 20 December 1804.

106. Jenson, *Beyond the Slave Narrative*, 103–106.

107. *Aberdeen Journal*, 28 November 1804.

108. *Lincoln, Rutland and Stamford Mercury*, 23 November 1804.

109. *Manchester Mercury and Harrop's General Advertiser*, 20 November 1804.

110. Laurel Brake and Marysa Demoor, eds., *Dictionary of Nineteenth-Century Journalism in Great Britain and Ireland* (Academia Press, 2009), 427.

111. *Morning Post*, 18 December 1804.

112. John Richard Moores, *Representations of France in English Satirical Prints, 1740–1832* (Basingstoke: Palgrave Macmillan, 2015), 88.

113. Stuart Semmel, *Napoleon and the British* (New Haven: Yale University Press, 2004), 111.

114. H. J. Spencer, "Jones, Stephen (1763–1827)," *Oxford Dictionary of National Biography*, online edition (Oxford: Oxford University Press, 2004), http://www.oxforddnb.com.libraryproxy.griffith.edu.au/view/article/15083

115. Linda Colley, "The Apotheosis of George III: Loyalty, Royalty and the British Nation 1760–1820," *Past & Present*, no. 102 (1984), 118.

116. Ralph A. Manogue, "The Plight of James Ridgway, London Bookseller and Publisher, and the Newgate Radicals 1792–1797," *The Wordsworth Circle* 27, no. 3 (1996), 158.
117. Ibid., 164–165.
118. *The Spirit of the Public Journals for 1805*, ed. Stephen Jones (London: James Ridgway, 1806), 51.
119. For more on this print and the manner in which it derided the 'legitimacy' of Napoleon's emperorship, see Semmel, *Napoleon and the British*, 107–108.
120. The idea that Napoleon was reborn as an infant emperor was echoed in satirical prints at the time: Moores, *Representations of France*, 87.
121. Jones, *Spirit of the Public Journals*, 38–42.
122. Ibid., 38–49.
123. For an overview of the development of the mock elections and their place in British culture at the end of the eighteenth century see John Brewer, "Theater and Counter-Theater in Georgian Politics: The Mock Elections at Garrat," *Radical History Review* 22 (1980), 7–40.
124. Jones, *Spirit of the Public Journals*, 53–54. Stuart Semmel argues that Dimsdale's election not only critiqued Napoleon but also called into question British politics and Britain's own traditional claims to legitimate, hereditary rule: Semmel, *Napoleon and the British*, 118–120.
125. It is worth noting that there is evidence that this poem was circulated in both the British and American press as well. See *Morning Post*, 26 November 1804.
    *The Portfolio*, 17 August 1805.
126. Moores, *Representations of France*, 87.
127. Jones, *Spirit of the Public Journals*, 61–62.
128. Gerald Newman dates the "English quest for National Identity" as occurring between 1750 and 1830: Gerald Newman, *The Rise of English Nationalism: A Cultural History, 1740–1830* (New York: St. Martin's Press, 1987), 127.
129. Colley, *Britons*, 6.
130. Moores, *Representations of France*, 88.
131. *The Female Revolutionary Plutarch, Containing Biographical, Historical, and Revolutionary Sketches, Characters and Anecdotes. Volume One* (London: John Murray, 1806), title page.
132. S. Burrows, "Goldsmith, Lewis (1763/1764?–1846)", *Oxford Dictionary of National Biography*, online edition (Oxford: Oxford University Press, 2004), https://doi-org.libraryproxy.griffith.edu.au/10.1093/ref:odnb/10923
133. *Female Revolutionary Plutarch*, 13–19.
134. Ibid., 25, 63.

135. Ibid., 99–111.
136. Ibid., 109.
137. Ibid., 105.
138. Ibid., 119–121.
139. Some historians have claimed that reports of Heureuse Félicité hiding white colonists to save them from the 1804 massacres were in fact true: Joan Dayan, *Haiti, History and the Gods* (Berkeley: University of California Press, 1998), 47.
140. *Female Revolutionary Plutarch*, 135–136.
141. Dubois, *Haiti*, 50.
142. In Britain, see for example: *Morning Post*, 1 January 1807; *Newcastle Courant*, 10 January 1807. In America, see: *Connecticut Gazette*, 10 December 1806.
143. *Newcastle Courant*, 10 January 1807.

CHAPTER 3

# President Christophe and Commercial Legitimacy

After Dessalines's death, Henry Christophe—a fellow leading figure of the Haitian Revolution—was named his successor. Almost immediately, Christophe met strong political opposition from Alexandre Pétion, another commander during the Revolution. From the beginning of 1807, a number of civil wars broke out as Christophe and Pétion battled for supremacy and each attempted to unite Haiti under their own proposed government. Newspapers reported on the turmoil as they described the chaotic battles that were "attended with much bloodshed".[1] Reports such as these were often filled with inaccurate suggestions that Christophe had been killed, with some reports claiming with equal inaccuracy that his death had come as a result of his attempts to establish himself as the new Emperor of Haiti.[2] In fact, Christophe eventually named himself 'President and Generalissimo' of the north of Haiti while Pétion—believing that Christophe aimed to emulate Dessalines's autocratic form of governance—established a separate Republic of Haiti with his followers in the south of the country.

With Christophe firmly established as the leader of northern Haiti by the end of 1807, the majority of American and British pro-trade supporters looked to Christophe as the more viable Haitian leader with whom a commercial alliance could be formed. The fact that Christophe was decidedly against any commercial or political dealings with France was particularly pertinent at a time when both Britain and America were keen on landing blows to French attempts to form commercial or military bases

© The Author(s) 2020
J. Forde, *The Early Haitian State and the Question of Political Legitimacy*, Palgrave Studies in Political History,
https://doi.org/10.1007/978-3-030-52608-5_3

71

near American shores, or those of Britain's colonies. Moreover, it should not be overlooked that at the time, Christophe's northern region was the largest and wealthiest in Haiti—a fact of which American and British traders were acutely aware.[3]

That American and British supporters focused more on Christophe than his counterpart in the south may also have been reflective of Christophe's strategy of actively seeking to elicit support from America's and Britain's governments and media. From the beginning of his time as leader of the north, Christophe looked to demonstrate to the political powers of the wider Atlantic world that Haiti was a stable, independent state, and one that could offer secure and favourable commercial terms. Christophe's strategy involved proclamations that attested to Haiti's stability and prosperity, and these were widely circulated within the newspapers of America and Britain. Although eliciting support for the new Haitian state from America's government continued to be an uphill struggle, there seemed to be a window of opportunity for the two Haitian leaders to gain support for their respective governments from Britain, despite the civil war between Christophe and Pétion. Significantly, Christophe was rather more successful than Pétion in securing the support of influential governmental figures, both within Haiti and Britain—figures that had the potential to bend the ear of key players within Britain's government and the British press, and this appears to have translated to British newspapers and periodicals devoting significantly more attention to Christophe than Pétion.

Julia Gaffield has argued that the strategies employed by Christophe to secure diplomatic recognition from British officials—and indeed within the Atlantic world as a whole—"reflect an international context in which ongoing warfare among European empires informed the actions of these governments and created openings for the new nation of Haiti".[4] Similarly, American and British representations of President Christophe were reflective of transatlantic dreams and anxieties of international political relationships and the alliances needed for America and Britain to prosper. In particular, the way in which Christophe's presidential title appeared to attract initially such favourable depictions of both himself and the northern Haitian state more generally, was indicative of American and British beliefs of the most suitable form of post-revolutionary political leadership. This support for Christophe's presidency would eventually wane, but this again must be understood within the wider context of alternative agendas for America's and Britain's governments. Ultimately, support or derision for President Christophe was dependent not only on prospects for trade, but also a desire among observers for America and Britain to be aligned with political leaders that would reflect favourably on their own countries, and who would serve as evidence of the need for governments and leaders to encompass the qualities and virtues espoused by American and British political commentators at the beginning of the nineteenth century.

## AMERICAN REACTIONS TO PRESIDENT CHRISTOPHE

From the moment Christophe was touted as the successor to Dessalines, the title he would take and the form of government that would be adopted was a central point of interest for a number of American newspapers. As historians have noted, although Americans on both sides of the political spectrum trumpeted American republicanism as unique and the most enlightened form of Atlantic governance in the early 1800s, anxieties remained as to whether America's leaders would be able to fulfil the promise shown since its revolution. With this in mind it became particularly important, especially for Republicans, that America's leaders continued to distance themselves from Old World ideologies of effective political leadership and to further the argument that the Atlantic political tide was shifting in favour of more progressive and democratic forms of governance.[5] In this context, the titles adopted by other post-revolutionary nations, especially those in the New World, were of particular significance.

Christophe was known to have been a close aide of Dessalines's, and it seems that this proximity to Dessalines's Old World dynastic model worked against him in the depictions that were drawn up by the American press. A number of reports emphasised Christophe's alignment with Emperor Dessalines as they speculated on how Haiti's new political leadership would be shaped. Newspapers such as the *Connecticut Gazette* claimed that Christophe was "aspiring to the office of Emperor of Hayti" while others still—such as the *New York Spy*—claimed that Christophe was looking to "frame a constitution to appoint him Emperor of Haiti".[6] Reports such as these were often in direct contrast to reflections on Pétion, who was said to be "taking the side of the people" in his development of a "new republican constitution".[7] In this sense, Christophe was positioned directly against the apparently republican aspirations of his rival.

This perception of Christophe as an imperial heir-apparent nevertheless changed for a number of American observers when news filtered through that he had in fact rewritten Dessalines's imperial constitution, naming himself in the process "President and Generalissimo" of Haiti. If Christophe's adoption of a presidential title was in part motivated by a desire to project an image of more stable governance to international audiences, then this seemed to achieve moderate success in the American press. A number of American newspapers affirmed Christophe's presidential status, while other reports also printed Haiti's new constitution.[8] In reality Christophe's was an "all-powerful presidency", which afforded him almost complete political control of the north of Haiti.[9] However, this was something that was not picked up on—or simply ignored—by a number of newspapers that suddenly wrote approvingly of a president who promised to "preserve the liberty of the country".[10] Although such depictions certainly stopped short of offering unconditional praise to Haiti's new head of state, in most cases Christophe's presidential title was respectfully observed. Reports spoke of the "dignity" of President Christophe and of his "devotion to the public good".[11] Whereas Dessalines's emperor title had been used as evidence of his self-serving nature and predilection for accumulating vast wealth, American newspapers claimed that president Christophe was paid a fixed salary—as with America's own president—and the amount was apparently common knowledge to the public.[12] In these ways, a number of American newspapers were able to suggest that Haiti's leader demonstrated enough credentials to be deemed a legitimate and viable president.

Such depictions of a dignified presidential Christophe offered a stark contrast to the apparent tyranny and despotism of Dessalines's emperorship, as attested to by a number of American newspapers. Perhaps more importantly, Christophe's presidential title aligned with Republicans' belief that Old World, dynastic forms of governance had no place in progressive post-revolutionary states, thereby making it more acceptable for some observers to reflect on Christophe and Haiti more favourably. As Gordon Wood has argued, at this time Republicans believed that the secret to world peace was "to get rid of monarchy and establish republics"— something that was now exemplified in Haiti through Christophe's and Pétion's turn to republicanism.[13] This was also a time when foreign trade was becoming increasingly more crucial to the prosperity of the American republic, but was becoming increasingly difficult to secure with the ongoing wars of the European powers. In this way, the adoption of a presidential form of political power in the prosperous region of a New World nation so close to America presented American merchants with a unique opportunity to promote trade with a foreign nation that in turn aligned with Republicans' ideological agenda.

Affirmations of the apparent stability that Christophe's mode of government had brought northern Haiti served the interests of those who opposed the trade embargo between America and Haiti that had been introduced by Jefferson in 1806 and that would last until 1810. By depicting Christophe in a positive light, commentators called into question the embargo by suggesting that trade with Haiti would be safe and prosperous for American merchants.[14] Christophe's constitution became a key symbol of this stability and, more generally, of his political legitimacy for newspapers that wanted to support a commercial relationship with the Haitian president. Mercantile newspapers such as New York's *Mercantile Advertiser* outlined directly the advantages of Haiti's new northern government, leading the newspaper to claim that Christophe's constitution "appears to be dictated by a policy both liberal and wise—Wise because it points and recommends the most salutary objects of national wealth and prosperity, viz. agriculture, industry, military discipline and sound morality—liberal, inasmuch as it inculcates, towards the nations and individuals who may hereafter trade with the state, the principles of generosity and justice". The *Advertiser* concluded that should Christophe follow such principles, Haiti would "enjoy a virtuous and permanent repose".[15] In this way, Christophe's presidential title and constitution found a receptive audience, particularly among American newspapers with commercial trading interests.

Even newspapers that were normally pro-Jefferson, such as the *Eastern Argus*, seemed to question the American president's continuing trade embargo with Haiti by portraying Christophe's constitution as laying the foundations for favourable trading conditions. The *Argus*'s summary of Christophe's constitution wrote approvingly that "order is to be maintained, military service required…divorce forbidden, marriage honored, [and] agriculture encouraged", thus portraying the constitution as a tool through which stability in Haiti could be achieved.[16] By highlighting the constitution's focus on the sanctity of marriage, newspapers such as the *Argus* suggested that Haiti's president held morality in high regard— something that would translate to a trustworthy commercial partner. *The Argus* also focused more directly on the question of trade by highlighting articles in the constitution that alluded to the protection of foreign merchants and that "weights and measure [would be] fixed".[17] By speaking favourably of the conditions that President Christophe had created for commercial relations, the Jefferson-supporting *Argus* demonstrated that the question of trade with Haiti was a contentious one, even within the Republican party.

Suggestions that Christophe could be a legitimate trading partner with America extended into some of the country's most well-read periodicals, including Charles Brockden Brown's *American Register*. Notably, Brown was an opponent of Jefferson's embargoes of foreign nations, and his 1807 edition of the *Register* (of articles published from 1806–1807) contained a report of Haiti from the start of 1806 that suggested Christophe was a leader to be trusted, albeit with caution. The report was an account of events that were alleged to have occurred towards the beginning of 1806. Although the editorial notes conceded the "imperfect" nature of the report, the *Register* clearly saw no harm in suggesting that a Christophe-led Haiti could be advantageous to American interests.

It is important to note that the *Register*'s report could hardly be considered as fully praiseworthy of Haiti, and it in fact detailed alleged further killings of white inhabitants of the island by Dessalines in the final month of his reign. The report clearly played to Brown's predilection for gothic literature as it portrayed French residents savagely murdered and hacked to pieces in the most grotesque manner by Haitian soldiers and labourers—a clear nod to the gothic scenes of Haiti that permeated American publications in light of the 1805 killings. The *Register*'s report, however, suggested that Christophe stood apart amid the chaos. Christophe was said to have acted out of "pure humanity" when apparently disobeying Dessalines's orders by refusing to send white residents to work on rectifying forts in the interior of the country. Instead, Christophe allegedly allowed the residents to remain with their properties, and he even invited some of them to the grand balls "in superior style" that he used to host. In doing so, the report affirmed that Christophe was a leader removed from the violence of his predecessor, and one who had the capacity to act cordially—and even protectively—of white residents of the island.

The same report did, however, detail Christophe's own apparent ferocity when hearing that some of the white residents had escaped the island, an act that allegedly saw these perceived deserters executed, at the behest of Christophe. In this sense, the report was far from a glowing portrayal of the Haitian leader. But the report also claimed that although Haitian troops had allegedly rioted during this period—leading to further violence against white inhabitants—this had occurred without Christophe being present, and that under his command this wouldn't have happened at all.

By alluding to Christophe's humanity, his apparent ability as a leader to maintain law and order, and his desire to protect white inhabitants who treated him well, the *Register* suggested that he was a leader with whom commercial relations could be established—albeit a leader that needed to be treated with caution.

To further support this idea, the report ended with two letters: one allegedly written by Christophe to the American merchants on the island, and their response. Christophe's letter suggested that he was legitimately concerned about the welfare of American merchants, and he apparently reaffirmed his stance that everyone would be protected, provided they abided by the laws of the island. The letter written in response—apparently on behalf of a number of merchants—confirmed that the merchants had no reason to be afraid of the Haitian government. Rather, the merchants claimed, they knew that the disturbances were the work of "mobs" and that such groups were also found in America and were therefore no reason for undue alarm. For the writer of the report, these letters were evidence that stories of violence on the island were reason for merchants to exercise caution and to abide by the laws, but that trade under Christophe would still be a possibility worth exploring, if America's own government would afford them the opportunity.

It would not be long before American allusions to political and commercial friendship with the Haitian government would be tested, however. By 1808, stories began to emerge in the American press that Christophe was becoming hostile to American merchants. Mercantile publications such as the *New York Commercial Advertiser* now began to speak of the "British born" Christophe and his "partiality towards the English, as well as his contempt for the Americans", something which was "apparent on every occasion".[18] The allusion to Christophe's alleged Britishness was no doubt intended to be framed within the context of stories of the impressment of American sailors and naval officers by British forces continuing to enrage the American public at this time. With British impressment at the forefront of so many Americans' minds—and the foundation for so much outrage—stories of the Haitian leader acting in a similar manner would not be easily ignored.

In light of such stories, any notion of overt support cooled, and only a couple of years later, the distinctly more threatening prospect of explicit contempt towards Americans from the Haitian president would be exacerbated by claims that Christophe had in fact detained a number of American ships—apparently in retaliation of the American government seizing

78    J. FORDE

Haitian vessels. These reports admitted that the American seizure of ships bound for Haiti gave Christophe "some excuse" for his retaliation. But they nonetheless predicted that the Haitian leader would soon "commit his depredations without deigning to give a reason for his conduct".[19] Thus, such reports attempted to cement an image of a Haitian leader acting outside the parameters of conventional commercial and political conduct. But perhaps more importantly, Christophe's seizures came at a time when Americans were resentful of the European powers' (particularly Britain's) perceived lack of respect for the American republic. The humiliation that some Americans felt at the hands of foreign powers had been an issue from the Barbary Wars and centred largely on Britain's apparent contempt, so much so that for republicans it would be cited as one of the most important reasons for the War of 1812. Therefore, the reactions against Christophe at this time need to be understood within a wider context of continuing outrage at America's alleged mistreatment from foreign powers and anxieties concerning their independence as a nation.[20]

The emergence of stories such as these mark a distinct shift in perception among American newspapers. Although reports could rarely be said to have lavished praise on Christophe before this, his presidential title—as well as his proclamations that suggested an openness to friendly foreign trade—certainly elicited at least a sense of neutrality among a large proportion of America's press. However, even mercantile publications such as the *New York Commercial Advertiser* evidently felt that any show of contempt towards American merchants meant that the Haitian head of state needed to be rebuked. This animosity would increase further as newspapers such as the *American Citizen* alleged that American vessels "have long been subjected, by this savage and blood thirsty chief, to capture" and that American seamen had been subjected to "imprisonment, to whippings, and to famine".[21] Other newspapers, such as *Poulson's Daily Advertiser* alluded to the imprisonment of American sailors while also claiming that Christophe took American cargoes "at his own prices, and pays, when, and how, he pleases".[22] This claim against Christophe was particularly pertinent as American readers would have been fully aware that the extortionate financial demands of a foreign leader acting with contempt towards American merchants helped to instigate the First Barbary War of 1801–1805.[23] Stories of Christophe's apparent cruelty emerged at a time when citizens of the young American republic believed that their government was afforded too little respect both at home and abroad.[24] In this context, stories of a foreign head of state seizing American vessels would have been a particular affront to American national pride.

While reports such as these suggest a genuine disdain for Christophe's perceived dislike of Americans, they also seem to have been motivated by an apparent lack of protection from the American government towards American merchants. Although America's official prohibition of trade with Haiti had ended in 1810—the same year that these reports emerged of Christophe's alleged treatment of American merchants—James Madison's government still refused to officially recognise Haiti's sovereignty. As Julia Gaffield highlights, this meant that merchants "did not have the typical diplomatic means to resolve conflicts or disputes that arose during their economic ventures".[25] *Poulson's Daily Advertiser* claimed in its report that in contrast to Americans, British merchants were able to trade "in the best manner they can", while the *American Citizen* lamented that the American seamen imprisoned and tortured by the Haitian government were "unprotected" by their own government.[26]

Reports that lambasted the Haitian head of state were—at least in part—constructed to highlight the perceived inaction and lack of care afforded to American merchants from their own government. By emphasising the apparent despotism and cruelty of the Haitian leader, pro-trade newspapers could better attest to the need for the American government to keep a watchful eye over its merchants. Stories of Christophe's alleged cruelty allowed American newspapers to conclude that the Haitian leader no longer embodied the virtuous nature of a republican presidency, and that he was therefore no longer deserving of such a title. These reports in turn served to delegitimise Christophe as a political leader, but, ironically, the protection that such publications craved would have been best secured by American diplomatic recognition of the Haitian state and of Christophe himself. Nevertheless, such reports instigated a general move to deny Christophe's presidential title and to refer to him instead as the "black Emperor" or with racialised imperial titles such as "his sable highness Christophe" or the "sable demagogue".[27] Such titles were evident from the beginning of Christophe's reign, but they certainly increased in number around this time. Stories of Christophe's un-presidential behaviour were now widely circulated in the American press. His decision to rename Cape Francois as "Cape Henry" was viewed as an act of vanity, which meant that these reports no longer alluded to President Christophe, but rather someone who was "styling himself President".[28] Christophe was

80    J. FORDE

now presented to American readers as a "cruel" and "cunning" leader, with a "despotic" government and whose "word is a law".[29]

To better frame Christophe as an illegitimate suitor to the virtues of a republican presidency, American newspapers aligned denunciations of the Haitian leader with Napoleon—an equally illegitimate claimant to enlightened political leadership. Echoing the ways in which American newspapers aligned Dessalines with the French emperor, Christophe's leadership was now framed in an analogous way. And these denunciatory reports served to discredit both political leaders, as well as to distance America's form of government from France's and Haiti's own post-revolutionary styles of governance. Reports of the seizures of American ships led newspapers to conclude that Christophe "treats our flags with the same indignity, that his Brother Emperour [sic] does in Europe". Although Christophe was said to have responded in retaliation to American actions, newspapers warned that he would act with increasing despotism "like his brother Napoleon".[30] Such reports accordingly drew on memories of the early promise of Napoleon's republican vision—one that descended into despotism. This same fate was clearly predicted to befall Christophe. These reports, therefore, exposed a clear fear of the prospect of a post-revolutionary leader operating with as much freedom and tyrannical autonomy in the New World as Napoleon was doing in Europe. As a result, suggestions that President Christophe was a leader with whom America should become friendly almost disappeared completely towards the end of his presidency.

## British Receptions of President Christophe

From the end of Dessalines's reign, British newspapers reported on the struggle for power between Christophe and Pétion and emphasised the perceived chaos that was enveloping the new nation.[31] Central to these reports were assertions that the instability in Haiti was evidence of the political dystopia found in post-revolutionary societies more generally. The *Salisbury and Winchester Journal*, for example, saw the fighting as proof of the unstable and volatile nature of post-revolutionary states, leading to the conclusion that such bloodshed was to be expected from governments "founded on such principles and hastily put together".[32] The news that Christophe had taken charge of northern Haiti—and the publication of his presidential constitution only a few months later—prompted a similar reaction from the *Caledonian Mercury*. The *Mercury* judged that this new constitution "seems to be very well in theory" but saw in it a parallel with France in which "so many similar systems were brought forward…all of which looked very well upon paper, but ended in nothing but mischief and misery". Therefore, the *Mercury* concluded, "the Haytian Constitution is not likely to be more solid and substantial" than any forms of governmental legislation that had been proposed in France. For the Whig-leaning *Mercury*, the political aftermath of the French Revolution had set a precedent that Haiti would surely follow, and the examples set in both countries served to strengthen its conviction that "political constitutions of any value are not the creation of the collective wisdom of any one period, but must be the work of time, long experience, and those alterations and improvements which can only result from practice and reflection". In truly patriotic fashion, for the *Mercury* the best example of a constitution derived from a traditional, permanent and stable form of government was Britain's constitutional monarchy, "which has rendered it the admiration of the world".[33]

In this context, Haiti's post-revolutionary status posed a potential risk to Christophe's early attempts to secure sovereign recognition from the British government and the British public. However, voices which cast doubt on the value or stability of Haiti's new constitution were soon drowned out by the acceptance that Christophe generally found in Britain at the beginning of his presidency. Only months after news of his presidential title and new constitution was circulated widely among British news sources, positive depictions of the new Haitian head of state began to emerge.[34] Newspapers such as the *Morning Chronicle* reported stories of "President Christophe", the "humane Chief" whose status was such that volunteers reportedly swore to "live and die by him".[35] Other newspapers enthusiastically published reports reputedly sent direct from Haiti that described Christophe as the "friend of humanity, the man who loves his country and who obeys its laws".[36] Popular periodicals such as the *New Annual Register* reported on the ongoing hostilities in Haiti by clearly aligning with Christophe because of his "valour, humanity and good sense".[37] While this level of enthusiasm for the president was hardly abundant, British newspapers at this time generally did seem to accept Haiti's new leader and routinely referred to the president in a respectful, albeit restrained, manner. Therefore, reports that addressed Christophe in this way are evidence that some observers were anxious to see the new Haitian leader treated with a certain amount of respect, dignity and, perhaps more importantly, with recognition of his political legitimacy.[38]

At the heart of a number of respectful depictions of Haiti's new leader was the potential of a prosperous trading relationship between Britain and the Haitian state. Gaffield's work has highlighted the fact that in the early years of Christophe's leadership, Britain remained Haiti's best hope of establishing a prosperous commercial relationship—a relationship that the Haitian government hoped would evolve into official recognition of Haiti's sovereignty from the British government. However, as Gaffield demonstrates, despite the best efforts of Christophe and British merchants, British ministers were unwilling to recognize formally the Haitian state.[39] Despite this, Britain allowed trading with Haiti to continue, and British merchants continued to agitate for official diplomatic recognition from the British government in order to better protect the commercial interests that existed in Haiti and to better promote the prospect of future commercial endeavours with the young Haitian state. As a part of this early campaign to promote trade, a number of newspapers clearly saw the need to present Christophe as a fair and viable political leader—and, importantly, one who was particularly biased towards Britain and her commercial interests.

Christophe's agency in gaining this support cannot be overlooked, and he was largely successful in securing the assistance of key figures that had the potential to promote his and Haiti's legitimacy as viable trading partners. In particular, despite being approached by both Haitian presidents, Jean Gabriel Peltier sided with Christophe. Peltier's newspaper, *l'Ambigu*, was apparently very influential for foreign audiences and in "shaping international and local opinion."[40] In October 1807, Peltier also wrote a memoir to the British minister Robert Stewart detailing the advantages of a treaty between Britain and Haiti, as well as the commercial dangers to Britain of not signing such a treaty. A key message of the memoir was the advantageous nature of Christophe's character, the legitimacy of his reign, and the illegitimacy of Pétion's apparently-rogue government. While there is little evidence of direct mention of the memoir in British newspaper reports at this time, the positivity with which Christophe was received suggests that Peltier's propaganda campaign received a wider audience than perhaps he had first anticipated.

A number of British newspapers at this time actively looked to legitimise the Haitian president in their promotion of trade with the Haitian state. The *Morning Post*, for example, predicted that news of Christophe's apparent openness to trade with commercial nations would be positively received by its readers. The *Post* printed reports written by members of

Christophe's government that depicted Haiti as a safe place with which to trade.[41] At the heart of reports such as these was the idea that Christophe was "decidedly in the interest of England", as opposed to Pétion who was "supposed to have an understanding with Bonaparte".[42] The story that Christophe was in fact of "British birth", and the fact that his government was "composed of men who have had the honour to serve his British majesty", further strengthened the idea that the northern president was someone with whom the British could, and should, do business.[43] Reports such as those in the *New Annual Register* emphasised their eagerness for a treaty of commerce to be established with Christophe, even while the civil war with Pétion continued to rage.[44]

The fact that potential trade opportunities were a decisive factor in the depictions of Christophe and his government was exemplified by the reporting found in the *Caledonian Mercury*. Where the *Mercury* had earlier responded with scepticism of Christophe's government, only a couple of years later its tone changed decidedly. By 1809, the newspaper asserted that the Haitian president possessed "a steady and determined spirit, not elated with success, nor depressed with adversity" and that the "patience and perseverance" of Christophe had instilled "confidence...into the public mind". The *Mercury* claimed that "nature" had given Christophe "all those essential qualities of body and mind, which could give vigour and effect to his government". More than this, the *Mercury* admitted that its favouritism of Christophe over Pétion was ultimately because it believed it was Christophe who could give the "best guarantee of the British interests in that part of the world".[45] This marked a significant reversal from the early doubts of the *Mercury* of the permanency and value of Christophe's first constitution. Instead, the newspaper now published proclamations of the Haitian president, including Christophe's 1809 speech in celebration of the anniversary of Haitian independence—a speech which the *Mercury* concluded would "reflect the honour on any statesman".[46]

For some publications, the legitimacy of Christophe's presidency—and therefore support for trade relations with the Haitian leader—mostly centred on his apparent plans to implement political and social stability within northern Haiti. Reports in *The Annual Register* wrote approvingly of Christophe's decision to take the "modest title of the president of the Hayti" and stressed that the Haitian president held "a regard to the true interests of his country". This extended to the apparent designs of his new government to "repair the havock [sic] and devastation of Hayti [sic], by the establishment of just laws, social order, [and] a freedom of trade". The

*Register* rather bizarrely attempted to assert England's agency in the apparent progress of Haiti under Christophe by claiming that Christophe's faith in the "personal character of the English" extended to his desire in establishing commercial relations with "the only people that had stood forth of regular government and law". That Haiti's stable government was apparently an indirect result of England's own governmental virtues was an interesting approach to eliciting public support for a commercial alliance with Christophe. But the *Register* also suggested that England's government already had reasons to view Christophe on friendly terms by claiming that he had imprisoned Haitians who had planned to export Haiti's revolution to Jamaica. This led the *Register* to conclude that "[it] was impossible for the British government to be otherwise than on good terms with such a neighbour". By alluding to British colonies as neighbours of Haiti—and by suggesting that Christophe had the power to stop or allow Haiti's revolutionary spirit to influence is allies—the *Register* was able to insist that without an alliance with the new Haitian state, the British government would be placing its colonies in extreme peril, and that they too could be subjected to such revolutionary upheaval.[47]

Central to the *Register*'s attempts to legitimise an alliance with President Christophe was the glowing portrayal of his 1807 constitution. As Sibylle Fischer has demonstrated, constitutions were an important display of sovereignty from Haiti's early governments, and this is something that publications such as the *Register* were attuned to as they argued for the legitimisation of Christophe's government.[48] The *Register* reported fondly that the constitution was "founded on a moral and religious basis" and that it "breathes a spirit of moderation, justice [and] political wisdom". Christophe was portrayed as having the vision necessary to secure Haiti's political and economic future—something reflected in his constitution, which encompassed "enlarged views of the true interests of Hayti, in its foreign and its internal relations". For the *Register*, the constitution was evidence of the minimal risk involved with trading with the Haitians: property was secure and the report seemed to approve of the death penalty for murder. Such was the *Register*'s enthusiasm for Christophe's constitution, that it aligned Christophe with the venerated Toussaint for his "patriotism, virtues, and talents, for government, as well as war"—virtues that were apparently evident in Christophe's "code".

The positivity with which the *Register* reported on the constitution is evidence of how pro-trade supporters sought to legitimise the notion of a trade alliance with Haiti. But it also reflects a wider belief from some

3 PRESIDENT CHRISTOPHE AND COMMERCIAL LEGITIMACY    85

British observers of who were the types of political leaders with whom Britain should be aligning themselves. In addition to printing commentary on Christophe's code, the *Register* also printed a proclamation by Christophe in which he denounced the "rebel" Pétion. In language extremely similar to that used by British loyalists to scorn Napoleon, the proclamation attacked Pétion for exposing his people to "massacre" in order to serve his own ambition, and it claimed that the "CANNIBAL Petion shed such deluges of blood". Accusations of ambition at any cost were commonplace in British attacks of Napoleon, as were portrayals of the French revolutionary leader as blood thirsty and cannibalistic. In this way, the *Register* clearly saw Christophe's proclamation as a potential avenue for further support and sympathy from British loyalists. Indeed, in its commentary on the Haitian constitution, the *Register* claimed approvingly that it had been written collaboratively, with a number of advisers having a hand in it. This was an important suggestion as this was one way to distance Christophe from the claims of absolutism that formed the basis of British denunciations of leaders such as Napoleon. In this way, the Haitian leader was again portrayed as a legitimate leader, and one whose friendship would reflect well on Britain's claims of honour and virtue in its international political dealings.

An 1809 article found in John Aikin's periodical *The Athenaeum* perhaps best exemplifies both the desire among some British observers for trade relations with Christophe at this time and the importance of asserting the Haitian president's legitimacy in eliciting this support. As editor of *The Athenaeum*, Aikin had previously published positive accounts of support for the new Haitian state, including an 1807 obituary of Dessalines that passionately defended the emperor's character, honour and achievements as leader of the nation state. After Christophe came to power, it is clear that Aikin continued to view Haitian independence in a positive light, and he more strongly advocated the need for a political and economic olive branch to be extended to the Haitian president in the April 1809 edition of his influential periodical. Where Aikin had personally penned the 1807 obituary to Dessalines, this report on Christophe allegedly came in the form of a letter from a priest who resided in Cape Francois. Whether or not the letter was genuine, the format of such a report gave it an air of credibility in its promotion of the present situation of the Haitian state. The letter stated that its purpose was to present an authoritative account of the "moral and domestic situation of the island".[49]

The letter looked to appeal to the interests of British merchants by stressing that Haiti was in a prosperous state, with the author claiming that in Cape Francois he was "in the midst of the most perfect abundance". Haiti was portrayed as a "terrestrial Paradise", one that was abundant in produce and resources. The author even cheekily referred to reports of the Prince of Wales's growing penchant for debauchery by claiming that "The Prince of Wales could not live better than we do". The author claimed that the promise of pay for his own work had been "fully realised" with no complications, thereby asserting the trustworthiness of Haitians when engaging in commercial partnerships. By referring to Haiti's apparently abundant resources, the high standard of living for those residing there, and the integrity of its citizens, the letter looked to persuade British merchants to "lose no time" in "forming a mercantile establishment here". The author warned merchants that other traders would soon establish their businesses on the island, and he urged British merchants to act hastily, asserting that the establishment of these businesses was inexpensive. There was also a suggestion that English goods had been too expensive for Haitian traders and that English merchants should consider reducing these costs for longer-term gains. This was, however, a minor possible downside in the overwhelmingly glowing portrayal of Haiti as a merchant's utopia and one that Britain needed to take advantage of.

Although the latter half of the report focused on appealing to British merchants in this way, the first half of the report preceded this by affirming Christophe as a viable, trustworthy and effective presidential leader. The letter constantly referred to the "general" and "president" in a respectful legitimisation of his titles. The author overtly suggested that the prosperity of the island as a whole was a direct result of the leadership of a president who "governs with great wisdom". The report highlighted the president's "probity" in a further assertion of the fact that merchants could trust the Haitian government in any potential commercial alliance. There were also numerous references to Christophe's sage economic management, and that he allegedly had no debts. The reference to being debt-free both legitimised Christophe as a leader who managed the public purse effectively and modestly, and it suggested to merchants that they would receive recompense immediately, which would have been an attractive proposition. This reference could also be read as another subtle criticism of the Prince Regent's use of public funds for his own personal pleasure, thereby providing British readers with an alternative model of political leadership to their soon-to-be king. The report also alluded to stability in

3 PRESIDENT CHRISTOPHE AND COMMERCIAL LEGITIMACY    87

Haiti and security for merchants because of Christophe's exemplary command of a respectful army—an army which, according to the report, would mean that Pétion would soon be "entirely destroyed" and that this would "contribute much to the general prosperity of the island". In this way, Christophe was legitimised as a president through the prosperity of the country, the organisation of military, and the general happiness found on the island, and this was obviously seen as key to promoting trade with Haiti more generally.

Only a couple of years after this early positivity, however, British newspapers soon began to paint a very different portrait of the Haitian leader. This shift in perception is again best exemplified by the depictions that began to emerge of Christophe in the pages of the *Caledonian Mercury*. Only a year after its glowing portrait of Christophe the "statesman", the *Mercury* was soon circulating reports of the "cruel" and "cunning" Haitian president. The Haitian government was now "despotic" and "Christophe's word is a law". The *Mercury* claimed that such was his tyranny, "when a criminal is brought before him…he orders him to be bayoneted on the spot". By the end of 1810, the *Mercury* would print reports from Haiti that even went so far to claim that Christophe had passed orders for Haitian troops to completely wipe out the lighter-skinned population of the country.[50] In this period, Christophe's image was also re-constructed by other newspapers and presented to the British public not as the "humane chief" but as the "rapacious" and "cruel" "Pirate".[51] This reversion to negative depictions of the Haitian leader demonstrates how quickly British perceptions of Christophe could shift in the early years of his rule.

A major factor in this increase in negativity towards Christophe within British newspapers was the emergence of stories that Christophe had seized American vessels and was treating merchants unfavourably and dishonourably. For example, the *Morning Post*—which, like the *Caledonian Mercury* had largely been receptive to Christophe until this point—now circulated reports from American newspapers of Christophe seizing American ships and coercing American sailors "into his service" and that he "strips and lacerates them and resorts to every violence which a ferocious tyrant can invent or inflict".[52] The *Caledonian Mercury* published similar stories titled "The Black Emperor of Hayti"—taken from the American press—that detailed the "contempt" with which Christophe apparently treated American merchants.[53]

Some years later British newspapers would in fact revel in Christophe's apparently preferential treatment of British merchants over Americans, but at this point in time they seemed alarmed at the political autonomy and even superiority that Christophe's seizing of the vessels represented. Only one year earlier the *Mercury* anticipated that Haiti and Britain would form a mutually beneficial commercial alliance.[54] However, by 1810 the *Mercury* had published a letter from Haiti which warned that "these blacks would give themselves airs if we would allow them"—therefore speculating that Christophe's Haiti was now operating independently to best serve its own interests.[55] Although Christophe's actions were against American merchants, they seemed to fuel fears of a black autonomous leader operating in the Atlantic—and, importantly, one operating under conditions that threatened both British commercial interests as well as the established racial hierarchy of Atlantic world politics. That the British navy was itself operating in a similar manner with the impressment of American seamen was an irony evidently lost on the authors of these kind of reports. Instead, it seemed that support for the black leader of Haiti was conditional on him acting in a milder and more moderate manner than the traditional (white) political leaders of the Atlantic. British loyalist writers were therefore keen to assert Britain's status as the ideological gatekeeper of what constituted legitimate political leaders overseas, and the conditions within they needed to operate to gain British approval.

Central to these denunciations of Christophe was a strategy that British observers had used against Dessalines some years earlier. By the 1810s, newspapers began to align Christophe with Napoleon to highlight the threat that these new, illegitimate leaders of post-revolutionary states posed to British commercial interests. Newspapers such as the *Morning Post* claimed that "CHRISTOPHE follows the example of NAPOLEON" in his seizure of the American vessels. As with Dessalines, the situating of Christophe as a threatening Other—along with Napoleon—relied on his political title. In this context, British newspapers began to attach more regularly the "Emperor" label to Christophe to frame him within this denunciation of post-revolutionary governance. Christophe was said to imitate "his brother NAPOLEAN [sic]" in the creation of lords and dukes and in the opulence of his government.[56] In reports of the ongoing conflict with Pétion's and Christophe's attempts to take over the whole of Haiti, Christophe's supposed thirst for expansion was rather dramatically aligned with that of Napoleon's. The *Chester Chronicle* even went so far as to place Napoleon's words directly in the mouth of the Haitian leader: "Christophe, imitating the language of another Emperor, gave out he intended to eat his Christmas dinner at Port au Prince!"[57] This alignment

## 3  PRESIDENT CHRISTOPHE AND COMMERCIAL LEGITIMACY    89

thus helped to reinforce the continuing British media campaign against Napoleon by asserting Christophe's legitimacy alongside that of the French emperor. Essentially, both leaders reinforced the other's illegitimacy. But, as with British depictions of Dessalines some years earlier, these representations also demonstrated a fear that Haiti's own postrevolutionary leader could go down the same path of destruction and conquest as his imperial brother—a path that could be disastrous to British commercial interests in the Caribbean.

## CONCLUSION

American and British writers that seemed to turn on Christophe—and that revisited claims of the Haitian leader's desire to reframe the northern Haitian state as an imperial form of government—would soon have felt justified when Christophe declared his intention to convert Haiti's republican government to a constitutional monarchy. But in the brief years of his presidency, the depictions of Christophe—and the contexts within which these were created—demonstrate how flexible transatlantic commentators were willing to be in their judgements of the Haitian leader. The prospect of commercial gain was often a key driver in American and British attempts to legitimise Haiti's northern president. This presidential title seemed to have afforded possibilities for commentators to claim that such support was not purely driven by a desire trade, but that it also aligned ideologically with both America and British perceptions of legitimate, effective governance. But when Christophe was judged to have operated with increasing aggression in the eyes of these commentators, even the commercial possibilities that would be opened up with an alliance with Christophe were not enough for newspapers and periodicals to continue to throw their weight behind the Haitian president. Rather, the need to evaluate and pass judgement on the parameters within which postrevolutionary leaders should operate—and to delegitimise those who acted outside of these boundaries—seemed to take precedence over calls for favourable commercial relationships to be formed.

## NOTES

1. *New York Spy*, 10 February 1807; *Caledonian Mercury*, 28 March 1807.
2. *Connecticut Gazette*, 11 February 1807; *Portland Gazette*, 16 February 1807; *Hull Packet*, 7 April 1807.

90  J. FORDE

3. Laurent Dubois, *Haiti: The Aftershocks of History* (New York: Metropolitan Books, 2012), 55.
4. Julia Gaffield, *Haitian Connections in the Atlantic World: Recognition after Revolution* (Chapel Hill: University of North Carolina Press, 2015), 1.
5. Gordon S. Wood, *Empire of Liberty: A History of the Early Republic, 1789–1815* (New York: Oxford University Press, 2009), 469.
6. *Connecticut Gazette*, 11 February 1807; *New York Spy*, 10 February 1807. Similar reports appeared in newspapers such as *Norfolk Gazette and Publick Ledger*, 9 February 1807; *Columbian Centinel*, 11 February 1807.
7. *Connecticut Gazette*, 11 February 1807; *The Democrat*, 14 February 1807.
8. See, for example: *Relf's Philadelphia Gazette*, 25 March 1807; *American and Commercial Advertiser*, 28 March 1807; *Poulson's American Daily Advertiser*, 2 April 1807.
9. Sybille Fischer, *Modernity Disavowed: Haiti and the Cultures of Slavery in the Age of Revolution* (Durham: Duke University Press, 2004), 227; Gaffield, *Haitian Connections*, 163.
10. *Mercantile Advertiser*, 24 February 1807.
11. Trenton Federalist 30 March 1807. Also published for example in *Republican Watch-Tower*, 3 April 1807; *Poulson's American Daily Advertiser* 2 April 1807.
12. *New York Commercial Advertiser*, 20 March 1807.
13. Wood, *Empire of Liberty*, 630.
14. For an overview of Jefferson's embargo and its largely hostile reception among northern merchants see Sara C. Fanning, "The Roots of Early Black Nationalism: Northern African Americans' Invocations of Haiti in the Early Nineteenth Century," *Slavery & Abolition* 28, no. 1 (2007), 66–67; Gaffield, *Haitian Connections*, 146–152.
15. *Mercantile Advertiser*, 31 March 1807.
16. *Eastern Argus*, 9 April 1807.
17. Ibid.
18. *New York Commercial Advertiser*, 20 January 1808.
19. *Evening Post*, 25 May 1808; *New York Herald*, 26 May 1810.
20. Wood, *Empire of Liberty*, 643.
21. *American Citizen*, 7 September 1810.
22. *Poulson's American Daily Advertiser*, 4 September 1810. For details of further claims made by American merchants about Christophe seizing ships and cargo in the 1810s see Julia Gaffield, "'Outrages on the Laws of Nations': American Merchants and Diplomacy after the Haitian Declaration of Independence," in Julia Gaffield, ed. *The Haitian Declaration of Independence: Creation, Context, and Legacy* (Charlottesville: University of Virginia Press, 2016), 171–173.

3 PRESIDENT CHRISTOPHE AND COMMERCIAL LEGITIMACY 91

23. C. B. Bow, "Waging War for the Righteous: William Eaton on Enlightenment, Empire, and Coup d'état in the First Barbary War, 1801–1805," *History* 101, no. 348 (2016), 701–708.
24. Linda K. Kerber, *Federalists in Dissent: Imagery and Ideology in Jeffersonian America* (Ithaca: Cornell University Press, 1980), 177–182.
25. Gaffield, "Outrages on the Laws of Nations," 171.
26. *Poulson's American Daily Advertiser* 4 September 1810; *American Citizen* 7 September 1810.
27. *Evening Post*, 25 May 1810; *New York Herald*, 26 May 1810.
28. *Evening Post*, 27 August 1810.
29. *Connecticut Mirror*, 3 September 1810: *Anti-Monarchist*, 5 September 1810.
30. This story was particularly widely reported. See for example, *Evening Post*, 25 May 1810; *New York* Herald, 26 May 1810; *Poulson's American Daily Advertiser*, 4 September 1810. Other newspapers reported on other seizures in the following months: *Columbian Centinel*, 30 January 1811.
31. See for example *Caledonian Mercury*, 28 March 1807; *Hull Packet*, 7 April 1807.
32. *Salisbury and Winchester Journal*, 30 March 1807.
33. *Caledonian Mercury*, 8 June 1807.
34. See for example, *Caledonian Mercury*, 1 June 1807; *Lancaster Gazette and General Advertiser*, 6 June 1807.
35. *Morning Chronicle*, 2 September 1807.
36. This same report was published in *Morning Post*, 1 January 1808; *Caledonian Mercury*, 4 January 1808.
37. *New Annual Register of the year 1807* (1809), 228–232.
38. It is worth noting that depictions at this time also tended to refer to the "rebel" and "cannibal" Pétion—often amidst rumours that he would soon strike up a trade agreement with Napoleon. See for example, *Morning Post*, 1 January 1808; *Caledonian Mercury*, 4 January 1808.
39. Gaffield, *Haitian Connections*, 155–175.
40. Ibid., 163.
41. *Morning Post*, 3 September 1807; 19 April 1808.
42. *Ipswich Journal*, 23 April 1808.
43. *Caledonian Mercury*, 20 June 1807.
44. *New Annual Register* of the year 1807 (1808), 348–349.
45. *Caledonian Mercury*, 3 April 1809.
46. *Caledonian Mercury*, 8 April 1809.
47. *New Annual Register of the year 1807* (1809), 228–232.
48. Fischer, *Modernity Disavowed*, 227–259.
49. *The Athenaeum: A Magazine of Literary and Miscellaneous Information* (London: 1809), 308–311.

50. *Caledonian Mercury*, 28 June 1810; 26 November 1810.
51. *Morning Post*, 18 July 1810.
52. Ibid.
53. *Caledonian Mercury*, 29 October 1810.
54. *Caledonian Mercury*, 3 April 1809.
55. *Caledonian Mercury*, 28 June 1810.
56. *Morning Post*, 6 May 1811.
57. *Chester Chronicle*, 1 February 1811. Port au Prince was the capital of Pétion's southern republic. This comment alluded to Napoleon's conquest of Vienna by Christmas of 1805, thereby suggesting that Christophe would follow Napoleon's lead and look to consolidate his power in the Americas.

CHAPTER 4

# King Christophe and the Question of Monarchical Legitimacy

By the middle of 1811, news had reached American and British newspapers that Henry Christophe had been crowned Henry I, King of Haiti in a ceremony performed with "great pomp" and a parade of over 10,000 Haitian troops in Cape Francois (present-day Cap-Haïtien). Before the day had concluded with a visit to the opera, the Haitian king had allegedly celebrated his coronation by riding all across the town to shower his new subjects with money.[1] Christophe's decision to transform the northern part of Haiti into a monarchy resulted in the establishment of the first and, as it would transpire, the only kingdom of Haiti. Exactly why Christophe abandoned his presidential status to become the self-proclaimed "first crowned monarch of the New World" has been the subject of increasing attention from historians.[2] Most notably, Sybille Fischer has discussed the "paradoxical" creation of Christophe's monarchy and his attempts to perform his legitimacy as a monarchical sovereign.[3] While historians had hitherto dismissed Christophe's monarchy as primarily emanating from "vanity", Fischer's work has demonstrated that the desire to consolidate and strengthen his power in Haiti and to assert racial equality with the other leaders of the Atlantic world were the motivating factors behind Christophe's change to a monarchical government.[4] In particular, it is now widely accepted that Christophe modelled his form of constitutional monarchy on the British example as part of his attempts to flatter Britain into officially recognising Haiti's independence.

© The Author(s) 2020          93

J. Forde, *The Early Haitian State and the Question of Political Legitimacy*, Palgrave Studies in Political History,
https://doi.org/10.1007/978-3-030-52608-5_4

The varying nature of depictions of King Christophe throughout his nine-year reign in American and British newspapers and periodicals highlights how the presence of a self-established hereditary monarchy in a post-revolutionary, post-colonial state clearly presented a significant number of challenges and opportunities to both supporters and opponents of Haiti at this time. Critics of King Christophe at times aligned him alongside the other self-created sovereigns of Europe—most notably Napoleon—to underline the illegitimacy of these self-created dynasties. Others, particularly in America, in fact underlined his monarchical status to expose the transparency and baselessness of traditional forms of monarchy (as exemplified in Britain).

Supporters, on the other hand, asserted that Christophe had an equal, if not better claim to legitimacy than the new European sovereigns such as Napoleon. Positive depictions such as these in Britain tended to praise Christophe for his decision to adopt a royal title, while American supporters excused his kingly status. In both cases, pro-Christophe accounts centred on the apparent progress Haiti had made under his guidance, thereby asserting the need for a sense of paternalism from heads of state—regardless of their mode of governance. Christophe's monarchical title thus became a significant heuristic tool for some observers by which to question the notion of legitimacy in Old and New World governments as well as to support the forms of government in their own respective countries. In turn, these calls to support or refute the Haitian monarch's claims to legitimacy contributed significantly to debates over whether the sovereignty of the Haitian state should be officially recognised by the governments of America and Britain.

Projections of Christophe's monarchical status—and American and British reactions to these depictions—need to be read in a wider context of transatlantic attitudes to traditional monarchies and post-revolutionary states in the 1810s. Christophe's monarchy was established in a period of time in which "a fundamental change occurred in the governing rules, norms, and practices of international politics".[5] American and British commentaries on the Haitian monarchy often had less to do with any real concerns for the progress of the Haitian kingdom itself and more to do with its value in supporting American and British political ideologies and modes of governance. Laurent Dubois has observed that Christophe's monarchy is often remembered as a kind of "historical joke", while Marlene Daut has pointed out that reports at the time often mocked the idea of a black monarchy.[6] While both observations are undoubtedly true, a significant number of contemporary representations of King Christophe often placed the Haitian monarchy in the centre of discussions of political legitimacy and the roles of monarchies in the Atlantic world in the early nineteenth century.

## A New World Monarch and American Perceptions of Legitimacy

Reports of Christophe's coronation as King of Haiti were circulated widely throughout the American press in 1811. Depictions of the newly created black court regularly emphasised Christophe's blackness in order to ridicule the apparent absurdity of a black king. Depictions of the "brilliant coronation" of "their sable majesties" made references to Christophe's "unchangeable ebony complexion and majestic form". Articles such as these adopted and mocked loyalist rhetoric to expose more fully the supposedly farcical nature of bowing to a black king. The "mighty Christophe" was allegedly adorned with a "golden crown" and the finest jewels while he sat on his "ivory throne". Exotic portrayals of "his colored majesty" undoubtedly played a significant role in this negative reception to a New World monarch—portrayals that were not as abundant during his presidency.[7] And so, if an autonomous black political leader could be tolerated for the purposes of trade, a black king was evidently more challenging to accept for an American audience. In this sense, Christophe's monarchical status would be equally, if not more, contentious than his race for American observers.

Christophe's new title meant that he was further aligned with his post-revolutionary imperial brother Napoleon, as some American newspapers looked for a conceptual framework within which to discuss this self-created New World king. In these reports, Christophe's apparent vanity and desire for imperial titles was a direct imitation of the French emperor. Newspapers such as the *New Jersey Journal* claimed that it was "difficult to tell which of the two, Christophe or Bonaparte, exceed each other in pomp and splendour".[8] Other newspapers such as *Poulson's Daily American Advertiser* drew parallels between the metaphorical birth of Haiti's king and the baptism of Napoleon's son—and the future King of Rome—which they stated "for splendour is full equal to the parade at Hayti".[9] Other reports insisted that the "plan of erecting a monarchy was in being a long time" but Christophe had "waited for the consent of the emperor of

France" before he proclaimed the Haitian monarchy.[10] The suggestion that the Haitian head of state looked for approval and permission from the detested Napoleon diminished Christophe's agency as a viable political leader, reducing him to a kind of mock monarch who was unable to display enlightened or individual political thought, and who instead waited for the approval of Europe's imperial leaders. But more than this, it allowed observers to question the legitimacy of both Christophe and Napoleon by drawing comparisons and exposing the apparent absurdity of replacing republican forms of government with the trappings of imperial government. In this sense, both Christophe and Napoleon asserted the other's illegitimacy as leaders of post-revolutionary states.

The question of Christophe's legitimacy would soon find an even more pertinent resonance only a couple of years after his coronation. By 1812 America was again at war with Britain—a conflict that would last until 1815. Jon Latimer has noted that by 1812, aside from a "pro-British Federalist minority" there was in fact "little to moderate" the "passionate" anti-British sentiments that had continued from America's revolutionary war.[11] As such, America's decision to go to war in part centred on the desire of Republicans to cement a republican national identity for America—an identity that had been threatened ever since independence from both the British and American Federalists.[12] Historians have argued that the War of 1812 "permanently altered the structure of American politics" and, in particular, led to a re-evaluation and reassertion of the superiority of America's republican form of government.[13] According to Gordon Wood, the culmination of the war "finally" established for Americans "the independence and nationhood of the United States that so many had previously doubted".[14] A large number of Americans at this time believed that the British monarchy not only represented a threat to America, but to the very concept of republicanism globally.[15] Therefore, American national identity was heightened as a result of their war—an identity that focused on America's otherness to the despotic and tyrannical hereditary dynasties of the Old World, as exemplified by Britain.

In the time during America's bitter struggle against Britain, but particularly after the war's end in 1815, denunciations of hereditary dynasties and the ideologies they asserted could be found with even more regularity in American newspapers. With hostilities between their old colonial masters reopened, American publications disdainfully mocked traditional claims to political power. In particular, Republican newspapers such as the *Essex Register* printed articles that rhetorically questioned what constituted a "legitimate" head of state.[16] In their eyes, the absurdity of Old World claims to legitimacy could be best exemplified by the situation in Britain. If the English monarchy was "truly legitimate" then, the *Register* asserted, "madness is a quality of legitimacy, since, in virtue of the legitimate claim, the old king, George III, continues to reign notwithstanding he is insane". The *Register* went on to question whether an English king— particularly one who was very publicly perceived as insane at this point—could still be a "legitimate" leader simply because of his hereditary title. The same report further wondered what else could be said of the Prince Regent, who was proof that "drunkenness, seduction, and undisguised salacity, are qualities of a legitimate monarch".

For other pro-Republican newspapers, Britain's new war against America was further proof of the tyranny and thirst for conquest of hereditary monarchs. The *National Advocate*, a Tammany newspaper, surmised that if the Prince Regent was seen to be avenging his father's loss of the American colonies in the War of Independence, in doing so "the HEREDITARY IDIOT evinced the legitimacy of his royal descent, and the legitimacy of his royal virtues".[17] Republican publications such as the Alexandria Herald questioned the basis of hereditary rule and the notion of royal blood as they outlined the scandalised lineage of the British monarchy—one that they claimed was tainted by the illicit affairs of its monarchs with prostitutes and servants.[18]

In addition to the impact that the War of 1812 had on political narratives, questions of legitimacy and the actions of Europe's dynasties were scrutinised even more intensely in America by 1815. In this year, Napoleon was defeated for a final time by the European allies, and the resultant Congress of Vienna aimed to restore and reinforce the political ideologies of traditional and monarchical forms of governance. Americans—particularly, but not exclusively, Republicans—perceived this meeting of "self-created august legislators" as an act that restored conservative and traditional power in Europe. This was seen to be especially the case with the restoration of the Bourbon monarchy in France, which was described in one newspaper as "the most scandalous abuse that ever has been made...of human reason among an enlightened people".[19] By perceiving this "conservative reaction" in Europe, "Americans were coming to believe that their democracy was all the more peculiar and significant".[20] In reaction to the Congress of Vienna, Republican-leaning newspapers in particular poured scorn on British and French claims to liberty and freedom to assert that these monarchies in contrast were in fact "crushing the rights of the world to elevate the usurped authority of sceptres".[21] Despite the alleged aims of the Congress to unite Europe once more and restore peace and order, such reports argued that "Europe can never know peace, or repose, or happiness, so long as the present inhuman and unnatural dynasties exist; so long as *legitimacy* has either its present meaning or power".[22] Republican supporters situated American republicanism directly opposite the "monstrous principles of Monarchy, or what is now falsely styled 'legitimacy'", arguing that these dynastic forms of power had "enslaved and degraded Europe, and threaten to bind the civilised World in chains".[23]

The War of 1812 led American observers to depict the republican movements in Spanish America in the 1810s as evidence of the virtues of republicanism. According to Caitlin Fitz, this prompted a "wave of nationalism" among American observers as they imagined "the Western Hemisphere as a happily independent republican community at a time when Europe seemed to be crumbling under the weight of dynastic alliances and monarchical tyranny".[24] Whether a continuation of Christophe's presidency and his republican mode of governing would have meant that Haiti would have been included in this celebration of republicanism is uncertain. What is clear is that his adoption of monarchy meant that in general Haiti would not only be excluded from celebratory narratives or republicanism, but Christophe's kingdom would be used by some Americans as a model of the oppressive nature of monarchy.

Representations of Christophe in America at this time, therefore, need to be considered within the political atmosphere in which they were constructed, although a number of negative reports of the Haitian king undoubtedly were motivated by the monarch's race. Newspapers such as Georgetown's *The Messenger*, for example, claimed that Christophe's "imitation" of monarchy was "proof" that "negroes were a species of monkey", while other newspapers claimed that Christophe "aped royalty".[25] As a result of the War of 1812 and conservative events in Europe, however, a majority of Americans on both sides of the political spectrum had come to believe that their nation remained as "the only beacon of republicanism...in a thoroughly monarchical world".[26] At a time then when American criticisms of Europe's dynasties was at a fever pitch—and such denunciations were increasingly tied into Americans' assertions of their own national identity—garnering support for a Haitian monarchy supposedly imitating such models of power would have been particularly challenging. After all, if some newspapers at this time claimed that "all the solemn farces which have been played off man, that of hereditary kings is the most silly", then how could newspapers offer concurrent support for the Haitian monarch?[27]

From as early as 1812, a number of both Republican and Federalist newspapers publicly stated their wish to see the removal of the newly founded Haitian monarchy from the Atlantic stage. Federalist-leaning publications such as the *New-England Palladium* went as far to report rather hopefully on the death of Christophe in 1812 and, more importantly, the death of his "Imperial Government".[28] Other pro-federalist newspapers such as the *Hallowell Gazette* framed Christophe as a tyrannical despot unworthy of his title, claiming that he "inspires terror in the capital whenever he shews [sic] himself in public".[29] Whether reports such as these were evidence of Federalists turning their backs on traditional forms of power, or whether Christophe's monarchy was an affront to the sanctity of these forms, is unclear. Either way, his presence was certainly unwelcome.

But the value that demonizing the Haitian king held, was most exploited by Republicans who wished to reinforce their dislike of Old World forms of political power. The *True American—published* and edited by James J. Wilson, future Democratic-Republican senator—stated that it recognised the presence of "the first crowned monarch of the New World", while wishing "this is the last".[30] Where President Christophe had earlier found pockets of support, the Haitian monarch was now suddenly caught in a Republican tide of overwhelming animosity towards kings and the very concept of royalty. The image of "that monster, Christophe, the soi-disant king of Hayti" became seared in the minds of the readers of pro-Republican publications.[31]

The image of a tyrannical King Christophe, therefore, allowed some American observers—particularly Republican-leaning ones—to not only call into question the legitimacy of Christophe's rule, but also that of the hereditary dynasties of Europe. In this way, Christophe was aligned with European monarchs, and his legitimacy as a king was asserted to expose the perceived absurdity of claims that monarchism represented a superior form of political leadership. The Haitian king was said to be "resolved to be behind hand with no monarch, Oriental or European," and American newspapers with Republican sympathies thus subjected him to the same savage rhetoric as his brother sovereigns, such as the "lunatic" George III or the "bloated idiot" the Prince Regent.[32] As scholars have highlighted, newspapers tended to italicise Christophe's royal titles in order to mock them and to call into question their legitimacy.[33] But, in fact, this was in keeping with reports that did the same with the titles of Europe's monarchs. As such, Christophe achieved a sense of parity in the disdain he elicited.

As well as emulating these European monarchs, newspapers such as *The Republican* framed Christophe as the epitome of the corrupting nature of imperial titles and the "trappings of royalty" as he was "as jealous of his royal titles as any white legitimate in any part of the world".[34] In these reports, Christophe's perceived imitation was not simply a point of ridicule, but it represented a genuine desire from within the New World to adopt the maxim of constitutions such as Britain's which asserted the "king can do no wrong"". Therefore Christophe, "seeing no reason why the tribute of infallibility should not as well belong to a king of Hayti as to a king of England", demonstrated for sections of the Republican press the infectious trend for monarchies not only in Europe but now threatening to take hold in the New World—a trend that was the opposite of American political identity, and one of which some editors and journalists were clearly fearful.

While attacks on Christophe in American newspapers were consistent with an anti-monarchical agenda, the publication that possibly made most use of the Haitian monarchy as a vehicle for derisions of royalty and notions of legitimacy was the widely read *Niles' Weekly Register*. Founded in Baltimore in 1811 by Hezekiah Niles, the paper "achieved a wide and deservedly high reputation".[35] Although the *Register* was said to not side with a particular party on social and political issues, Niles's Anglophobia and derision for all forms of monarchy was clearly apparent, particularly in editions published in the aftermath of the War of 1812 and the restoration of conservatism in Europe by the mid-1810s.[36] Niles left no sense of ambiguity when, in an article scorning the Congress of Vienna, he proclaimed: "I hate all monarchies".[37] The British—the "dear friends" of legitimacy—were a particular focus of attack in the *Register*, as Niles blamed Britain's social and economic "distresses" at this time on their attachment to royalty.[38] Niles wrote approvingly of Napoleon's brief ousting of the French monarchy in the Hundred Days War, believing that "his establishment on the throne will do more than anything else I can think of, to put down the foul doctrine as to the 'legitimacy of princes'—a doctrine the most hateful of any that has affected the human race".[39]

With Napoleon soon removed from power once more and the Bourbons restored again, Niles turned to King Christophe to call into question the notion of hereditary legitimacy and to chastise those who supported it. The *Register* sought to directly align Christophe with his "brother sovereigns" in order to underline the alleged absurdity of monarchical legitimacy.[40] The *Register* reported on the celebrations of Christophe's anniversary in 1816 by summarising that they were done "with a pomp and manner...to make us laugh at legitimacy".[41] Reports in the *Register* at times drew on this "laughter" by emphasising the blackness of Christophe and his court and by relying on racist ideologies of the time. One such report, described by Marlene Daut as "all-out mockery", depicted the Haitians as "acting royalty" and detailed the members of Christophe's court: "the countess of Lime Punch...the baroness Big Bottom...count Quince-jelly".[42] As Daut asserts, reports such as this were designed to mock the concept of a black monarchy and to "link Christophe's blackness to imitation, robbery, treachery, and jealousy", thereby delegitimising the very notion of a black hereditary monarchy.[43]

Although these reports undoubtedly relied on negative racial perceptions to mock the Haitian court, they were also designed to mock the concept of royalty as a whole. The explicit lesson of Haiti was that if even the "poor despised negroes" could establish a monarchy (and by this time have sustained the institution), then clearly this proved the baseless and transparent nature of hereditary monarchy.[44] The *Register*'s report concluded, therefore, that it hoped its depiction of Christophe's court would be viewed "as a curiosity of royalty, as for the benefit of all who desire 'to laugh and to be fat' at the fools and knaves who applaud it—black or white".[45] These kinds of reports served a dual purpose. Not only did they discard any serious contemplation of Christophe's monarchy and authority, as Daut suggests, but they also served to undermine the significance of legitimacy and tradition so often used by supporters of hereditary monarchies. In essence, these reports were not simply designed to mock the presence of a black monarchy in the New World, but to expose the frivolity of monarchies everywhere.

In order to manipulate representations of Christophe to contribute to this anti-monarchical discourse, the *Register* looked to assert Christophe's tyrannical nature, while simultaneously claiming his legitimacy as a monarchical sovereign. A number of reports published by the *Register* often painted a picture of Christophe as an irrational, vengeful monarch with the "fury of a tyger".[46] But, for the *Register*, the Haitian monarchy was not a site of exceptional cruelty; rather, it was an insight into the commonplace world of monarchical tyranny. The *Register* reported that, under the

Haitian monarchy, the "people are wretched—grievously oppressed. His word is law. His nod is fate," and King Christophe "claims both people and territory as his own property".[47] But at the same time such reports asserted Christophe's legitimacy and that he had "an equal right to exclaim with Lear: "I'm every inch a king"". In the face of continuing reluctance of European countries—as well as America—to recognise his imperial title, Christophe had "a right to maintain his dignity as any" and ultimately he was "more truly a legitimate king than three fourths of them".[48] The idea that the Haitian monarchy's claim to sovereignty was in fact "much better founded…than many of those who have subscribed to the 'holy league'" was a constant theme in the *Register* at this time.[49] Other reports drew on parallels between the Queen of Haiti and Princess Charlotte of Britain and asked readers of the *Register* to determine "whether the *Haytian Queen* or the heir apparent of the *British throne*, exceeds in splendour".[50] However, when these reports asserted that "[n]one of the European legitimates surpasses him in the most princely qualities", the purpose was not only to present Christophe as a social and political other to the citizens of the early American republic but simultaneously as an "equal" to the tyrannical monarchs and emperors of the Old World.[51]

## AMERICAN DEFENCES OF KING CHRISTOPHE

By the time that reports such as the ones found in Niles's *Register* were being circulated, Christophe would have undoubtedly been aware of the increasingly negative press in America relating to his character and his kingdom. Similarly aware of the power of the American press in attempting to foster support for the recognition of the sovereignty of the kingdom of northern Haiti, Christophe's secretary—Baron de Vastey—set about publishing a number of pamphlets and books that were designed to defend passionately both the Haitian Revolution and Christophe's regime. Vastey was a mulatto Haitian, educated in France and who became known as "the most prominent voice of post-independence Haiti".[52] Much has been said elsewhere asserting the significance of Vastey's writing, which was often and purposefully circulated among American and European audiences. And, as a number of scholars have observed, most of Vastey's writings contained defences and justifications of both Christophe's reign and his adoption of a monarchical government.[53] In particular, Doris Garraway has argued that Vastey's defence of Haiti's monarchical system was "an attempt to argue for its belonging within the modern Atlantic world".[54]

Vastey wrote against the racist depictions of Christophe and his court, and he attached this fear to a prevailing and ruling ideology of "white privilege" and the fear of a black king.[55] He defended the adoption of monarchy as the only suitable form of government for Haiti, and he simultaneously criticised republicanism as an unstable form of governance—as seen in the allegedly chaotic republic of Pétion. As Marlene Daut observes, these writings were important not just for European audiences but also to an American one largely scathing of Old World monarchies and any imitation of them. Vastey clearly saw the importance of justifying Christophe's mode of government in order to secure approval from British and American audiences that would then hopefully transfer into support for Haitian recognition. Daut also claims that this was largely successful in America as northern newspapers "began internalizing Vastey's own understanding of the meaning of Haitian independence for the [Western] hemisphere".[56] Certainly, as Daut asserts, American newspapers appeared to be more supportive of Christophe's monarchy from 1816—possibly because of a growing awareness among American audiences of Vastey's work. However, Doris Garraway claims that there is in fact little evidence of detailed, sustained engagement with Vastey's work in American newspapers until after his death in 1820. Whether Americans immediately "internalised" Vastey's arguments or not, what is clear is that despite the negative and resentful reporting of publications, such as Niles's *Weekly Register*, Christophe certainly found pockets of support during the mid-1810s.

From 1816, reports began to emerge in American newspapers—largely those with Federalist sympathies—that tried to counter the claims that Christophe was the epitome of monarchical tyranny. Such reports would have strengthened calls for the American government to formally recognise the Haitian state—something which, in turn, would help to secure and promote the commercial interests of American merchants. Newspapers such as the *Hampden Federalist* thus claimed that the Haitian king was "at peace with the world".[57] Others criticised the derision of Christophe based on his title by claiming that both governments of Haiti sat comfortably side by side, and that both Christophe and Pétion practised "the axiom of the poet: 'For forms of government lets fools contest / That which is best administered is best'".[58]

The extent of Christophe's tyranny was questioned by reports of his "shrewd and judicious" form of governing. While there were concessions to the "imperfections" of his government, the Federalist-supporting *Albany Gazette*, for example, stressed the need that "some allowance" needed to be made because of the "heterogeneous nature of those materials which he has had to mould into order and subordination".[59] Other Federalist reports instead focused on Christophe's "achievements" and the "progress" Haiti had made under his leadership. It was said that Christophe was "wisely providing for the civilization and improvement of his country", that he had been "very liberal in his patronage of science," and that he had "richly endowed a number of seminaries and public schools".[60] In this way, reports tried to replace the image of Christophe the cruel with Christophe the benevolent.

This positivity towards Christophe was not intended to offer support for monarchies everywhere. In some cases, it was quite the opposite. For newspapers such as the *Albany Gazette*, Christophe's endeavours to fortify Haiti's defences, to educate all Haitians (including, importantly, children), and his supposed successes in implementing law and order in Haiti offered a direct contrast to the "chaos" found in Europe. According to the *Gazette*, France was "environed by hostile armies", while England was the site of constant "tumults and riots". And while "these disgraceful events" were "marking the history of the present day in those governments", Americans apparently "read of no outrages, no riots" in Christophe's Haiti—leading the *Gazette* to wonder: "Would not the government of France shrink from a comparison with the government of Hayti?"[61]

Rather than these reports lending themselves to ideological debates of legitimacy, they served a distinct practical purpose. Alongside reports of education and military defences in Haiti flourishing under Christophe, other accounts asserted more directly the commercial stability and opportunities found in Haiti. American readers were told: "The commerce of the world [France excepted] is invited to [Haiti's] luxuriant shores".[62] Newspapers with Federalist sympathies seemed to be particularly keen on promoting Christophe's kingdom as a legitimate and secure political power with which to trade. Although trade between America and Haiti had been legal since 1810, the numerous embargoes on American trade with Haiti had served a damaging blow to American merchants in the Caribbean. As a result, British merchants had profited considerably in the region.

Equally damaging to American merchants had been the numerous trade embargoes with Britain and its colonies that were enacted during the War of 1812. In the aftermath of the war, by 1816 it appears that a number of American newspapers—largely Federalist publications—viewed the Haitian kingdom as a potential solution to the woes of America's international merchants and promoted Haiti as a lucrative commercial partner. Publications such as the *Hampden Federalist* and the *Hallowell Gazette* claimed that "[c]ommerce and the culture of the soil was improving in his dominions" and that, as a result, the Haitian economy was in such a prosperous state that Christophe could "show more money than the Bank of England".[63] These same reports attested to the growing ease with which merchants would be able to conduct business with a population that was being educated in English, as well as French, "for commercial and political purposes".[64] Some newspapers sought to neutralise memories of the 1804 massacres by reporting that in Haiti "whites are [as] equally protected and respected as the men of colour".[65] Even *Niles' Weekly Register* demonstrated the multiplicity of Haiti's political value by publishing —at the same time of its denunciations of Christophe's monarchical title—reports that claimed a white person could travel in Haiti "with as much security as I could have done in any part of Great Britain".[66] Such reports were direct responses to accounts of Christophe's alleged contempt of American merchants—a claim that was exacerbated by stories of Americans being hanged by the Haitian king that emerged by the beginning of 1816.[67] But according to Niles's *Register*, as long as foreign merchants abided by Haitian laws (which were "equitable", "founded on the basis of justice" and "rigidly" enforced) and paid their taxes (which were "reasonable") then Haiti was a site of commercial opportunity and safety because although Haitians were "resolved to live free or perish", they were equally "desirous to live in friendship with all men".[68]

Such allusions to the peaceful and secure nature of Christophe's kingdom would have supported the call for the American government to formally recognise Haiti—recognition that would lead to better conditions in which American merchants could operate. Within such positive depictions, the question of Christophe's legitimacy as political sovereign and his position in relation to other Atlantic world leaders played a significant role. Newspapers such as the *Albany Gazette* aligned Christophe with the post-revolutionary leaders of Latin America and questioned why editors around the country were "enlisted in favour of the pretended patriots of South America" and yet "the hand of friendship and assistance" was not extended to their "brethren of St. Domingo".[69] The *Gazette* claimed that by denying Haiti's agency, this was a direct affront to the American maxim of equality among all men. The report suggested that this approach to

Haiti was indicative of hypocrisy in the reporting of American politics and particularly in allusions to the meaning of republicanism. Although both "Christophe and Petion rebelled against that monster '*Legitimacy*'", the paper decried the lack of support for Haiti from their republican neighbours, and it concluded by suggesting that the silence among America's newspapers on the subject came from the fact that "St. Domingo at the time of the rebellion, belonged to the father of republicanism, Bonaparte—and having remained silent upon the subject so long, they are now ashamed to agitate it".[70] As observed by the *Gazette*, the reluctance of American newspapers to frame Haiti's struggle for independence within celebrations of the independent movements in South America most likely stemmed from "the circumstance of their skin being a shade or two darker than that of the Spaniards". Other reports supported the stance of the *Gazette* by stating: "if we open a negociation [sic], it must be on a footing as we would establish with any other nation".[71]

Although these kinds of reports were rare, they demonstrated a willingness among some American observers to situate Haiti directly alongside the other trading nations of the Atlantic world. These commentaries sought to distance the Haitian king from reports that aligned him with the monarchs of the Old World by framing him within discussions that celebrated the revolutionary leaders of Latin America. Such depictions in turn called on memories of America's own revolutionary past and the struggles of its leaders to establish independence in the hostile political world of the Atlantic. Christophe's titles and the apparent legitimacy of these were, therefore, a constant point of contention in America throughout his reign. Across the Atlantic, depictions of Christophe and the Haitian monarchy would be similarly dependent on the unique socio-political domestic conditions in Britain and would be equally contentious and contradictory in their nature.

## British Reactions to the Emergence of a New World King

When news emerged of the coronation of a black king in the Caribbean—and one who apparently styled himself on the British sovereign—British conservative newspapers reacted negatively to news that their own cherished form of monarchy had been mimicked. If Christophe had hoped that his turn to monarchy would increase his popularity in Britain, and that this would translate into diplomatic recognition of Haiti from the British government, this initially backfired in the British press.[72] British newspapers sneered at the "spectacle" of a black monarchy and the presence of a "sable monarch". Christophe's blackness reduced him to a primal and volatile figure who was said to be "thirsting after the baubles of regal splendour".[73] For others—such as the loyalist *York Herald*—Christophe's kingly status made a mockery of the traditional form of monarchy on which Britain had been built. His adoption of monarchical practices was apparently "amusing enough", but much more serious for the newspaper was when "this would-be-Sovereign had the audacity to rise up, and drink to—'*His Brother* the King of Great Britain.'"[74] For the *Herald*, copying Britain's form of governance was one thing, but to allude to any closeness or direct alignment between the Haitian and British monarchies was a step too far and too close for comfort. Reports claimed that the Haitian king was not only violent but a "determined enemy" of the British, and some publications even very publicly wished for "an end to the Imperial Government of St. Domingo, and its sable Dukes, Count Marshals &c."[75] According to newspapers such as the *Observer*, Christophe's followers affectionately referred to their monarch as the "'Avenger of the African Race'", thereby depicting the presence of a black sovereign as a potential threat to British interests in the Caribbean.[76] Other reports looked to continue the narrative that Haiti would inspire the slaves of Britain's colonies to revolt as Christophe was said to have been looking to export the spirit of the Haitian Revolution throughout the Caribbean.[77]

The rhetoric found in reports such as these, and the lack of positive reactions to his coronation, certainly point to a reluctance among the British press to conceive of and accept a black monarch. Indeed, at times these reports directly expressed indignation at the subversion of racial hierarchy that the Haitian monarchy represented. As with British depictions of Dessalines, however, these reports cannot be read only through the prism of a British fear of the presence of a black imperial sovereign. They also need to be considered in conjunction with the anxieties of a British population that continued to debate the concept of legitimate political rule—a debate that had been sparked by the upheaval of traditional hierarchies throughout Europe and the formidable rise of Napoleon. Despite rare exceptions, British radicals and reformers largely ignored the Haitian monarchy in their writing, perhaps because they thought it best to avoid the issue of a post-revolutionary society apparently choosing to style itself on the very monarchy they opposed.[78] But where radical writers clearly saw little value in the Haitian monarchy to further their political causes, the Haitian king became a regular fixture in loyalist writings in the 1810s. Christophe, the illiterate ex-slave who had risen to control the wealthiest colony in the New World, was often derided as part of a more general loyalist narrative aimed at denying agency or legitimacy to these new forms of power. In other words, Christophe's blackness, rather than being the reason for these negative depictions, became for some observers a tool with which to deride post-revolutionary leaders in general, particularly those who dared to claim an imperial title.

The Glorious Revolution of 1688 meant that the question of post-revolutionary legitimacy and the rights of kings had been a constant point of contention in Britain. William III's revolutionary succession meant that the topic of where Britain's monarchical government derived its legitimacy from was a highly contentious topic throughout the eighteenth century. Loyalists and reformers debated—often with each other—the legacy of England's revolution and where Britain's monarchical government ultimately derived its own legitimacy.[79] By the end of the eighteenth century, British radicals increasingly looked to the events of 1688 in their calls for political reform and to assert their right to publicly question a government and monarch that was seen to be acting outside of the parameters of the nation's constitution.[80] With the emergence of Napoleon's dynastic form of governance in the 1800s, English loyalists had to find a way to deride the French emperor without calling into question the basis upon which the English monarch and the House of Hanover had been deemed legitimate.[81] For loyalist writers, therefore, the newly created Haitian kingdom became a way to underline the apparent illegitimacy of Napoleon's imperial title in a way that reduced the risk of England's own monarchy being dragged into the debate.

In the early years of Henry I's reign, the self-created nature of his imperial title was constantly emphasised in British reports that sought to delegitimise the Haitian sovereign.[82] A number of these reports at the same time denied the Haitian sovereign a kingly title and aligned him alongside his political "brother" Napoleon.[83] This imagined fraternity also extended to the nature of the absolutist rule of the "Black Emperor", who was said to have acted with unbounded cruelty towards his subjects, and who expected obedience from them to the point of subservience.[84] Reports such as these were almost identical to conservative narratives that attacked the tyrannical nature of Napoleon's leadership, while at the same time reminding British readers that such tyranny was thankfully missing from their own more inclusive constitutional monarchy.[85]

## Abolitionists and the Troubling Agency of King Christophe

Although British negativity towards Christophe's monarchy would remain for the first few years of its existence, representations of King Christophe increased significantly in both volume and positivity from the mid-1810s. This has been largely attributed by historians to the influence of British abolitionists.[86] Within the first few years of his reign, Christophe set about trying to improve his popularity in Britain by looking to secure British abolitionists as key advocates of the Haitian monarchy. Christophe's aides printed copies of his proclamations and other state papers in English and sent them to William Wilberforce and Thomas Clarkson—two of the foremost leaders of the British abolition movement. Clarkson responded particularly enthusiastically, leading to a period of correspondence between the Haitian king and British abolitionists that would last until Christophe's death in 1820. In this time, abolitionists provided advice and guidance to the Haitian king of how to best secure prosperity for the nation.[87] They also assisted Christophe in his plans to implement an education system accessible to all members of Haitian society by providing educational resources, including teachers, and Christophe would eventually implement these plans with remarkable success.[88]

The work of historians such as David Geggus has shown how Haiti became "a crucial test case for ideas about race and about the future of colonial slavery" for British abolitionists.[89] Abolitionist publications reflected this renewed interest in Haiti and responded positively to Christophe's overtures in the 1810s as they depicted the apparent progress found in Haiti as proof of the capability for the moral improvement of a post-slave society. But reports such as these were often framed within narratives that praised the apparent progress of the Haitian state more generally, with few direct references to Christophe. The kinds of books and pamphlets by supporters of abolition that were produced about Toussaint Louverture some years previously were never constructed for Christophe. James Stephen even chose to edit and republish his "history" of Toussaint Louverture in 1814 rather than engage with the current leader of the Haitian state.[90] Likewise, whereas Wilberforce privately claimed to pray for the Haitian king on a daily basis, he at the same time instructed fellow abolitionists to "keep Haiti in the background" until it was better able to "stand on its own two legs"—this in itself a telling indicator of how anxious key abolitionists figures were of the public perception of Haiti and its current leader.[91] Possibly for these reasons, while abolitionists undoubtedly supported Christophe and aimed to aid him in a number of ways in his efforts, public appraisals of the Haitian king in the form of articles or literary texts were notably missing at this time.

The reason for abolitionists' trepidation at publishing their own panegyrics on the Haitian king is perhaps best exemplified in an anti-abolition pamphlet that emerged in 1816 and would be widely distributed and discussed in both British and American newspapers. Joseph Marryat—a London merchant, Member of Parliament for Sandwich, and an agent for Grenada—published a pamphlet that was designed to offer a rebuttal to perceived attacks made against him by abolitionists and, in particular, by James Stephen. Marryat was an important mouthpiece for West Indian planters, and earlier in 1816 he had published his *Thoughts on the Abolition of the Slave Trade*—a publication that was the focus of much criticism and derision by abolitionists. In his second pamphlet—*More Thoughts*—Marryat sought to defend his original ideas on the folly of abolishing slavery in the British colonies, while simultaneously offering the same kind of character assassination to British abolitionists to which he believed he had been subjected. A central part of this attack on the abolitionist group was the assistance and support they had given—and continued to give—the Haitian monarchy.[92]

In *More Thoughts*, Christophe's monarchical status was pivotal to Marryat's scathing attack on the abolitionists. Marryat described a supposed meeting among the abolitionists and the "friends of the African and Asiatic Society" at a London tavern.[93] The meeting was advertised in British newspapers in March 1816, and Marryat's account of the meeting was published soon after. Three years later, Marryat's son would employ George Cruikshank to etch a satirical interpretation of the event. The print evokes the chaos that Marryat imagined in his 1816 pamphlet and has been aptly described by Temi Odumosu as a "visually arresting display of coarsely rendered caricatures, representing its subjects as lewd, misshapen, and unruly".[94] Key to Marryat's and Cruikshank's criticisms of the meeting was the alleged celebration of the King of Haiti by British abolitionists. And as Odumosu has argued, Marryat was particularly scathing of the idea

# 4 KING CHRISTOPHE AND THE QUESTION OF MONARCHICAL LEGITIMACY 111

that the British abolitionists would assert Christophe's legitimacy as a monarch.[95]

Marryat placed Stephen at centre stage of this meeting as he claimed that the British abolitionist had proceeded to eulogize the Haitian king to the members of the society. Marryat was particularly scathing of Stephen's attempts to "vindicate" Christophe from accusations of vanity and a desire for the trappings of monarchy—a claim often made in negative depictions of Christophe and one asserted by Marryat in his pamphlet.[96] But for Marryat, more damning than this was Stephen's alleged belief that "King Henry of Hayti, the name by which he always spoke of this person...derived his title from a more legitimate source than the monarchs of Europe". According to Marryat: "This broad assertion was afterwards somewhat qualified by particularizing the Ex-Emperor of France, and the Kings of Spain and Naples; and contrasting their rights to the "golden circle"". In the pamphlet, Stephen not only supported Christophe but the Haitian monarch was his "immaculate favourite" as the reader was undoubtedly led to believe Stephen even favoured the Haitian king over the British monarch. Although at the beginning of the meeting toasts to the British monarchy were drunk "but, *without rising from their seats*", a toast to Christophe—made later in the meeting—was said to be drank with "the *whole company standing, with three times three, and enthusiastic acclamations*".[97] Whether true or not—and whether alcohol had played a role in this increased enthusiasm or not—Marryat saw the differences in the two toasts as evidence of where abolitionist supporters' allegiances truly rested.

The idea that British abolitionists asserted Christophe's legitimacy alongside and even possibly above the claims of the British sovereign was more serious than to simply "belittle" anti-slavery figures such as Wilberforce, as some have claimed.[98] This was a damning attack on the abolitionists and Stephen in particular—one that was borderline treasonous. Marryat's speculation that abolitionists displayed an allegiance for the Haitian monarchy over the British king led to the conclusion that the "doctrine of legitimacy laid down by Mr. Stephen on this occasion, is certainly not calculated for the meridian of the Congress of Vienna; nor even such as Mr. Wilberforce would have ventured to broach, at one of his visits to the Prince Regent".[99] The fear that support for Christophe's monarchical status could be interpreted by political opponents as an indictment of the British monarchy at this time could very well explain the reluctance by British political supporters of Christophe to speak publicly in favour of him. Marryat overtly suggested that support for the sovereignty of the

Haitian monarchy pointed to an element of radicalism in abolitionist politics from which abolitionists would have wanted to distance themselves. Stephen's supposed support for his "hero" Christophe even apparently extended to the prediction that "'the new black dynasty will in no distant time, subvert the relations of the western world'".[100] By placing support for political upheaval and subversion throughout the Western hemisphere in the mouth of Stephen, Marryat directly associated support for Christophe with a political radicalism that even sympathisers of Haiti would have found difficult to uphold. Marryat's attack is a good indicator of the kinds of criticisms that abolitionists were wary of and wanted to avoid, and perhaps answers why they themselves presented indifference to the volatile—and potentially damaging—subject of Christophe's legitimacy.

## The Haitian Monarchy and British Perceptions of Legitimacy

Although abolitionists did not publish their own articles or literature that directly asserted Christophe's legitimacy as a monarch, they would have undoubtedly been aware of the importance of such questions if Haiti was to gain the support from Britain that abolitionists knew would be so vital to its progress. As a result, abolitionists promoted displays of Christophe's legitimacy that had been created by the hands of others, but that served to paint the Haitian king in a favourable light. One good example of this was a painting by Richard Evans of *His Majesty Henry Christophe, King of Hayti*, which was displayed at the Royal Academy Exhibition in 1818. The painting was a gift from Christophe to Wilberforce, and it was most likely displayed to the public at the behest of the abolitionists, although this was not made explicit at the time.[101] The abolitionists were also almost certainly responsible for the publication and circulation of a number of texts written by Baron de Vastey—texts which not only passionately defended Haiti's sovereignty but also asserted the legitimacy of the Haitian monarch. Vastey's texts, Evans's painting and the circulation of Christophe's numerous proclamations and manifestos were crucial performances of the legitimacy of the Haitian monarchy. But, importantly, these were performances that allowed abolitionists to publicly keep their distance from the Haitian king.

4 KING CHRISTOPHE AND THE QUESTION OF MONARCHICAL LEGITIMACY    113

An even more direct defence of the monarchy's legitimacy had already been circulating in Britain before Vastey's writings and Evans's portrait came to light: Prince Saunders's *Haytian Papers*, published in 1816.[102] Prince Saunders was a well-educated, free African-American who taught in, and established, schools for African-Americans in Massachusetts.[103] In 1815, Saunders arrived in England in order to establish better links with, and assistance from, British abolitionists. At this time, Wilberforce and Clarkson persuaded Saunders to go to Haiti to provide diplomatic assistance and guidance to Christophe.[104] While in Haiti, Saunders wrote his *Haytian Papers* in order to promote more positive depictions of the Haitian state and of Christophe to a British audience. At the behest of Christophe, and with the encouragement of Thomas Clarkson, the publication of the text coincided with Saunders embarking on a number of speaking tours in Britain, and later the United States, that were designed to promote positive depictions of the Haitian state.

The primary function of Saunders's *Haytian Papers* was to assert the legitimacy of the Haitian monarch and to highlight the enlightened and liberal forms of governmental policy implemented by King Christophe. Saunders's text emphasised how Haitians were "blessed with a sovereign" that had the needs of the Haitian people at the heart of his policies and decisions.[105] A considerable section of the *Papers* was devoted to the "Narrative of the Accession of their Royal Majesties to the Throne of Hayti". In it, readers were told that under Dessalines's government and immediately after his assassination, "[i]nsubordination and licentiousness" were commonplace, "the public treasures were squandered" and that "dark and secret plots" were being conducted throughout the army and the people. However, Christophe—"[g]reat at all times"—was said to be aware of all of these problems and acted swiftly and decisively to counter them for the good of the Haitian people.[106]

Central to Saunders's attempts to court British favour was the explanation and justification of Christophe's adoption of a monarchical title. Saunders emphasised the fact that Christophe initially took up a presidential title as he attempted to improve the security of Haiti, as well as improving the schools, hospitals and agricultural practices of the state. However, despite these "good deeds of the government" Saunders presented a picture of a restless, ill-disciplined state under Christophe's presidency. The repeated use of the presidential title in this part of the text asserted the idea that Christophe at least tried to use this mode of government before the adoption of monarchy—possibly a concession to a British audience

114    J. FORDE

which was still unsure whether to be flattered or offended by this imitation of traditional monarchy. Even though Christophe apparently acted always in the interests of the people, the threat of internal revolution constantly lingered. Saunders insisted on the "insufficiency" of the presidential title, which the people "had invested him in calamitous times" and that Christophe needed to adopt a title with more authority and power in order to instil the stability and discipline necessary for Haiti's economic and social improvement—thereby speaking to British loyalist affection for the stability of monarchy.[107]

The fact that Christophe was a self-created monarch was recognised in Saunders's writing as Christophe's adoption of monarchy was depicted as having little to do with the sovereign himself. Rather, "the declared opinion of the most respectable and enlightened citizens was in favour of placing Henry on the throne". Saunders claimed that the "happy news" of Christophe's coronation was "received with unbounded transports of affection and joy".[108] The portrayal of Christophe as a reluctant monarch, and the unbridled joy of Haitians at this new of form governance, was a conscious effort to write against any negative depictions of a supposedly illegitimate sovereign. Christophe's title was presented as not only necessary but also deserved due to his bravery in war and his vigorous attempts at improving the welfare of his citizens.

Saunders also sought to legitimise Christophe's nomination by depicting his personal conduct as befitting a traditional monarch. Christophe's example was one that apparently influenced the "re-establishment of manners" throughout the north of Haiti and reinstalled a sense of order and calm throughout the state. This led Saunders to conclude that Christophe was proof that "good manners are the attendants of good monarchs, and constitute the glory of their reign; as, on the other hand, from licentiousness come bad princes, to the disgrace of their government".[109] Whether the latter part of this quote was a thinly veiled swipe at the debauchery of the Prince Regent is impossible to ascertain. But if it were, it would represent an acute awareness on the part of Saunders of the British public's disdain for the heir to the British throne. And more than this, it demonstrates the significance Saunders placed on the performance of both legitimate and acceptable monarchical forms of rule, particularly for a British audience.

While the circulation by abolitionists of works such as Saunders's undoubtedly had a positive impact on depictions of Christophe by the mid-1810s, it is important not to overstate their influence. By the time

Saunders's text was published in Britain in 1816, its assertions of the legitimacy of the Haitian monarchy would be read by a largely already-receptive audience as appraisals of the Haitian monarchy had started to appear in British reports before audiences had had a chance to read Vastey or Saunders. In an 1814 article considering the "Politics of the New World", the *Liverpool Mercury* concluded that Christophe demanded respect as a sovereign because it was he who "knows as well as any European governor, what is really beneficial to his people, and feels far more than such a governor would do, that it is his duty to perfect those institutions, that relate so directly to their happiness".[110] Periodicals such as the *New Annual Register* likewise claimed that "the measures of this sovereign displayed a wise and enlightened policy" and that his proclamations were "in point of eloquence and force of reasoning…not inferior to the most celebrated state papers of the most eloquent and enlightened nations".[111]

As such, positive receptions to the Haitian monarchy were not simply reflective of abolitionist backing of the Haitian king. They were also a direct product of the political climate in which they were created. Positive reactions to King Christophe emerged at a time when British loyalists loudly proclaimed the merits of constitutional monarchies to counter and mitigate increasing political agitation at home and political upheaval abroad. In the early 1810s, loyalists had initially framed King Christophe in denunciatory narratives of Napoleon and the notion of self-created dynasties. With the capture of Napoleon and the restoration of conservative forms of political power in Europe by the mid-1810s, however, representations of the Haitian king were suddenly re-appropriated as a means to project loyalist celebrations of traditional forms of political power, as exemplified by the Kingdom of Haiti.

By the mid-1810s, radical movements had re-emerged in England with a forcefulness that alarmed conservative commentators. And key to this growing movement was the support that Napoleon's claims to legitimacy (even posthumously) began to find within radical publications. In response, a "wave of loyalist pamphleteering" emerged in the hope of averting "the spectre of revolution".[112] Although the reputation of monarchy in Britain generally "fluctuated wildly over time", the latter part of George III's reign in the 1810s was a high point for the popularity of the British monarchy, and it became "more celebrated, more broadly popular and more unalloyedly patriotic than it had been for a century at least."[113] The British government sought to capitalise on this by promoting the "cult of monarchy", even though loyalists often varied widely in their assertions of the conditions to which monarchical governments should adhere.[114] Most of these commentators, however, consistently argued that constitutional monarchical rule was the most solid foundation for any form of governance, and as such they responded favourably to constitutions adopted by figures such as the new king of the Netherlands—constitutions that had "strong monarchical authority" at their core.[115] By the end of 1814, Napoleon had been defeated, and the resulting Congress of Vienna had in effect re-established the strength of hereditary monarchical rule throughout Europe. In this climate, British loyalists trumpeted the merits of traditional, dynastical forms of power with increasing confidence.

By the mid-1810s, Haiti's constitutional monarchy emerged as a significant point of reference in loyalist narratives regarding the legitimacy and superiority of Britain's form of monarchical government. Within such reports, Christophe's legitimacy began to be asserted more vociferously. In these reports, Christophe's previous image as a despotic emperor was recast as a legitimate monarch who proved worthy of his title. Whig newspapers such as the *Chester Chronicle* received the symbolic performances of his legitimacy through his royal adornments with more enthusiasm than other publications had in the early years of his reign. The *Chronicle* described the Haitian king's pageantry as "beautiful" and "superb" as part of its praise for the Haitian kingdom, in turn allowing the newspaper to assert its Whiggish principles by asserting the legitimacy of a head of a constitutional monarchy.[116]

Loyalist newspapers such as the *Morning Post* also praised the Haitian monarch at a time when the publication was becoming increasingly praiseworthy of the British Prince Regent. This meant that positive portrayals of the Haitian king helped the *Post* to advocate the merits of monarchical rule more generally, thereby hoping to counter increasing agitation and unrest towards the increasingly unpopular heir to the British throne. The *Post* published Christophe's "Manifesto of the King"—a document intended to assert the Haitian king's own legitimacy on the Atlantic stage, and one that confidently proclaimed the benefits of a king to his nation.[117] Proclamations from Haiti that praised the restoration of the Bourbon monarchy and aligned Haiti's monarchy with the dynasties of Europe were also printed by the *Post*.[118] Although little commentary was offered on these proclamations, the *Post*'s inclusion of them suggests that the newspaper was supportive of the Haitian kingdom's alignment with its dynastic siblings in Europe. *The Post* wrote approvingly that Christophe was "the pattern of every royal excellence" and that he was determined to

## 4 KING CHRISTOPHE AND THE QUESTION OF MONARCHICAL LEGITIMACY 117

make "his kingdom and reign respected for its strength, resources and love of justice".[119] In this way, King Christophe became a key figure within a celebratory climate of monarchical governments.

Within such celebratory narratives, Christophe's affairs were depicted to be "as well conducted as in the best organised government in the world".[120] Other reports went even further to claim that Christophe's conduct and numerous proclamations not only proved black capability for political leadership, but that the Haitian king would "put to the blush some of the [w]hite legitimates of the holy alliance, whose main object appears to be, to suppress every trace of that spirit of popular freedom in the old world; which they see with such alarm, spreading itself in spite of their congresses and hired Cossack, over every region of the new world".[121] Reports such as these, therefore, elevated Christophe from an imitator of European monarchy to one who was in fact leading the way for other monarchs to follow.

These positive portrayals of the King of Haiti served multiple purposes for loyalist observers at this time. First, for conservative writers who wanted to counter radical narratives that had increasingly anti-monarchical messages at their core, the King of Haiti became proof of how a noble monarch can reflect the virtues of a nation to an international audience. Christophe's proclamations were described as being "in point of elo-quence and force of reasoning...not inferior to the most celebrated state papers of the most eloquent and enlightened nations," thereby asserting Christophe as a statesman who deserved to be revered internationally.[122] Christophe performed the duties of a sovereign respectfully by receiving foreign diplomats "with all the respect due to an Ambassador," in turn paving the way for his nation to secure profitable international relations.[123] Haiti's impressive military fortifications were also praised in sections of the British press and were depicted as evidence of Christophe's ability to pro-tect his subjects from any foreign force.[124] Narratives such as these depicted the absence of a hereditary lineage as secondary to the king's conduct and the ways in which he served as a symbol of the strength and nobility of his nation.

Positive portrayals of Christophe also served a distinct purpose for moderate conservatives who wanted to outline the duty of care a monarch should show to his subjects. Newspaper such as the *Liverpool Mercury*—founded by the Liberal-leaning Egerton Smith—concluded that Christophe demanded respect as a sovereign because it was he who "knows as well as any European governor, what is really beneficial to his people,

118   J. FORDE

and feels far more than such a governor would do, that it is his duty to perfect those institutions, that relate so directly to their happiness."[125] Periodicals further asserted that King Christophe was acting towards the advancement of his nation and that "the measures of this sovereign displayed a wise and enlightened policy."[126] Reports such as this drew on positive associations with the paternalistic (and by now much celebrated) George III, while also alluding to the unpopularity of the Prince Regent— something that stemmed largely from the Regent's perceived incompetent leadership and the neglectful care of his subjects.[127] Whig newspapers such as the *Caledonian Mercury* framed the Haitian kingdom as evidence of the benefits of constitutional monarchical rule, but at the same time asserted that that a large part of this praise was because the Haitian king "never loses sight of the good of his kingdom and the happiness of his people"—a timely reminder for the Prince Regent.[128] By this time, the Haitian monarch was frequently portrayed as a "beloved" king responsible for the happiness of the "tranquil" nation.[129] Reports such as these aimed to place Christophe at the centre of Haiti's apparent progression, particularly when they recognised that it was the "[s]overeign himself" who "encouraged the foundation of schools".[130]

British newspapers therefore framed Christophe in celebratory narratives of monarchical governance, but which also outlined how a monarch should behave for his own reputation, for the happiness of his subjects, and for the stability of the nation. In this way, positive depictions of Christophe served to underline why France should celebrate the demise of Napoleon and the implementation of its own constitutional monarchy, to remind Britons of the level of paternal care that could and should be afforded by monarchical forms of government, and to remind supporters of the Prince Regent that birth right alone was not enough to legitimise wholly a monarch's reign.

Such positive portrayals of the Haitian king would have benefitted newspapers that called more vocally for a commercial relationship to be firmly established with the Haitian kingdom. Reports of "richly laden" merchant vessels leaving Cape Henry sat alongside depictions of the "tranquil and happy" Haitian state; all of which painted an overall picture of a nation "full of loyalty to its Sovereign, and enthusiastically attached to its new Constitution, its laws, and independence".[131] The fact that Christophe not only desired commercial relations with Britain but that he could provide security for them was key in these reports. The Haitian king apparently treated English merchants "with respect" but Americans "with every

## 4 KING CHRISTOPHE AND THE QUESTION OF MONARCHICAL LEGITIMACY    119

mark of scorn"—something that would have pleased loyalists still hurting from England's defeat in the War of 1812. Other reports dismissed claims that the Haitian king was looking to trade with France and suggested that the Haitian king held contempt for the French. Such newspapers were eager to stress the strength of Christophe's army and the impregnability of his fortresses in the face of potential foreign invasion. In other words, British investments would be in safe hands.[132]

Despite the popularity of the Haitian king within the British press, Christophe and his court were decidedly absent in literary texts produced by English writers, even in pro-Haitian abolitionist narratives produced in the 1810s.[133] A notable but often under-appreciated example of this was the positive affirmation of Christophe's monarchy in James Barskett's *The History of the Island of St. Domingo, From its First Discovery by Columbus to the Present Period*.[134] Little is known about Barskett, but his defence of the Haitian monarch in a literary text was a unique contribution to the portrayals of Christophe in this time. Barskett offered a passionate defence of Christophe's monarchical title by asserting that the "pompous title of emperor" was refused by king and that the eventual establishment of monarchy on the island was said to be "the opinion of the people at large". The title was framed as a necessity as it was "the only mode of government adapted to their country". The titles of Toussaint and Dessalines were dismissed as inappropriate for the time in which Christophe was operating, and the implementation of a monarchical system was "received by the people at large with general satisfaction".[135] Even more than this, Barskett used stories of Christophe's implementation of a national education system, and his apparent willingness to answer petitions, as a way to suggest that the Haitian monarch was surpassing Britain's own Prince Regent as a truly paternal leader of his nation.[136]

Barskett was concerned with depicting the Haitian monarch as a political leader who was not only doing what he could for the good of his people, but who also displayed the necessary character and diplomatic skills to be included in international political relations. Barskett published Christophe's Royal Almanack of 1814 in the appendix with some insightful commentary and praise. In particular, Barskett was complimentary of Christophe's Code Henry—a series of laws announced shortly after his coronation which were designed to regulate "commerce, civil proceedings, the police, agriculture, and the military".[137] Despite the fact that these laws forced Haitians to labour on plantations, Barskett declared that the principles of the Code were "laid in justice, equity, and humanity".[138]

Christophe was said to be trusting of his court and cabinet and was shown to be reasonable in his dealings with France.[139] Barskett drew parallels between Christophe and the still-revered Toussaint, particularly in their "moderation and temper".[140] Also, and possibly most importantly for foreign political observers, Christophe was said to encourage friendly trade relations with foreigners, and even in his dealings with the antagonistic French he was said to be calm and reasonable.[141] In these pages, Barskett sent a clear message to his British audience that King Christophe could, and should, be approached as a legitimate sovereign—and, crucially, one who could open lucrative avenues of commerce for the British.

Despite the mass interest in Haiti that seemed to consume the British press in the mid-1810s, the presence of a Haitian monarchy would become a source of contention once more by 1818. By this time, stories of Christophe's apparent cruelty and despotism began to reframe the Haitian monarch in British newspapers. Particularly damaging were reports that Christophe had imprisoned and murdered merchants with little cause or judicial process and that he had even placed Archbishops under house arrest.[142] An even bigger blow to Christophe's reputation was the emergence of a report by the late 1810s that a British merchant in Haiti had been subjected to torture by thumb screws, under Christophe's orders.[143] Although some British reports tried to counter such negative depictions of the Haitian king by reminding readers of his progressive attitudes towards education, Christophe's reputation in Britain would be in ruin by the end of the 1810s.

## CONCLUSION

King Henry I of Haiti was a fluid, changing and contradictory figure in imaginations on both sides of the Atlantic. Although these depictions were often subject to the common racist rhetoric of the time, observers constructed representations of Christophe—and of the Haitian monarchy in general—to suit a variety of alternative agendas in both Britain and America in the early nineteenth century. The way in which these depictions were shaped and re-shaped time and time again is representative of the volatile political landscape of the Atlantic world in the early nineteenth century. In particular, acceptance of the legitimacy of Christophe's monarchy was a constant source of contention and an issue that was particularly susceptible to the wider context of Atlantic world politics in the 1810s.

## 4 KING CHRISTOPHE AND THE QUESTION OF MONARCHICAL LEGITIMACY 121

The presence of a black, ex-slave who was the self-created monarch of a post-revolutionary state represented a paradoxical political figure in both America and Britain. In America, public declarations of support became exponentially more difficult after Christophe's coronation. In this sense, support for the Haitian king to promote more favourable commercial opportunities became secondary to the opportunity of denouncing the monarch to better attack the ideological foundations of monarchical governments everywhere. American republicans derided the fact that Christophe seemed to style himself on the British monarch as part of a more general narrative of scorn for the hereditary dynasties of the Old World. But Americans with mercantile interests saw the importance of supporting the Haitian king and legitimising his sovereignty in the hope that the American government would officially recognise Haiti's independence—a recognition that could have led to better conditions for American merchants in the Haitian state. These depictions therefore excused Christophe's imperial title as they sought to legitimise the Haitian's monarchy sovereignty. Such assertions managed to simultaneously criticise forms of Old World monarchy by claiming that Christophe was succeeding in the betterment of his country in ways that Europe's dynasties had failed. Whether American observers attacked or supported the presence of the Haitian state, the perceived legitimacy of its monarch was key to such discourses.

In Britain, the presence of yet another self-created, post-revolutionary imperial leader became less confronting after the subjugation of Napoleon and the restoration of traditional forms of governance in Europe. In this more stable political atmosphere, British observers were afforded greater opportunities to declare support for both the king and for trading with the Haitian kingdom. Praise for the Haitian monarch drew on the popularity of Britain's own sovereign as depictions of Christophe asserted the virtues of caring, paternal monarchs and the benefits they can bring to their citizens. Critics of the Haitian king would express disdain at the perceived imitation of the British monarchy by a black political figurehead. However, the level of support Christophe found in Britain suggests that his adoption of monarchy found a receptive audience among British loyalists keen to assert the superiority of their mode of leadership in Atlantic world politics. In this way, the Haitian monarchy was as central to narratives of the virtues of monarchism—and of legitimate modes of governing more generally—as it was to discussions of race and the potential of post-slavery societies. When news emerged of Christophe's death by the end of 1820, the political value of the first and only King of Haiti continued to resonate for observers on both sides of the Atlantic.

## NOTES

1. *Aberdeen Journal*, 11 September 1811.
2. Christophe gave himself this title prior to his coronation in 1811: Laurent Dubois, *Haiti: The Aftershocks of History* (New York: Metropolitan Books, 2012), 61.
3. Sybille Fischer, *Modernity Disavowed: Haiti and the Cultures of Slavery in the Age of Revolution* (Durham: Duke University Press, 2004), 253.
4. Ibid., 245–259. For an example of this kind of dismissiveness, see Hubert Cole, *Christophe, King of Haiti* (New York: Viking Press, 1967), 191. This re-evaluation of Christophe has led other historians to draw similar conclusions as Fischer. Most notably, see Dubois, *Haiti*, 54–64.
5. Paul W. Schroeder, *The Transformation of European Politics, 1763–1848* (New York: Oxford University Press, 1994), vii.
6. Dubois, *Haiti*, 64; Marlene Daut, "The "Alpha and Omega" of Haitian Literature: Baron De Vastey and the U.S. Audience of Haitian Political Writing," *Comparative Literature* 64, no. 1 (2012), 56.
7. *The Tickler*, 31 July 1811; *Philadelphia Gazette*, 6 December 1811. Marlene Daut's work best highlights the confronting nature of Christophe's race for an American audience: Daut, ""Alpha and Omega","" 56–58.
8. *New Jersey Journal*, 30 July 1811.
9. *Poulson's Daily American Advertiser*, 23 July 1811.
10. *Philadelphia Gazette*, 20 August 1811.
11. Jon Latimer, *1812: War with America* (Cambridge: Harvard University Press, 2007), 5.
12. Gordon S. Wood, *Empire of Liberty: A History of the Early Republic, 1789–1815* (New York: Oxford University Press, 2009), 668–669.
13. Sean Wilentz, *The Rise of American Democracy: Jefferson to Lincoln* (New York: W. W. Norton & Company, 2005), 141.
14. Wood, *Empire of Liberty*, 699.
15. Russell L. Hanson, *The Democratic Imagination in America: Conversations with Our Past* (Princeton: Princeton University Press, 1985), 105.
16. *Essex Register*, 1 July 1815.
17. *National Advocate*, 9 Jan 1815.
18. See for example *Alexandria Herald*, 1 September 1815; *National Standard*, 20 September 1815.
19. *Weekly Aurora*, 2 August 1815; *The Enquirer*, 8 July 1815.
20. Wood, *Empire of Liberty*, 701, 725.

# 4 KING CHRISTOPHE AND THE QUESTION OF MONARCHICAL LEGITIMACY 123

21. *National Advocate*, 23 January 1816.
22. *New Jersey Journal*, 4 June 1816.
23. *Essex Register*, 6 March 1816.
24. Caitlin Fitz, "The Hemispheric Dimensions of Early Us Nationalism: The War of 1812, Its Aftermath, and Spanish American Independence," *Journal of American History* 102, no. 2 (2015), 357. For further insight into how the war provoked nationalist sentiments see Nicole Eustace, *1812: War and the Passions of Patriotism* (Philadelphia: University of Pennsylvania Press, 2012).
25. *Relf's Philadelphia Gazette*, 25 October 1816; *The Messenger*, 26 October 1816.
26. Wood, *Empire of Liberty*, 701.
27. *American Beacon*, 11 May 1816.
28. *New-England Palladium*, 24 November 1812.
29. *Hallowell Gazette*, 12 April 1815.
30. *The True American*, 24 February 1812.
31. *National Intelligencer*, 22 July 1816.
32. *Delaware Gazette and Peninsula Advertiser*, 23 March 1815.
33. See McIntosh and Pierrot, "Henry I," 129. See for example *The Northern Sentinel*, 19 July 1816.
34. *The Republican*, 20 June 1818; *Sun*, 3 December 1816.
35. Frank Luther Mott, *American Journalism: A History, 1690–1960* (New York: Macmillan, 1962), 188.
36. Ibid.
37. *Niles' Weekly Register*, 27 May 1815.
38. *Niles' Weekly Register*, 2 November 1816; 30 November 1816; 3 May 1817.
39. *Niles' Weekly Register*, 20 May 1815.
40. *Niles' Weekly Register*, 12 April 1817.
41. *Niles' Weekly Register*, 2 March 1816.
42. Daut, ""Alpha and Omega"," 56.
43. Ibid.
44. *Niles' Weekly Register*, 4 January 1817.
45. *Niles' Weekly Register*, 19 November 1816.
46. *Niles' Weekly Register*, 12 October 1816.
47. *Niles' Weekly Register*, 13 June 1818.
48. *Niles' Weekly Register*, 22 November 1817; 30 May 1818.
49. *Niles' Weekly Register*, 22 November 1817.
50. *Niles' Weekly Register*, 22 June 1816.
51. *Niles' Weekly Register*, 13 June 1818.

52. Doris L. Garraway, "Empire of Freedom, Kingdom of Civilisation: Henry Christophe, the Baron De Vastey, and the Paradoxes of Universalism in Postrevolutionary Haiti," *Small Axe* 16, no. 3 (2012), 10.
53. Vastey has been the subject of an increasing amount of scholarly work in recent years, including: Marlene L. Daut, *Baron de Vastey and the Origins of Black Atlantic Humanism* (New York: Palgrave Macmillan, 2017), Chris Bongie, *The Colonial System Unveiled* (Liverpool: Liverpool University Press, 2014). Three of Vastey's texts were published in English: *Reflexions on the Blacks and Whites: Remarks Upon a Letter Addressed by M. Mazeres, ... to J.S.L. Sismonde de Sismondi* (London: F. B. Wright, 1817); *Political Remarks on Some French Works and Newspapers Concerning Hayti* (London: n.p., 1818); *An Essay on the Causes of the Revolution and Civil Wars of Hayti, Being a Sequel to the Political Remarks Upon Certain French Publications and Journals Concerning Hayti* (Exeter: Western Luminary Office, 1823). For an overview of the circulation of these texts in both Britain and America, and Vastey's defences of the Haitian monarchy within these texts, see: Daut, ""Alpha and Omega"; Sara C. Fanning, "The Roots of Early Black Nationalism: Northern African Americans' Invocations of Haiti in the Early Nineteenth Century," *Slavery & Abolition* 28, no. 1 (2007), 70–71.
54. Garraway, "Empire of Freedom," 5.
55. Daut, ""Alpha and Omega"," 56.
56. Ibid., 57.
57. *Hampden Federalist*, 7 March 1816.
58. *American Beacon*, 27 June 1818.
59. *Albany Gazette*, 17 July 1817.
60. *Hallowell Gazette*, 24 February 1818; 1 July 1818.
61. *Albany Gazette*, 10 April 1817.
62. *American Beacon*, 27 June 1818.
63. *Hampden Federalist*, 7 1816; *Hallowell Gazette*, 1 July 1818.
64. *Hallowell Gazette*, 1 July 1818.
65. Ibid.
66. *Niles' Weekly Register*, 12 October 1816.
67. *National Intelligencer*, 30 January 1816.
68. *Niles' Weekly Register*, 12 October 1816; *American Beacon*, 27 June 1818.
69. As will be discussed in more detail in the fifth chapter, it is important to note that the revolutions of Spanish America were largely supported in America by the mid-1810s, though Haiti was often excluded from such celebrations: Caitlin Fitz, *Our Sister Republics: The United States in an Age of American Revolutions* (New York: W. W. Norton & Company, 2016), 87.
70. *Albany Gazette*, 2 December 1817.

4 KING CHRISTOPHE AND THE QUESTION OF MONARCHICAL LEGITIMACY    125

71. *Niles' Weekly Register*, 22 November 1817.
72. For discussions of how Christophe constructed a regal image—largely to secure support from the British government—see: Karen Racine, "Britannia's Bold Brother: British Cultural Influence in Haiti During the Reign of Henry Christophe (1811–1820)," *The Journal of Caribbean History* 33, no. 1 & 2 (1999), 127–132; McIntosh and Pierrot, "Henry I," 138–142.
73. *Liverpool Mercury*, 21 February 1812.
74. *York Herald*, 7 September 1811.
75. *Caledonian Mercury*, 7 January 1813; *Liverpool Mercury*, 18 October 1811; *Caledonian Mercury*, 19 October 1811.
76. *Observer*, 13 October 1811.
77. *Liverpool Mercury*, 27 September 1811.
78. For an exception to this silence in radical writing, see James Forde, ""A soldier of fortune": Henry Christophe, British loyalism, and the troubling question of political legitimacy," *Atlantic Studies* 16, no. 2 (2019), 207–208.
79. The 1688 revolution was a highly significant frame of reference throughout the eighteenth century in parliamentary and public discussions of political principles: H.T. Dickinson, "The Eighteenth-Century Debate on the 'Glorious Revolution'," *History* 61, No. 201 (1976), 28–45.
80. Kathleen Wilson, "Inventing Revolution: 1688 and Eighteenth-Century Popular Politics, " *Journal of British Studies* 28, no. 4 (1989), 374–388.
81. Semmel, *Napoleon and the British*, 108.
82. A number of newspapers in the immediate years after his coronation made reference to Christophe's self-created status: see for example *Bury and Norwich Post*, 26 June 1811; *Caledonian Mercury*, 7 January 1813.
83. *Morning Post*, 6 May 1811.
84. *Cheltenham Chronicle and Gloucestershire Advertiser*, 20 February 1812.
85. Moores demonstrates how loyalists satirised Napoleon's alleged tyranny: John Richard Moores, *Representations of France in English Satirical Prints, 1740–1832* (Basingstoke: Palgrave Macmillan, 2015), 87–88.
86. Geggus, "Haiti and the Abolitionists," 121–123; Racine, "Britannia's Bold Brother," 128–130.
87. The correspondence between Clarkson and other abolitionists with Christophe and his aides can be seen in Earl Leslie Griggs and Clifford Holmes Prator, *Henry Christophe & Thomas Clarkson: A Correspondence* (New York: Greenwood Press, 1968).
88. For more information on Christophe's plans for education in Haiti and the help he solicited from British abolitionists for assistance with these plans, see Karen Racine, "Imported Englishness: Henry Christophe's Educational Program in Haiti, 1806–1820," in *Imported Modernity in*

126   J. FORDE

*Post-Colonial State Formation: The Appropriation of Political, Educational, and Cultural Models in Nineteenth-Century Latin America*, edited by Eugenia Roldán Vera and Marcelo Caruso (Bern: Peter Lang, 2007), 205–230.

89. Geggus, "Haiti and the Abolitionists," 114.
90. James Stephen, *The History of Toussaint Louverture* (London: J. Hatchard, 1814). This was originally published as *Buonaparte in the West Indies; or, the History of Toussaint Louverture, the African Hero* (London: J. Brettell, 1803).
91. Geggus, "Haiti and the Abolitionists," 123; 133.
92. Joseph Marryat, *More Thoughts, Occasioned by Two Publications Which the Authors Call "an Exposure of Some of the Numerous Mis-Statements and Misrepresentations Contained in a Pamphlet, Commonly Known by the Name of Mr. Marryat's Pamphlet, Entitled Thoughts, &C." And "a Defence of the Bill for the Registration of Slaves"* (London: J. Ridgway, 1816). News of the pamphlet also found its way into American newspapers. See *Boston Daily Advertiser*, 29 August 1816; *New York Courier*, 2 September 1816.
93. Marryat, *More Thoughts*, 99.
94. Temi-Tope Odumosu, "Abolitionists, African Diplomats and 'the Black Joke' in George Cruikshank's *the New Union Club*," in *The Slave in European Art: From Renaissance Trophy to Abolitionist Emblem*, ed. Elizabeth McGrath and Jean Michel Massing (London: Warburg Institute, 2012), 333.
95. Ibid., 345.
96. Marryat, *More Thoughts*, 102, 107–108.
97. Ibid., 100–102.
98. Odumosu, "Abolitionists, African Diplomats," 345.
99. Marryat, *More Thoughts*, 106.
100. Ibid., 120.
101. For discussions of this painting see Rosalie Smith McCrea, "Portrait Mythology? Representing the 'Black Jacobin': Henri Christophe in the British Grand Manner," *The British Art Journal* 6, no. 2 (2005), 66–68; McIntosh and Pierrot, "Henry I," 138–141. Both McCrea and McIntosh note that the painting was most likely commissioned by Christophe himself and it therefore demonstrates an acute awareness of the need to project an image of himself as a 'legitimate' king.
102. Prince Saunders, *Haytian Papers. A Collection of the Very Interesting Proclamations, and Other Official Documents; Together with Some Account of the Rise, Progress, and Present State of the Kingdom of Hayti* (London: W. Reed, 1816).

103. For an overview of Saunders's life, see Sara Fanning, "Prince Saunders," in *Encyclopedia of African American History*, ed. Leslie M. Alexander and Walter C. Rucker (Santa Barbara: Abc-clio, 2010), 519–520; Arthur O. White, "Prince Saunders: An Instance of Social Mobility among Antebellum New England Blacks," *The Journal of Negro History* 60, no. 4 (1975), 526–535.

104. White, "Prince Saunders", 528.

105. Saunders, *Haytian Papers*, v.

106. Ibid., 57–58.

107. Ibid., 115.

108. Ibid., 115–116.

109. Ibid., 112.

110. *Liverpool Mercury*, 7 October 1814.

111. *The New Annual Register or General Repository of History, Politics and Literature for the year 1814* (London: J Stockdale, 1815), 280.

112. Jennifer Mori, *Britain in the Age of the French Revolution, 1785–1820* (Essex: Longman, 2000), 80.

113. Colley, "Apotheosis of George III," 230, 195.

114. Linda Colley, "Whose Nation? Class and National Consciousness in Britain 1750–1830, " *Past & Present* 113 (1986), 181–182.

115. Brian E. Vick, *The Congress of Vienna: Power and Politics after Napoleon* (Cambridge: Harvard University Press, 2014), 244.

116. *Chester Chronicle*, 23 December 1814.

117. *Morning Post*, 7 December 1814.

118. *Morning Post*, 8 December 1814.

119. *Morning Post*, 13 August 1816.

120. *Morning Post*, 13 August 1816.

121. *Liverpool Mercury*, 3 April 1818.

122. *New Annual Register*, 280.

123. *Morning Post*, 15 January 1815.

124. *Trewman's Exeter Flying Post*, 8 December 1814.

125. *Liverpool Mercury*, 7 October 1814.

126. *New Annual Register*, 280.

127. Poole, *Politics of Regicide*, 142.

128. *Caledonian Mercury*, 8 October 1814.

129. *Morning Post*, 1 October 1814.

130. *Caledonian Mercury*, 29 November 1817; *Morning Post*, 22 November 1817.

131. *Morning Post*, 1 October 1814.

132. *Caledonian Mercury*, 23 June 1814; *Trewman's Post*, 8 December 1814.

133. The prominent abolitionist author James Stephen, for example, republished his *History of Toussaint Louverture* (1814), rather than engage with

the figure of Christophe. Stephen apparently planned to write a biography on Christophe, even going so far as to collect materials for the project, but for unknown reasons this never materialised. See Geggus, "Haiti and the Abolitionists," 125.

134. James Barskett, *History of the Island of St. Domingo, from Its First Discovery by Columbus to the Present Period* (London: Rest Fenner, 1818).
135. Barskett, *History of St. Domingo*, 336.
136. For a lengthier discussion of Barskett's text and his portrayal of Christope, see Forde, "A soldier of fortune," 212–214.
137. Griggs and Prator, *Henry Christophe*, 45.
138. Barskett, *History of St. Domingo*, 413.
139. Ibid., 367, 362.
140. Ibid., 333–335.
141. Ibid., 362.
142. *Morning Chronicle*, 22 January 1817; *Caledonian Mercury*, 30 January 1817.
143. This story was widely reported in Britain. See for example, *Hull Packet*, 18 March 1817. For an overview of the scandal, see Cole, *Christophe*, 236–238.

CHAPTER 5

# The Death of a New World Monarch in Transatlantic Republican Thought

Towards the end of 1820, American and British newspapers fervently circulated reports that Henry Christophe, King of Haiti, had ended his own life with a bullet to the heart. Although details were at first inconsistent and sketchy, newspapers and periodicals excitedly detailed the alleged particulars of the suicide of Haiti's first and only king. The events that had led to his death were of particular interest. Most accounts emphasised the fact that Christophe's troops had turned against him, apparently because of the increasingly cruel and self-serving nature of the monarch's rule. At the beginning of his reign, the king had displayed a genuine desire to improve the welfare of his subjects by establishing schools and colleges, and by looking to secure favourable trade agreements with other countries to protect the country's economic future. But the harsh conditions inflicted upon Haiti's agricultural labourers—conditions viewed by Christophe as necessary to the economic stability of Haiti—soon took their toll, and the tide of public opinion had turned decidedly against the king's favour prior to his demise.[1]

Reports speculated that Christophe's own aides and ministers had also grown frustrated, and that they viewed the king's form of rule as becoming increasingly autocratic in nature. Sensing this insubordination and hearing news that Christophe had suffered a stroke, which had rendered him paralytic, Jean-Pierre Boyer—Pétion's successor as president of the southern republic of Haiti—marched to the north to defeat Christophe, as well as to unite northern and southern Haiti under one republican form of

© The Author(s) 2020
J. Forde, *The Early Haitian State and the Question of Political Legitimacy*, Palgrave Studies in Political History,
https://doi.org/10.1007/978-3-030-52608-5_5

129

130   J. FORDE

government. Some of Christophe's troops apparently defected in order to assist in implementing this change in government.[2] As Boyer's soldiers and some of Christophe's own treacherous troops reached the gates of the king's magisterial fortress, Christophe decided to take his own life rather than suffer the indignity of his imminent demise. Some contemporaries—correctly, as it would transpire—considered the Haitian monarchy essentially ended with the death of Christophe: "the Monarchy of Hayti may be considered as having expired with Christophe".[3]

The manner of Christophe's death was more than simply a source of sensational gossip—rather, it became a key point of reference in American and British discussions about political legitimacy in the early 1820s. In particular, the death of Haiti's king became a celebrated cause among anti-monarchical commentators on both sides of the Atlantic. In these depictions, Christophe's demise was framed as a "revolution" against a tyrannical king. Representations of Christophe's death claimed that his subjects had rebelled against him and thus framed the king's demise as a revolutionary reaction to monarchical rule. In reality, Christophe's death was the culmination of a long civil war with the southern Haitian republic, and it represented a victory for Boyer's southern republic. Nevertheless, despite its inaccuracy, American and British opponents to monarchism framed the king's death as a revolutionary moment created by the people against the restrictive consequences of monarchical rule—a revolution that some observers believed held almost equal importance to the one that had established Haiti's independence some sixteen years previously.[4]

Within this chapter, the term "revolution" is used when discussing these events not to claim that these nineteenth-century observers were correct, but to help to outline the reasons why such terminology was used for their respective agendas. As well as newspapers and periodicals, figures from playwrights, to poets, to caricaturists all sought to glory in the death of Haiti's monarch and outlined it as proof of the tyrannical and fated nature of absolutist monarchical rule—often forgetting or ignoring the fact that on paper at least, Christophe's had been a constitutional monarchy, based on the British model. In the early post-Christophe era, the downfall of the Haitian monarchy became a significant focal point for both American republicans and British radicals in their assertions of how progressive forms of government should operate and how to best care for their citizens and the welfare of the nation.

Reports that celebrated the demise of Haiti's king should certainly be considered, in part, as race-based reactions by white observers to the removal of a powerful black figure from the political stage. A deeper analysis of the different depictions of the Haitian king's death, however, demonstrates that Christophe's race was only a partial factor in the positivity with which his death was received. Just as significant were the charged political climates of both Europe and the Americas in Atlantic receptions of the revolution against Christophe. Malcolm Chase notes that by 1820 there was a "growing internationalism within reform opinion" as reformers and radicals across Europe looked to reformist movements and actions abroad for inspiration.[5] The perceived rebellion against Christophe was certainly viewed through this international lens by a number of transatlantic observers. Christophe's death came at a time when revolutions throughout Europe and Latin America threatened to completely overturn the established political order in the Atlantic world. In this context, Haiti's own revolution against its king became a symbol for anti-conservative commentators of the universal hatred for regressive, archaic forms of political rule, and of the devastating consequences for rulers who refuse to listen to the needs of their people.

## AMERICAN REPUBLICANS AND THE DEATH OF A NEW WORLD TYRANT

Given the significant decline in popularity that Christophe had suffered in America by 1820, it is perhaps unsurprising that the vast majority of reports described enthusiastically the death of the monarch. Accounts of the demise of Haiti's king sometimes alluded to the death of the "black chief" as newspapers sought to deny Christophe his royal title once and for all and to celebrate the removal of a black political figurehead from the Atlantic stage.[6] Other reports emphasised Christophe's race by sarcastically alluding to "his Ebony Majesty", as the death of a black king was depicted with a sense of relief and even joy. Articles such as these claimed that the death of King Christophe "should afford great satisfaction" to American readers. These were undoubtedly racially charged reactions formed from the disgust of some American observers at the presence of a black monarchy and its perceived pretensions of power and sovereignty.[7] Reports in Republican newspapers wondered, with fake empathy, over "[w]hat is to become of her black Majesty the Queen [and] the little black Prince Royal [?]" as news sources sneered at the demise of the Western hemisphere's first black monarchy.[8] That this particular report was written during Mordecai Manuel Noah's editorship of the *National Advocate* is no coincidence. Noah at this time was strongly opposed to black theatre groups in New York and was a vehement opponent to black voting rights, claiming the black population of the state lacked the mental capacity required of such a privilege.[9] For an editor of a Republican newspaper with views of black people such as Noah, clearly the removal of the Haitian monarchy from the Atlantic stage could not have come soon enough.

American newspaper reports that placed Christophe's blackness at the heart of celebrations of the demise of the Haitian monarchy were nevertheless surprisingly few and far between. Instead, as with American depictions of him while he was alive, Christophe's royal status was often depicted with equal—if not greater—significance than his race as commentators enthused over the accounts of a revolution against monarchy in the New World. The political context within which news of Christophe's death was received was key to the construction of these reactions. Glowing portrayals of Christophe's death came at a time when Americans on both sides of the political spectrum continued to be further united in their derision of the dynasties of the Old World. American political thought at this time centred on a perception of the world as clearly divided between the repressive monarchism of Europe and the progressive republicanism of the New World nations. Despite this belief, insecurity in America abounded due to America's perceived weakness against the political powers of the Old World. This insecurity began to increase even further with the numerous congresses held among Europe's Holy Alliance—congresses that were intended to strengthen its union further and to cement the ideology of conservative, monarchical rule. Some Americans even feared that Europe's sovereigns would seek to establish "puppet monarchies" in the New World to further strengthen their power.[10]

Within this environment of disdain and, for some, fear of Old World models of governance, memories of Christophe's reign came to symbolise the oppressive nature of monarchism. And for American opponents of the archaic practices of Old World dynasties, his death came to signify the universal desire among people to be free from the tyranny of monarchical governance. As such, reports claimed that the abolition of the Haitian monarchy "will cause much conversation among the legitimates in Europe"; conversations that, some reports hoped, would be dominated by the fear that Europe's archaic forms of political leadership would soon be at an end.[11]

Hezekiah Niles's Anglophobic *Weekly Register* was at the forefront of American assertions that Christophe was "just as much entitled to his throne…as the best of them" and that, as a result, "his melancholy fate will excite the sympathies of the 'Holy Alliance'".[12] In other editions the *Register* claimed that the death of "Christophe the Cruel" had been met with unbounded joy by the Haitian public because they were finally free from the tyranny of monarchy.[13] This sentiment was echoed in a number of publications at the time. Reports of the "great rejoicing" of the Haitians and claims that they were "highly elated" were common rhetoric in newspaper accounts of the revolution.[14] These depictions not only encouraged American readers to share in this joy at the death of a king, but they also warned European monarchs to view the rebellion in Haiti with alarm and trepidation by portraying it as symptomatic of the revolutionary spirit sweeping across the Americas and Europe.

Central to reports that celebrated the demise of this New World monarch were the often-gruesome imaginings of his death. While some articles salaciously reported that his head had been cut off and placed on a pole by the revolting troops, the majority of depictions accepted—but reported with equal verve—the version of events that culminated in Christophe "blowing his brains out".[15] A common feature of these reports was the apparent indignities the king's corpse suffered. One such allegation was that Christophe's body "was left on the road for some days and was then carried to the edge of a wood, where it remained, partly naked".[16] Depictions found in the anti-monarchical *Niles's Weekly Register* asserted that Christophe's own troops had robbed his corpse of his jewels, including his crown. Even though this was reported to have cost 70,000 dollars, reports gleefully claimed that one of Christophe's own troops had sold it to an American merchant for a mere twelve dollars.[17]

Reports such as these revelled not only in this revolution against a king but also in the very physical and literal removal of the privilege of monarchical rule. In these depictions, the pomp of monarchy was literally laid bare, and the illusion of the trappings of royalty were exposed to the American public. Newspapers cemented the image of the ex-king of Haiti abandoned by his troops, lifeless and naked on the side of the road while cries of "'Vive la Liberte'" echoed around him.[18] As Niles' *Register* would feign sympathetically: "Alas! poor royalty".[19] In this way, the revolution against King Christophe afforded anti-monarchy observers the opportunity to gloat over the death of a sovereign and the end of his monarchical regime.

American reports of the end of the Haitian monarchy often contained rumours—that would later be correctly verified—that both northern and southern Haiti would soon be united under one republican government. As such, a number of depictions sought to position the revolution against the Haitian monarchy within a pro-republican narrative that ultimately underlined America's own political superiority in the face of the powers of the Old World. In this light, Christophe's demise was portrayed in equally glowing terms by some sections of the American press. The death of Haiti's monarch was framed, by some newspapers at least, as a "Revolution in favour of Liberty".[20] For reports such as these, the alleged uprising against Christophe meant that Haiti's real revolution had occurred—and one that, crucially, Americans could more comfortably support. Whereas the 1791–1804 revolution involved the destruction of the plantation system and the deaths of white army officers, colonists, and civilians, the Haitians' ousting of a monarchical figure in 1820 allowed American newspapers to now respond more enthusiastically to events in Haiti.

Newspapers on both sides of America's political divide used Christophe's death to attack the character of the monarch and to laud Haiti's liberation from the chains of monarchy. Reports remembered the Haitian ex-king's "ferocious disposition" and that the "principles of morality were no guide to him". For these reasons, such reports asserted, Christophe's reputation in America "has been neither favourable to him as a man or a monarch", and the fact that his death resulted from a rebellion against him served to justify such opinions.[21]

But Christophe's death seemed to hold a particular pertinence for Democratic-Republicans at this time, and this enthusiasm is best exemplified by the writing that appeared in the Republican governmental mouthpiece, the *Daily National Intelligencer*. Writing in November 1820, the *Intelligencer* looked forward to an "entire subversion of the imperial regime" and predicted that "nothing…will arrest the Republican progress" in the Haitian state.[22] If Americans continued to believe that their own revolution had paved the way for a universal liberation of tyranny, Christophe's death was further proof. The newspaper clearly framed Christophe's death as a revolution of the people, and it stressed that Haitians had not only overthrown the monarchy but were "hastening to embrace" a republican form of government—proof that, even for ex-slaves, liberty under a monarchical regime was nothing more than a fallacy.[23] Reports such as these often ignored the fact that Haitians in the south of the country had in fact been living under a republican form of government for over a decade—first under Pétion's presidency, and continuing under Boyer's. This was likely to enable a simple narrative to thrive—one that placed Christophe's death as a moment of final liberation of the Haitian ex-slaves. Remembering the despotic nature of the Haitian king, reports such as those found in William Duane's *Weekly Aurora* enthusiastically predicted that "[s]hould [Boyer's] plans succeed...we shall soon be presented with a new era in the progress of liberty and independence".[24] For a Republican such as Duane, Christophe's death was clearly a celebratory moment, and one that was evidence of the universal desire for the type of liberal governance as practised by America's own Democratic-Republican government.

In general, for a number of American observers Christophe's death symbolised the reluctance of peoples to live under sovereign rule. At a time when the legitimacy of America's republican form of government continued to be questioned on the global political stage, the fall of the Haitian monarchy was presented symbolically as a changing of the guard from the restrictive nature of Old World forms of governance to the inclusiveness of republicanism. That this rebellion against a king should occur in the New World was all the more significant because it helped to solidify Americans' belief that this was a geo-political space that could position itself as a distinct entity from Old World political beliefs—a position that could see the American republic thrive.

## British Radical Perceptions of a New World Revolution

In the immediate aftermath of Christophe's death, the fallen Haitian king found more favourable reflections of his reign in British memories than in American ones. Although such positive reports were far from abundant, they were a significant point of departure from the majority of representations of the monarch that were produced in Britain towards the end of the 1810s. Although Christophe's reputation was almost completely destroyed in Britain by this time, after his death more articles could be found that wrote approvingly of the monarch's attempts to establish schools, roads and hospitals; particularly because these attempts were made in consultation with British abolitionists. Some went so far as to claim that he had been "animated with a desire to advance the conditions of his subjects". Such reports conceded to the truth of stories of his cruelty, but they simultaneously asserted that this had often been necessary and that he had retained "no bad idea of the duties of a monarch in so rude a society".[25] Others even claimed that Christophe had confided to a British officer that "he knew he was considered a tyrant, but that it was necessary to [be] so; the people would be more fit for liberty hereafter"—thereby offering an excuse for Christophe's tyranny after his death that was largely absent in British loyalist reports towards the end of his reign.[26]

British newspapers that asserted their outrage at the Haitian king's tyranny in the later years of his reign were largely a result of stories that Christophe had affronted British and American merchants in Haiti. After his death, however, Christophe's despotism towards his own people was evidently seen as more acceptable in a number of British depictions. These memories of Christophe's reign certainly did not celebrate the king's perceived tyranny. Even reports such as those found in the *Imperial Magazine* that sought to defend the late king claimed that he had been a "great lover of power" and at times had acted as a "perfect tyrant". But these representations still asserted the necessity of his severe rule for the progress of the post-slavery state by claiming that it was "exceedingly doubtful" whether the Haitians could be governed in a more liberal manner, or whether they would "degenerate into perfect savages...without having some severe regulations established among them".[27]

As historians have highlighted, even British abolitionists in the 1810s and 1820s stopped short of promoting a free-labour ideology in their calls for the emancipation of slaves. Instead, a number of abolitionists attested to the necessity of a more gradual form of abolitionism—one that would secure slaves' freedom, but only under strict and regulated governance. It has been argued that this was because abolitionists generally believed that slaves "required a long transition to absorb proper work habits, religion and civilization". Free labour, therefore, "would be superior when and only when the slow-growing plant of 'true liberty' overcame, through 'gradual amelioration', the slave's indolence and licentiousness".[28]

Supporters of gradual emancipation pointed to the economically successful nature of Christophe's reign to demonstrate the advantages that strict governance could bring to ex-slaves, who were deemed unsuited to and ill-equipped for more liberal forms of leadership. In the immediate aftermath of the Haitian monarch's death, some periodicals ran lengthy obituaries that alluded to Christophe's cruelty, but asserted that he was "just in his dispositions".[29] For conservative publications such as the increasingly popular Tory periodical, *Blackwood's Edinburgh Magazine,*

Christophe's alleged "earnestness to advance the public welfare" was apparently enacted "too impetuously for the rough and unhinged condition of his new subjects"—a telling lesson for more radical abolitionists who were agitating for the immediate and total emancipation of slaves in British colonies.[30] Even more liberally minded publications such as the *Monthly Magazine*, or *British Register* concluded that the Haitian king's severity had been necessary and that he had still "attended to the welfare of his subjects".[31] These depictions ultimately offered justifications for Christophe's severe mode of rule that were largely absent while he was alive, but which acted as a warning against immediate emancipation.

Despite these appraisals of his form of rule, other British newspapers were more unsympathetic to the memory of the Haitian monarch. Some reports emphasised Christophe's race as they referred to the revolution against his "dusky Majesty", and they seemed to revel in the chaotic end to the black king's reign.[32] Even writers such as William Wordsworth— who had hitherto written poetry in support of Toussaint Louverture and who had expressed sympathy for Haitian refugees—now openly mocked the demise of the black monarchy in writings such as "Queen and Negress Chaste and Fair", a poem which sought to ridicule the arrival of Christophe's wife and daughters to Thomas Clarkson's household in England after the death of the Haitian king.[33]

Newspaper depictions and literature often framed Christophe's death as a fitting—and for some amusing—end to the carnivalesque sideshow that had been the Atlantic world's first black monarchy. The satirical and vociferously Tory *John Bull* would later claim that Christophe's brother had been spotted queuing at the offices of London's Mendicity Society—a charity established to keep beggars off the streets of London.[34] Stories such as these indicate a desire among some British loyalists to both mock the presence of a black monarchy on the Atlantic stage and to revel in its demise. This, in turn, suggests that despite the appraisals for Christophe that appeared in loyalist publications from the mid-1810s, his presence never sat wholly comfortably with British conservative observers.

These kinds of depictions certainly demand to be read as race-based reactions to the removal of the presence of a black monarch in the Atlantic world—a presence that a number of British loyalist observers clearly found confronting. As with American reports of the Haitian king's death, however, Britain's own concerns regarding political leadership and questions of legitimacy played an equally crucial role in how Christophe's death was depicted in the early 1820s. In particular, by this time British loyalists had become increasingly eager to detach Britain ideologically from the so-called Holy Alliance. As historians have demonstrated, by the 1820s British loyalists tended to portray their own constitutional monarchy as the political system that best counteracted the absolutist, repressive tendencies of the Holy Alliance, as well as the extremities of American republicanism.[35] A number of conservative British publications, therefore, framed Christophe's death within narratives that warned against tyrannical forms of monarchical rule—and which in turn celebrated Britain's own constitutional monarchy—by emphasising that the Haitian king's demise had come as a direct consequence of the severe modes of rule he had adopted. In reports such as these, and unlike those that saw some merit in his harsh forms of governance, his tyranny was far from justified. Rather, it was portrayed as a form of rule that should be universally rebuked and which justified his unruly end.

Conservative periodicals—such as Walter Scott's *Edinburgh Annual Register*—reminded readers that Christophe had "exercised a sway entirely despotic" and that he had "long been odious to his subjects, for the capricious tyranny which marked every part of his administration, and the deeds of bloody cruelty with which it was often stained".[36] For devout tories such as Scott, Christophe's alleged despotism rendered him an unfit and illegitimate monarch, and it served to remind British readers of the sanctity of their own monarchy. Christophe's death, other reports summarised, was a direct result of his actions as he "fell a victim to the disaffection excited by his own enormities".[37] In this way, the revolt against the Haitian monarch was projected by British news sources as an example of the self-defeating nature of repressive forms of rule, as practiced by Europe's despotic sovereigns—but a practice that was, importantly, far removed from Britain's cherished constitutional monarchy.

Loyalists, therefore, used Christophe's death to remind readers of the more liberal and progressive nature of Britain's own monarchy. British radicals, on the other hand, would use the demise of the Haitian king to draw parallels with Britain's own oppressive political regime. As historians have noted, throughout the 1810s the voices of Britain's working classes were muted considerably, and government policies of repression were a constant feature of the political landscape.[38] In particular, the Peterloo Massacre in 1819, in which military authorities charged into tens of thousands of protesters calling for parliamentary reform and killed 15 people, served to strengthen British radicals' portrayal of a British government intent on stifling any liberal or reformist voices.[39] In the wake of Peterloo, a number of prominent radicals would more vocally proclaim their belief that if the British public did not fight for a turn to a republican form of government, they would be left with a mode of military despotism.[40]

The 1819 Gagging Acts and the subsequent imprisonment of a number of prominent radical figures were actions designed by the government to quieten reform movements, and they were relatively successful in doing so.[41] But from 1820, the radical press received a vital shot in the arm with the news of successful revolutions in European regions such as Portugal and Naples—revolutions that were depicted in radical publications as a blow to oppressive regimes and restrictive political ideologies everywhere.[42] And so when news of the successful revolution against the Haitian monarchy emerged by the end of 1820, some radical observers sought to frame the events in Haiti in a celebratory narrative of anti-monarchy rebellion, and it served as a tantalising and powerful point of reference in radicals' calls for major political reform in Britain. In essence, if political revolutions occur when hopes for reform are quashed, a number of British radical observers looked to events in Haiti in 1820 to underline further the kind of revolutionary movement that could and should take place when citizens are subjected to governmental oppression.[43]

The poignancy that the latter days of Christophe's reign held for some British radical observers in this charged political atmosphere was captured in J. H. Amherst's often-overlooked play from 1821, *The Death of Christophe, Ex-King of Hayti*.[44] Although little is known about Amherst, the play is remarkable for its portrayal of monarchical tyranny, of the virtues of republican revolution, and for its regicidal undertones at a time of such hostility towards both the British government and monarch. Amherst was responsible for a number of plays staged at the Royal Coburg in the early 1820s, and *The Death of Christophe* was first performed here on 29 January 1821.[45] The Coburg's capacity—said to be approximately 3800—was one of the largest of London's theatres at the time, and Amherst's play was performed here for a number of weeks in 1821.[46]

The play is noteworthy for a number of reasons, not least among them that it is the earliest known on-stage characterisation (in English) of two of Haiti's leading political figures—Christophe and Boyer. With Amherst's portrayal of the revolution against Christophe appearing on stage only months after news of Christophe's death had reached British audiences, the uprising in Haiti was evidently an event that Amherst believed had captured the imaginations of the British public. The play was revived in 1822 and yet again in 1825, when the lead role of Christophe was played

140    J. FORDE

for the first time by a black actor—the American, Ira Aldridge.[47] Although it is impossible to attest to audience numbers for the play, the fact that the Coburg was willing to revisit Amherst's drama on multiple occasions appears to be testament to its enduring popularity and resonance with British audiences.

The Royal Coburg is said to have been one of the most unique and exhilarating playhouses in London during this period, despite the fact that the theatre had been the victim of increasing litigation that restricted the performance of shows deemed unsuitable by the Examiner of Plays—a governmental official whose responsibility it was to decide which theatrical productions were acceptable.[48] The Coburg was one of a growing number of illegitimate theatres in London that had opened during such strict regulation, and it apparently avoided litigation through its staging of burletta and pantomime—forms which were allowed by the Examiner.[49]

The Coburg managed to avoid this litigation enough to become known as the "Blood Tub" due to its preference for bloody and violent productions, and the theatre gained a reputation for plays that commented on politics and issues of morality.[50] The Coburg's dislike of George IV became increasingly apparent, and it was prosecuted in 1820 for its production of *King Richard III*—a dramatisation of the infamous story of a successful rebellion against a British king.[51] This was in keeping with like-minded theatres in London at this time which staged productions that sought to criticise monarchical rule and traditional forms of political power. These included Drury Lane's 1821 production of *Don Giovanni*—a play that, according to some historians, audiences would have recognised as a satire of the Regent—and numerous productions of *Jack and the Beanstalk* with its allusions to giant-killing.[52] Outside of London, and therefore outside of the jurisdiction of the Examiner of Plays, other theatres put on dramas such as *Coriolanus*, thereby bringing to the stage the story of a successful revolution against a tyrannical government.[53]

Historians have suggested that the Coburg's audiences of plays such as *Coriolanus* would have been well aware of the political messages implicit in such productions, and the same must certainly be said of those who witnessed Amherst's portrayal of the revolution against the Haitian monarchy.[54] The death of a black New World king who invited little sympathy from Britain's ruling classes offered the Coburg a unique opportunity to stage a play that overtly celebrated a revolution against a monarch—an opportunity that was routinely denied to the Coburg and London theatres in general at a time of increasingly autocratic regulation.

Despite appearing at such a renowned venue and in the midst of a plethora of politically charged productions throughout London, surprisingly little attention has been paid to Amherst's *Death of Christophe*.[55] In particular, the way in which the play acts as a celebration of the overthrow of monarchical rule and as a warning against stifling public calls for reform is often overlooked in discussions of the play. Most significantly, Amherst's play brought to the stage the demise of an unfeeling, oppressive monarch at a time when disdain for the British king was at a high among radical audiences. The play, therefore, is a pertinent example of the value that Christophe's death had for proponents of more radical politics in England at this time.

From the very beginning of the play, Christophe's tyrannical nature was asserted as he was described as "a tyrant that disgraces human nature". The monarch was referred to throughout the play in a variety of guises. He was said to be "hard-hearted"; "the resemblance of the devil"; "the tyrant who lives but on his peoples [sic] misery"; and "the scourge of mankind". Amherst even alluded to the well-known thumb-screw scandal that helped to turn British opinion against Christophe by including a scene in which an alleged revolutionary was tortured using the "singing screws". The scene reminded audiences of accusations in the British press in the late 1810s that Christophe had approved of the use of torture against British merchants.[56] In these ways, Christophe the tyrant—a figure well known to the British public by 1821—lived up to his reputation in Amherst's play.

Rather than simply reaffirming Christophe's lack of popularity, however, the play should also be considered in the context of the social unrest in Britain that was directed at the new British monarch and at the increasingly oppressive and restrictive measures of the British government—both targets for growing vitriolic criticism in British radical circles. By 1820, reformers and radicals largely viewed Britain's political leadership as "a form of tyranny posing as a form of self-rule".[57] The unpopularity of the Prince Regent had intensified after his public pardoning of the officials complicit in the Peterloo Massacre. Radicals and reformers saw this as further proof of the Regent's lack of care for the welfare of his subjects, and this significantly amplified the antipathy towards him. Prominent radical writers such as Robert Wedderburn and Richard Carlile wrote even more vociferously against the Regent's actions in the aftermath of Peterloo and optimistically depicted his perceived support of the events in Manchester as the beginning of the end of support for monarchism among the British

142   J. FORDE

public.[58] Within this increasingly anti-monarchical context, Amherst's unsympathetic treatment of a fallen tyrannical king had a receptive audience by the early 1820s.

A detailed analysis of the play suggests that Christophe's race was deliberately downplayed to enable the criticism of despotic political power to be universalised and to resonate more powerfully with its British audience. Amherst explicitly depicted a monarch out of touch with the needs of his people and unwilling to listen to calls for reform. The very first time the famed Haitian monarch appeared to the audience was when they witnessed his idea of justice as he dealt with a petitioner by shooting him on the spot—an act the king justified to his wife as a "warning lesson" to "those rebellious subjects who would abuse their monarch with perpetual petitionings".[59] This was a pertinent issue for British reformers, who had by this time become increasingly frustrated with the British government's refusal to discuss their own petitions throughout the 1810s.[60] Prominent radicals such as Hunt and Cobbett from the 1810s had vocally promoted the power and significance of petitioning. Since his time as Regent, however, George IV had constantly ignored petitions and calls for reform—something that led to such indignation among some ultra-radical observers that they openly projected regicidal imaginings as a result.[61] In addition, the accusation that Christophe was only willing to answer petitions if they arrived with some form of bribery was a further ongoing point of concern for British reformers exasperated with the continuing system of 'Old Corruption' in British politics—a political system in which governmental and public funds were used to further the self-interest of Members of Parliament.[62]

In Amherst's play, King Christophe embodied a corrupt mode of leadership by responding to any threat of insurrection or agitation with oppression and the imprisonment of anyone whom he felt had the "spirit of rebellion" within them. This was a striking parallel to the increasingly harsh sentences that were handed down to British radicals accused of sedition or blasphemy. Christophe was portrayed as being happy for such "reptiles" to "rot in dungeons" and anyone who questioned his form of governing was threatened with a similar fate, or worse.[63] Ultimately, Christophe was depicted in the play as a monarch struggling to deal with the currents of rebellion sweeping through his kingdom—a narrative with a domestic pertinence that would not have been lost on the Coburg's radically leaning audience.

5 THE DEATH OF A NEW WORLD MONARCH IN TRANSATLANTIC... 143

In contrast to the waning popularity of the British monarch—and the government as a whole—at this time, George's wife, Caroline, continued to enjoy a significant amount of support, particularly among the British working class. For years Queen Caroline had been publicly accused of adultery by her husband and his ministers, leading to her exile in Europe from 1814. George's attempts to discredit and divorce her in anticipation of his coronation in 1820 became known as the Queen Caroline Affair. But the attempts by George IV and his ministers to isolate Caroline from the public domain and to defame her character only served to intensify support for the British queen—and opposition to the king—among British radicals.[64] For reformers, the treatment of the queen served as an explicit example of the level of oppression and corruption at work in both Parliament and the monarchy.

The majority of the actors, staff and audiences at the Coburg were very public supporters of Queen Caroline—so much so that when one of its most prominent comedians took to the stage one evening in November 1820 he succeeding in raising three cheers for the victimised queen.[65] The pro-Caroline nature of the Coburg was such that the queen allegedly visited the theatre on at least one occasion in 1821.[66] Whether Caroline was aware of Amherst's play at the same theatre in the same year as her visit is of course unknown, but she would have likely found his depiction of the Haitian monarch's wife favourable to say the least.

Amherst's portrayal of Christophe's wife in the *Death of Christophe* displayed an acute awareness of this support for the estranged wife of George IV as he presented the figure of the Haitian queen as analogous to Queen Caroline. Christophe's wife—named "Alraida" in the play—was portrayed throughout as a rare voice of reason and one who tried to save the king from his impending fate, despite his harsh treatment towards her. The virtues of Alraida provided a direct contrast to her tyrannical husband and allowed the Haitian king's wife to be cast as someone who embodied the virtues that should be found in a monarch, but that were often lacking—in much the same way that British radicals portrayed Caroline in the early 1820s.[67] Alraida allowed Amherst to more subtly underline the inhumane and uncompassionate nature of monarchs. In her very first scene, the queen's caring nature provided a stark contrast to the king, especially when she begged him to consider the welfare of his subjects and directly asked him "[w]here can they fly but the monarch for relief?". Alraida implored the king to "gain [the people's] love"—something that George IV was failing ever more to do in Britain at this time.[68] The caring nature of Alraida was exemplified in the final scene of the first act when she tried desperately to save the life of an elderly blind prisoner that Christophe had demanded be shot on accusations of treachery. By the end of the play—with Christophe's demise all the more certain—it was Alraida who again provided the empathy and foresight that the king lacked, instructing him that "the people...will never more be thine", if he continued on this path of tyranny.[69]

*The Death of Christophe* presented British audiences not only with the portrayal of a tyrannical king falling on his own sword, but also with an image of Haitians as the architects of their own liberty in an age of oppression—something that, the play suggested, qualified them as legitimate recipients of the virtues of a more liberal form of government. The Coburg apparently had a penchant for dramatisations of struggles for freedom from political oppression. As well as restaging Amherst's play multiple times in the early 1820s, the theatre also presented its audience with a drama that positively portrayed the Greek fight for independence in 1823.[70] The staging of plays that celebrated revolutionary movements abroad, such as the revolution in Greece, was in keeping with the celebratory tone with which British radicals spoke about the European revolutions of the early 1820s. For example, in British alehouses in 1820, radicals applauded and toasted the revolutions of Portugal and Naples, while they simultaneously attacked the oppressive policies of the British government.[71]

Amherst's play sought to contribute to this rhetoric by situating the rebellion against Christophe and its liberal undertones alongside the European revolutions of the early 1820s. Although this alignment was not explicit, the narratives presented in the play spoke to universal themes of political reform and liberal revolution. Ultimately, Amherst used the troops who fought against Christophe as mouthpieces to promote the necessity of political upheaval and to serve as a rallying cry for the glorious nature of revolutionary movements. In the very first scene of the *Death of Christophe*, one of Boyer's soldiers spoke of troops who "may conquer in the cause of humanity or die bravely fighting for the rights of liberty". This same soldier scolded those who were opposed to or showed indifference to the revolution by asserting that "in the hour our liberties are threatened they neither deserve house nor home who wont [sic] absolutely stand forward to defend both".[72] Even though the presence of Boyer was sparse (Amherst instead focused his attention on Christophe's court and the troops of Boyer) Haiti's new leader emerged to the audience at the beginning of the play and addressed his troops by claiming that:

...our cause is that of human nature[.] no eloquence is needed to shew [sic] the policy or justice of aiming to exterminate a monster trampling on the rights of fair humanity and mercilessly weltering in his subjects [sic] blood. The universal cry is raised against Christophe[,] before whom age is no protection, infancy no power to move to pity. Onward Gentlemen, the eye of heaven is on us smilingly—our country-men regard us with hearts all filled by glorious hope and expectation...the universal voice must in the end prevail and crush to nothingness the mean and selfish wretches who delude the Monarch and oppress the people.[73]

In this way Amherst framed the fight against Christophe as one that was more universally recognised as one in the name of liberty. Importantly, with memories of Peterloo still fresh in the minds of British audiences, passages such as these highlighted the notion of a revolution from below and the importance of popular activism in affecting meaningful political reform. The rebellion against Christophe was shown to embody the same liberal ideas as those found in the revolutions of Europe and in British radicals' dreams of political reform. Amherst's play therefore sought to legitimise the Haitians' struggle to liberate themselves from the stranglehold of monarchical oppression—a struggle being witnessed throughout Europe, and one that some radicals hoped would gain traction in Britain.

The parallels between the fated king of Haiti and the threat of rebellion found in Europe and Britain were highlighted more explicitly in a print by the renowned radical printer and publisher, John Fairburn. Dated February 1821—only one month after Amherst's play hit the stage—Fairburn's *The Ghost of Christophe Ex-King of Hayti, appearing to the Un-Holy Alliance!!* (Fig. 5.1) depicted Christophe in an equally less than flattering light.[74] Fairburn drew attention to Christophe's blackness with caricaturised facial features, and the ex-monarch was depicted as an exotic version of Old World monarchy. More than this, the Haitian king's death was clearly depicted as one that benefited the country as a whole. In the background, a black figure proclaims joyously "Tank God de d___n tyrant be dead and poor slave be at liberty". The figure appears to be in the process of standing up from the kneeling position and is therefore highly evocative of the famous "Am I not a Man and a Brother?" medallions of the British

**Fig. 5.1** John Fairburn, *The Ghost of Christophe, ex-King of Hayti, Appearing to the Un-Holy Alliance!!*, 1821 (British Museum, 1935,0522.12.175)

abolitionist movement of the late eighteenth century.[75] Christophe's death, apparently, was the final act of emancipation for which Haitians were waiting.

By drawing on this famous image of abolitionism, Fairburn clearly suggested that the subjects of such an oppressive regime as Christophe's were no better off than slaves, thereby drawing a distinct link between those in Caribbean slavery and the labouring classes of populations living under monarchical rule. In this respect, Fairburn's print was quite unique in the way that it aligned the struggles of the Haitians under Christophe's rule with the working classes of Europe's dynasties. Radical writers such as William Cobbett had written disdainfully of Caribbean slaves as they felt that England's own working classes were being neglected by abolitionist concerns. Fairburn, on the other hand, clearly saw the value in depicting Haitians with slightly more empathy as he warned more generally of the state of serfdom that existed under monarchical regimes.

In his print, Fairburn presented Christophe's death as a fable akin to the one presented in Amherst's play. The character and actions of the fallen Haitian monarch were explicitly aligned with those of the members of Europe's Holy Alliance, as well as the British monarch. The ghost of the Haitian king emerges to the monarchs of Europe as blood pours from the self-inflicted wound from his pistols. Christophe offers the weapons to the European monarchs, declaring: "Unworthy members of a cursed league, take those and die and follow if thou canst a tyrant's fate". That Christophe's fate was the one that would follow all monarchical tyrants is emphasised by the lack of physical distance between Haiti and Europe—a distance shortened by Christophe who strides between the continents. By inviting the European monarchs to share in Christophe's fate, Fairburn further emphasised the idea that the populations of Britain and Europe were being subjected to the same kinds of oppressive regimes as that of Christophe's Haiti.

Fairburn optimistically hoped that the death of the Haitian king would be the catalyst for a change in the ways of Britain's own monarch. In the print, George IV sits with a discarded "Plan of Reform by John Bull" at his feet. However, the presence of the ghost of the fallen Haitian king leads him to repent his negligence of his subjects and wife—and to consider ridding himself of the corrupt ministers around him—by proclaiming: "By all the glorious points upon my Stars_by all the glory of my tripple Crown I like not this, Black King…be off—the Holy League I'll quit[,] reform my life[,] Kick off my Ministers[,] and love my wife". In this way, Fairburn optimistically saw the death of the Haitian monarch as a lesson for Europe's increasingly oppressive monarchical regimes—a lesson he hoped would be heeded by Britain's own sovereign.

Articles that appeared in Richard Carlile's radical publication *The Republican* in the early 1820s also asserted the importance of Haiti's latest fight for liberty. Carlile was a prominent voice in British radical circles and a staunch advocate of republican principles.[76] "Principled, passionate and personally reckless", Carlile's writing by the end of the 1810s had become increasingly anti-monarchical, and from the late 1810s he had been at the centre of a resurgence in the promotion of Paineite republican ideology as British radicals increasingly leaned towards "an outright commitment to revolutionary republicanism".[77] This made him a prime suspect in the British government's crackdown on radical publications and it was a position that eventually caught up with Carlile at the end of 1819, when he was imprisoned for six years for printing works of Thomas Paine.

Carlile's first real engagement with Haiti came with a report on the death of Christophe that appeared on 15 December 1820 in *The Republican*.[78] Unsurprisingly, the report was unsympathetic to the demise

148    J. FORDE

of a king who was "not deficient in all the necessary qualifications to make a monarchical despot". Carlile did, however, offer some praise for the ex-king by claiming that he had been a "great patron of education" and that his "sole object was the improvement of the negro world"—leading Carlile to assert Christophe's legitimacy as a monarch and one who had "ruled his kingdom with more ability than any of his European brothers".[79]

Despite such concessions to the positive impact of Christophe's rule, in this article Carlile reserved larger praise for the rebellion against the Haitian monarchy. In keeping with Fairburn's depiction and its parallel between monarchical rule and slavery, *The Republican* claimed that the revolution against Christophe had resulted in the "further emancipation of the negroes of Hayti". For Carlile, Haiti was proof that "the popery of monarchy can no longer be tolerated", and that it could "only be considered the bauble and relic of the darkest times which the progress of knowledge has taught us to reject". In this way, the demise of the Haitian monarchy represented hope that the insurrections such as those found in Europe would continue their march—something that Carlile optimistically predicted that the "allied banditti of kings" in Europe were powerless to halt. Carlile was less optimistic about the potential for meaningful political change in Britain, but Haiti's revolution and its abolition of monarchy appeared to provide a genuine source of comfort because "[w]hilst we are almost sickened by hope deferred at home, our languor is occasionally dissipated by the success of the advocates of liberty, and the friends of the human race abroad". Carlile's message was clear: while Englishmen foolishly "affect an attachment to monarchy", the Haitians were proof not only of the universal desire for progressive and republican ideals, but also of the capacity of the common man to implement this change.

Only a month later, Carlile's "A New Year's Address to the Reformers of Great Britain" re-emphasised his praise for the new Haitian republic by asserting that it "promises a fine example to all the West India Islands, in the abolition of monarchical despotism and the establishment of the Representative System of Government, with an elective presidency as the executive". Carlile felt comforted by Haiti's unified turn to republicanism, and he even went so far to claim that it had "amply dispelled the gloom of our more immediate interests at home". By the end of 1820, George IV had failed to pass a bill through Parliament that would have allowed him to divorce Queen Caroline and to strip her of her royal title. Carlile therefore sought to align the success of the Haitian revolutionaries with the perceived "triumph" of Queen Caroline over "the conspiracy against her life and honour" leading Carlile to proclaim that "[we] have conjointly worked us half a revolution".[80] In this way, Carlile began to explicitly align the revolutionary events in Haiti with the undercurrent of rebellion in Britain and to portray Haiti as a source of inspiration for those who agitated for political reform.

## Conclusion

The extent to which radicals such as Carlile or Fairburn truly admired the Haitians that had overthrown their monarch is of course contentious and coated in ambiguity. What is apparent, however, is that the uprising against King Christophe—and the monarch's subsequent demise—genuinely captured the imaginations of radical and republican thinkers in both America and Britain. For some Americans, a people's revolution against the Haitian king served as evidence of the archaic nature of monarchical rule, and it was used as proof of the desire of peoples everywhere to live under republican forms of government. This in turn reinforced American national identity as the leading Atlantic world nation in its approaches to legitimate and progressive political leadership. For British radicals and reformers, the death of the self-made New World king became a symbol of the brittle foundations upon which monarchism was built and exposed the power that the public should harness if their sovereign is neglectful in his or her duties. Not all radicals were necessarily anti-monarchy, but as the case of Christophe proved, monarchs should be held accountable for their actions, or they should suffer the consequences—no matter how extreme the end result. In the immediate aftermath of Christophe's death, depictions of the leader of the uprising against the king—and his plans for a new, unified form of government for the Haitian state—would excite the imaginations of American republicans and British radicals to an even larger extent.

## Notes

1. The coercion of Haitians to cultivate the grounds on which they had served as slaves was an aspect of the leadership of Louverture and Dessalines as well, but Christophe's regime is renowned for enforcing this plan with particular severity. This—and the ways in which Haitians navigated and resisted forced labour—is documented masterfully in Johnhenry Gonzalez, *Maroon Nation* (New Haven: Yale University Press, 2019).
2. *Observer*, 11 December 1820; Dubois, *Haiti*, 85–86.

3. *Jackson's Oxford Journal*, 9 December 1820.

4. It is important to note that this chapter does not intend to argue that this rebellion against Christophe deserves equal status with the 1791–1804 Revolution. However, the term "revolution" will be used not only as it most aptly describes the way that Christophe's own subjects turned on him, but also because this is how his death was viewed and described by the majority of American and British observers.

5. Malcolm Chase, *1820: Disorder and Stability in the United Kingdom* (Oxford: Oxford University Press, 2013), 166.

6. *City of Washington Gazette*, 7 November 1820.

7. These race-based reactions against Christophe from commentators outside of Haiti would largely continue until well into the twentieth century. Since then, Christophe's rule has been treated to more thoughtful considerations of his reign: see for example Aimé Césaire's 1963 play, *The Tragedy of King Christophe* (Evanston: Northwestern University Press, 2015).

8. *National Advocate for the Country*, 17 November 1820.

9. Samuel A. Hay, "Escaping the tar-and-feather future of African American theatre," *African American Review*, 31, no. 4 (1997), 617.

10. Eliga H. Gould, *Among the Powers of the Earth: The American Revolution and the Making of a New World Empire* (Cambridge: Harvard University Press, 2012), 213; Jay Sexton, *The Monroe Doctrine: Empire and Nation in Nineteenth-Century America* (New York: Hill and Wang, 2011), 58.

11. *National Advocate for the Country*, 17 November 1820.

12. *Niles' Weekly Register*, 11 November 1820.

13. *Niles' Weekly Register*, 25 November 1820.

14. *Cohen's Lottery Gazette*, 30 November 1820; *Boston Recorder*, 25 November 1820.

15. *National Gazette*, 14 November 1820; *City of Washington Gazette*, 7 November 1820.

16. *New Hampshire Sentinel*, 25 November 1820; *Cohen's Lottery Gazette*, 30 November 1820.

17. *Niles' Weekly Register*, 10 February 1821.

18. *Boston Recorder*, 25 November 1820.

19. *Niles' Weekly Register*, 10 February 1821.

20. *National Gazette*, 26 January 1821.

21. *The Atheneum; or, Spirit of the English Magazines*, 1 May 1821, 93; *Poulson's American Daily Advertiser*, 10 February 1821.

22. *Daily Intelligencer*, 11 November 1820.

23. *Daily Intelligencer*, 11 November 1820.

24. *Weekly Aurora*, 4 December 1820.

25. *The Traveller*, 7 December 1820.

5 THE DEATH OF A NEW WORLD MONARCH IN TRANSATLANTIC...    151

26. *The Gentleman's Magazine and Historical Chronicle, July to December 1820*, vol. 90 (1820), 565–566.
27. *Imperial Magazine*, vol. 3, no. 30 (1821), 746–748.
28. Seymour Drescher, *The Mighty Experiment: Free Labor Versus Slavery in British Emancipation* (Oxford: Oxford University Press, 2002), 108.
29. *The Traveller*, 7 December 1820.
30. *Blackwood's Edinburgh Magazine*, vol. 9, no. 51 (1821), 267; Blackburn, *Overthrow of Colonial Slavery*, 423.
31. *Monthly Magazine, or British Register*, vol. 51, no. 350 (1821), 93.
32. *The Traveller*, 7 December 1820.
33. This poem has been described by Marcus Wood as "stupidly unpleasant". For an analysis of the poem—and Wordsworth's change of opinion since his writing on Toussaint—see Marcus Wood, ed. *The Poetry of Slavery: An Anglo-American Anthology, 1764–1865* (Oxford: Oxford University Press, 2003), 231–237.
34. *John Bull*, 10 December 1821. For an overview of the establishment of the Society and its aims see M. J. D. Roberts, "Reshaping the Gift Relationship: The London Mendicity Society and the Suppression of Begging in England, 1818–1869," *International Review of Social History* 36, no. 2 (1991), 201–231.
35. Sexton, *Monroe Doctrine*, 63.
36. *The Edinburgh Annual Register for 1820*, vol. 13 (1823), 323–325; *The Annual Register, or a View of the History, Politics and Literature of the Year 1820* (1822), 244.
37. *The Monthly Review, or Literary Journal...January to April, inclusive, 1821*, vol. 94 (1821), 443.
38. Malcom I. Thomis and Peter M. Holt, *Threats of Revolution in Britain: 1789–1848* (London: Macmillan, 1977), 29–39.
39. Chase, *1820*, 52. For a detailed analysis of how Peterloo became such a central frame of reference in British imaginations in 1819 see James Chandler, *England in 1819: The Politics of Literary Culture and the Case of Romantic Historicism* (Chicago: University of Chicago Press, 1998).
40. James Epstein, *Radical Expression: Political Language, Ritual, and Symbol in England, 1790–1850* (Oxford: Oxford University Press, 1994), 105.
41. The Gagging Acts, passed in December 1819, punished those who were deemed to have written or published anti-establishment material.
42. Mark Jarrett, *The Congress of Vienna and Its Legacy: War and Great Power Diplomacy after Napoleon* (London: IB Tauris, 2013), 239; Chase, *1820*, 166–168.
43. Thomis and Holt, *Threats of Revolution*, 62.
44. Houghton Library, Harvard University, TS 3111. 225, J. H. Amherst, *The Death of Christophe, Ex-King of Hayti: A Drama in Three Acts* (1821).

152   J. FORDE

45. David Worrall, *Harlequin Empire: Race, Ethnicity and the Drama of the Popular Enlightenment* (New York: Routledge, 2015), 71.
46. Ibid., 69.
47. Tabitha McIntosh and Gregory Pierrot, "Capturing the Likeness of Henry I of Haiti (1805–1822)," *Atlantic Studies* 14, no. 2 (2017), 142; Bernth Lindfors, *Ira Aldridge: The Early Years 1807–1833* (Rochester: University Rochester Press, 2011), 89–92.
48. John Larpent held this position from 1778–1824. For an overview of his time as Examiner of the Plays see David Worrall, *Theatric Revolution: Drama, Censorship, and Romantic Period Subcultures 1773–1832* (Oxford: Oxford University Press, 2006), 103–132.
49. Worrall, *Harlequin Empire*, 67–68.
50. Jane Moody, *Illegitimate Theatre in London, 1770–1840* (New York: Cambridge University Press, 2007), 34.
51. Chase, *1820*, 73.
52. Chase, *1820*, 74.
53. Moody, *Illegitimate Theatre*, 108.
54. Chase, *1820*, 75.
55. David Worrall has supplied the most extensive discussion of the play, particularly focusing on the lack of any notable race-based criticism of Christophe: Worrall, *Harlequin Empire*.
56. David Geggus, "Haiti and the Abolitionists: Opinion, Propaganda and International Politics in Britain and France, 1804–1838," in *Abolition and Its Aftermath: The Historical Context, 1790–1916*, ed. David Richardson (London: Frank Cass and Company Ltd, 1985), 125.
57. Chandler, *England in 1819*, 30.
58. Steve Poole, *The Politics of Regicide in England, 1760–1850: Troublesome Subjects* (Manchester: Manchester University Press, 2000), 154.
59. Amherst, *Death of Christophe*, Act 1, f. 19.
60. Marcus Wood, *Radical Satire and Print Culture, 1790–1822* (Oxford: Clarendon Press, 1994), 97; Thomis and Holt, *Threats of Revolution*, 39.
61. Poole, *Politics of Regicide*, 143–148.
62. Philip Harling, "Parliament, the State, and 'Old Corruption': Conceptualizing Reform, C. 1790–1832," in *Rethinking the Age of Reform: Britain 1780–1850*, ed. Arthur Burns and Joanna Innes (Cambridge: Cambridge University Press, 2003), 98.
63. Amherst, *Death of Christophe*, Act 2, f. 14.
64. Epstein, *Radical Expression*, 110.
65. Worrall, *Harlequin Empire*, 68.
66. Worrall, *Theatric Revolution*, 196–217.
67. For an overview of how British radicals supported Caroline and used her as a symbolic figure in their denunciations of George IV and of the British

monarchy in general see Iain McCalman, *Radical Underworld: Prophets, Revolutionaries and Pornographers in London, 1795–1840* (New York: Cambridge University Press, 1988), 162–177.

68. Amherst, *Death of Christophe*, Act 1, f. 20.
69. Amherst, *Death of Christophe*, Act 3, f. 4.
70. Worrall, *Harlequin Empire*, 68.
71. Chase, *1820*, 166–168.
72. Amherst, *Death of Christophe*, Act 1, f. 7.
73. Ibid., f. 11.
74. For a rare discussion of this print, see Rosalie Smith McCrea, "Portrait Mythology? Representing the 'Black Jacobin': Henri Christophe in the British Grand Manner," *The British Art Journal* 6, no. 2 (2005), 66–70.
75. Marcus Wood has highlighted how the image became synonymous with the anti-slave trade movement and was reproduced in literature, on newspaper headings, and even in ceramic figures: Marcus Wood, *Blind Memory: Visual Representations of Slavery in England and America, 1780–1865* (Manchester: Manchester University Press, 2000), 22. It is also worth noting that in the 1810s the image was also appropriated by other British radicals to suggest that Britain's working classes were no better off than the slaves of the Caribbean: Marcus Wood, *Radical Satire and Print Culture, 1790–1822* (Oxford: Clarendon Press, 1994), 211–214.
76. For an overview of Carlile's life and his writing see Joel H. Wierner, *Radicalism and Freethought in Nineteenth-Century Britain: The Life of Richard Carlile* (Santa Barbara: Greenwood Press, 1983).
77. Chase, *1820*, 18.
78. This is a publication that James Epstein has aptly described as "one of the most outstanding radical journals of the nineteenth century": Epstein, *Radical Expression*, 109.
79. *The Republican*, 15 December 1820, 564–565.
80. *The Republican*, 1 January 1821, 3.

CHAPTER 6

# The Promise and the Threat of Boyer and Haitian Republicanism

King Christophe's death in 1820, and the resulting political system adopted in Haiti from that point on, would go on to shape Haitian politics for decades to come. Shortly after the king's death, despite some early resistance from troops that remained loyal to Christophe, Jean-Pierre Boyer proclaimed a unified Haitian republic and appointed himself the president—a title he would keep for another twenty-three years. This period in charge was the longest of any of Haiti's post-revolutionary leaders. Some historians have asserted the "remarkable stability" that Boyer initially brought to Haiti, especially after his bloodless annexation of neighbouring Santo Domingo (present-day Dominican Republic) in 1822.[1] Haiti initially became "politically more relaxed" under Boyer's early stewardship, particularly in contrast with the severe and autocratic forms of rule practised by Dessalines and Christophe.[2] Although Boyer would end up cultivating his own brand of despotic leadership, rumours of this would not reach American and British news sources until the mid-1820s, and so the apparent stability of the early 1820s was welcomed and even celebrated by a number of Boyer supporters in Britain and America.[3]

The positivity with which Boyer's Haiti was received by some can been seen in how it was promoted by organisations such as the American Colonisation Society as an opportunity for free African-Americans to start over and prosper (and in turn to alleviate the 'problem' for American white society of an ever-increasing free-black population in America).[4]

© The Author(s) 2020                                                   155
J. Forde, *The Early Haitian State and the Question of Political Legitimacy*, Palgrave Studies in Political History,
https://doi.org/10.1007/978-3-030-52608-5_6

Scholarly studies have underlined Haiti's significance as a symbol of freedom and inspiration for African-Americans throughout the 1820s and 1830s. Haiti's continuing independence—despite a lack of official recognition of its sovereignty from the American government—was promoted as a source of pride for free African-Americans trying to carve a political identity for themselves in a largely hostile climate in America.[5]

The impact of Boyer's early success in uniting Haiti under a republican form of government—and the promise this held in the imaginations for some—extended much further than the opportunity it presented to African-Americans, as well as white Americans with colonial aspirations. Although Boyer had been leader of the southern republic since 1818, it was after Christophe's death that he caught the attention more fully of transatlantic commentators. What united these figures was their attempts to celebrate Boyer, and Haiti's unified turn to republicanism, as proof of the virtuous nature of republican government. At a time when revolutions throughout Europe and the Americas threatened to completely overturn the established political order in the Atlantic world, Haiti's own implementation of republicanism became a key point of reference in a number of American and British political commentaries—narratives that were increasingly anti-conservative in nature. While the governments of both America and Britain continued to refuse to recognise the Haitian republic, transatlantic representations of Boyer in the early 1820s give a valuable insight into the nuances and complexities of American and British perceptions of the Haitian republic—perceptions framed by considerations of political legitimacy and the virtues of republican governance.

Reactions to the early years of Boyer's presidency were framed within a climate of anxieties of America's and Britain's ruling classes and wider populations. By the 1820s, Americans were witnessing the increasing power of their own federal government—one that by now lacked any real form of partisan resistance.[6] As such, historians have argued that some Americans began to fear the emergence of a central "tyrannical" form of government in their own country.[7] Other Americans were still wary of the potential internal threat posed by those who "stood alongside Great Britain, ready to undermine the republic from within".[8] American politics by 1820 had "faced a multi-faceted crisis", as the Panic of 1819 and the Missouri Crisis had "threatened the stability of the union by eroding both the power and authority of the federal government and the ties and sympathies between the states".[9]

Although the War of 1812 and its succeeding years had instilled a sense of American patriotism—particularly for its form of government—the political crises and tensions that converged in America by the late 1810s led Americans to once more view their republic as "internally vulnerable" and weak compared to the Old World powers that continued to dominate Atlantic world politics.[10] As Caitlin Fitz has highlighted, by the 1820s a large number of political observers viewed America as "a lonely republic bobbing alone in a churning sea of monarchy".[11] In this context, the emergence of a peaceful, unified Haitian republic allowed Americans to further underline the glory of republican governance and to reaffirm America's status as paving the way for these new forms of republican governments to emerge—a crucial shot in the arm for American Republicans at a time when public confidence in the federal government was at a low.

Britain was a similarly insecure political entity in the early 1820s as loyalists mourned the death of the popular George III. The deceased king's "simple personal piety" is said to have "elevated him in personal estimation" of the British public—a stark contrast with the debauchery associated with the lifestyle of his son, George IV.[12] Since his time as Regent, the British public had loathed to see the emergence of a sovereign who paid such little regard to his subjects and who seemed only to live for decadence and self-indulgence.[13] Historians have demonstrated how George IV's eventual coronation in 1821 was met in some parts of the country with deep public disdain and anger.[14] The Peterloo killings of 1819—along with the British government's decision to further restrict freedom of the press in light of these events—enabled radicals in the early 1820s to assert the "moral bankruptcy of aristocratic government" as a plethora of publications flouted Britain's sedition laws to print scathing commentaries of Britain's political elites.[15] This resentment towards the new British sovereign intensified with the harsh treatment of his estranged wife, Caroline, and in particular George's attempts to obtain a divorce between 1820 and 1821—something that British radicals seized on as a central part of their denunciations of the new British monarch.[16]

The British ruling classes were also anxious spectators to the revolutionary tide sweeping through Europe in the early 1820s. Revolutions in Greece, Spain, Portugal and Naples threatened to upend the established order in Europe—something that was written about with enthusiasm in radical-leaning publications.[17] British radicals saw the European revolutions as a potential catalyst for more universal political and social progress and vehemently derided the Holy Alliance for their attempts to negate this

158   J. FORDE

progress in the name of self-preservation. As Richard Carlile would conclude towards the end of 1820: "[Thomas] Paine thought he lived in the age of revolution, but the present moment better deserves the epithet".[18] In this political climate, news that Haitians had revolted against their king in favour of reform and a complete change of government was seized upon by a number of observers in Britain. British radical voices had hitherto largely ignored the topic of Haiti in their writing, possibly because Haiti's apparent successes during Christophe's reign would have disrupted their anti-monarchical narratives. However, the establishment of a republican form of government in Haiti presented an opportunity for radical voices in Britain to capitalise on these events as valuable reference points in their calls for political and social reform.

While the governments of both America and Britain continued to refuse to recognise the Haitian republic, the depictions of Haiti explored in this chapter give a valuable insight into the nuances and complexities of American and British perceptions of the Haitian republic—perceptions framed by considerations of political legitimacy and the virtues of republican governance. At a time of domestic political agitation in America and Britain, Haiti's turn to republicanism was celebrated by a number of different observers on both sides of the Atlantic—all of whom saw the implementation of a single unified republican government in Haiti as proof of the universal desire and need for progressive forms of governance to replace the dated modes of Old World approaches to political leadership.

## JEAN-PIERRE BOYER AND AMERICAN REPUBLICAN IMAGINATIONS

American reports of Boyer's victory over Christophe often contained rumours that both northern and southern Haiti would soon be united under one republican government, with President Boyer at its head. Such stories came at a time when American newspapers had been excitedly reporting the continuing successes of the republican revolutionaries of Spanish America. The American public responded to news of republics replacing Latin American colonies by naming livestock, towns, and even children after the revolutionary heroes.[19] As Fitz has demonstrated, by 1822 three-quarters of 4 July celebrations recorded in American newspapers included toasts to the newly established Spanish-American republics and their founders.[20] Fitz has further argued that Haiti was, in general,

6 THE PROMISE AND THE THREAT OF BOYER AND HAITIAN REPUBLICANISM    159

excluded from celebratory narratives that explicitly drew parallels among the revolutionaries of Spanish America and the United States because the black state had "gone too far".[21] Michael J. Dash also notes the continued lack of official recognition of Haiti from the American government despite the very public support for the revolutions in Spanish America. Dash argues that southern planters in the United States played a crucial role in ensuring that Haiti was "relegated...to a zone of negativity and absence" in the 1820s.[22] However, if in this time the Americas "increasingly seemed like a sanctuary for liberal republics; [and] Europe a final, desperate bastion for absolutist monarchy", then the positive depictions of Boyer's unification of Haiti that emerged must be viewed—at least in part—as a product of the championing of New World republicanism.[23]

Narratives that celebrated Haiti's unified turn to republicanism in general refused to explicitly align this revolution in Haiti with the other republican revolutions in Spanish America. Nonetheless, newspapers such as Philadelphia's *Weekly Aurora* claimed that Boyer's attempts to establish "republican institutions upon the ruin of the cruel tyranny which existed under the imperial government" was of paramount importance to America, "if not to mankind in general".[24] These kinds of pro-Haitian reports looked to frame the uprising in Haiti in a discourse that celebrated New World resistance to European political thought. Although Boyer's Haiti would not be overtly aligned with the new republics of Spanish America it was, nevertheless, framed in a more general celebration of the republicanism found in the Western hemisphere and a continued American denunciation of the repressive and archaic nature of Old World monarchies.

Newspaper reports that patriotically sought to underline the glorious nature of republicanism soon focused on the distinctly contrasting characters of the fallen Haitian king and Haiti's new republican saviour. Reports in Republican-supporting publications such as the *National Advocate* situated depictions of the republican leader Boyer directly opposite those of the "absolute and despotic" monarch.[25] In a stark contrast to the Haitians' apparent detestation of their king, Boyer's popularity was allegedly "unbounded", and early reports of his reign in Haiti spoke of "the Freedom which is enjoyed, and the republican justice which is practised".[26] Reports such as these commonly claimed that Christophe's family were now under the protection of Boyer—a striking contrast to the allusions to Christophe's inhuman and bloodthirsty nature that had been so common in the American press. Even when newspapers reported that Christophe's sons had been killed in Boyer's revolution, they also claimed that this had

160    J. FORDE

happened before Boyer had arrived at the palace, and that it would not have occurred under his guidance.[27] That these reports appeared in Republican newspapers such as the *Boston Recorder*, and anti-monarchical publications such as *Niles's Weekly Register*, is hardly surprising. While there was little evidence to support their stories, these depictions nonetheless underlined the paternal, humane and non-violent characteristics of republican leaders—something that, in turn, cemented their legitimacy, especially in contrast to monarchical heads of state.

This feeling of positivity towards the "Washington of Hayti" was common in American newspapers by the end of 1820.[28] The wave of celebration for Haiti's new republican leader prompted the *New York Literary Journal, and Belles-Lettres Repository* to publish a remarkable poem celebrating the republican spirit of Haiti's new head of state—the anonymous, 'To Freedom's Sons of St. Domingo'.[29] In it, Boyer was legitimised not only as a viable political leader, but crucially one who fitted the mould of exemplary republicanism:

> Proud the march of the free and brave,
> When they march to freedom—or the grave,
> Nor seek alone their lives to save,
>                   But Liberty.
>
> Proud is the warrior's sparkling eye,
> When tyrants hosts in terror fly
> Before the men who dare to die
>                   For Liberty!
>
> And proud are they, tho' white men scorn
> The jetty black which wraps each form,
> To follow in the battle's storm
>                   Brave Boyer!
>
> Proud is their look of conscious might,
> When they rush to the field of fight,
> Where thy banner is waving bright,
>                   Brave Warrior!

> Proudly thy name to earth's gone forth,
> To east, to west, to south, to north,
> None e'er can find, 'mong all their worth,
> > A Braver!

> Prouder than all that day shall be,
> When St. Domingo's sons are free,
> And thousand tongues cry "hail to thee,"
> > Our Saviour.

The poem was an explicit celebration of the Haitian uprising against its monarchy—one which had caused tyrants to flee and which proclaimed the virtues of freedom and liberty. More striking than this, however, is how two-thirds of the poem acted as a celebration of "Brave Boyer", the "Brave Warrior" and "Saviour". The poem's description of Haitians who "rushed to the field of fight" and followed their leader in the name of liberty, clearly called to mind American memories and celebrations of their own revolutionary heroes. Boyer's leadership and republican form of governance was depicted as the final act of freedom that Haiti's ex-slaves had yet to experience and was framed as the ultimate form of emancipation. The fifth stanza's assertion that Boyer's reputation and bravery could not be bettered throughout the world was a significant declaration, and the poem as a whole represents a particularly forceful celebration of Haiti's new leader and the perceived accomplishments of his revolution. By outlining the achievements of Haiti's republican revolution and the character of its leader, the anonymous poet clearly sought to legitimise Boyer's form of republicanism as one with which Americans should identify and align.

It is important to note that the figure of Boyer did not elicit as much enthusiasm as depicted in this poem from all American observers. For example, Carroll Smith-Rosenberg has demonstrated how Leonora Sansay's 1819 novel *Zelica*—a novel which, like her 1808 novel *Secret History; Or The Horrors of St. Domingo* is situated in the latter years of the Saint-Domingue revolution—portrayed Haitians and their leaders as undeserving of and unsuitable to the privileges of republican governance.[30] *Zelica* was published two years before the overthrow of Christophe and Boyer's succession, but a number of publications at the beginning of 1821 were clearly intent on communicating a similar message. These reports were hesitant to add their voices to these choruses of approval of Boyer,

162   J. FORDE

particularly as reports from Haiti contested claims that Boyer had brought tranquillity to the north and instead asserted that the overthrowing of Christophe had only resulted in outright chaos for the whole nation—reports that in turn denied Boyer's legitimacy as a republican president and Haiti's legitimacy as a republic.

This scepticism is perhaps best exemplified by the *National Gazette*'s early reports of the formation of Boyer's unified government. The *Gazette*'s editor, Robert Walsh, had by this time completed something of a political transformation. Previously a staunch Federalist and Anglophile who had contributed to anti-Republican publications such as Joseph Dennie's *Portfolio*, Walsh turned his back on support for Britain and its political system in the aftermath of the War of 1812, converting to a nationalistic supporter of America's form of republican government.[31] Walsh's praise for the virtues of republicanism did not, however, necessarily extend outside of America. It certainly did not extend to Haiti.

From as early as November 1820, the *Gazette* reported on Boyer's succession of Christophe with a sneering, mocking disdain. The newspaper likened Boyer's early proclamations in the aftermath of Christophe's death to those found during the French Revolution that alluded to liberty and equality, but that in reality would only bring the Haitians "cruel despotism, universal misery, iron yoke, vice, horrors, pain, [and] accumulated woe"—hardly the most ringing of endorsements for Haiti's new leader. The *Gazette* pondered sarcastically whether Haiti's "well-trained philosophical politicians will be able to comprehend all that is said". In a similar vein, a later report found in the *Gazette* in March 1821 also questioned whether Haitians had the "talents and education necessary" for the writing of Haiti's state papers. Boyer, described by the *Gazette* as a "usurper" and "military chief", had only succeeded in fanning the flames of "discord". As such, the *Gazette* predicted, Haitians would "break out at any moment into revolt". Although race was not mentioned overtly, the suggestion that the blackness of Haiti's government excluded them from republican legitimacy was explicitly clear.[32]

As opposed to being a united country under Boyer's government, other newspapers claimed that the nation-state was divided by race as mulatto Haitians were said to favour the republican form of government, while the black citizens of Haiti were said to be in favour of monarchy.[33] Newspapers doubted whether Boyer had the "energy and promptness" of Christophe to deal with such social and racial tensions. Perhaps more significantly, where some sources praised the president and enthused about his

6 THE PROMISE AND THE THREAT OF BOYER AND HAITIAN REPUBLICANISM    163

moderate temper and mild form of government as one befitting of this new republic, alternative depictions claimed that "his reputed mildness is not appreciated as a very estimable trait by such people as the Haytians".[34] As a result, such reports concluded: "All things appeared to be paving the way for some ambitious Chief to…wade through rivers of blood up to throne".[35] While mildness in government may be a positive trait in more civilised republics, Haiti was depicted as a site of political turmoil and incivility—and therefore an infertile land in which the fruits of true republicanism could grow.

Despite these negative depictions, in general Americans were presented with representations that were enthusiastic about Haiti's change in government and its new leader. Although a handful of reports were disparaging of the president, the majority sought to legitimise Boyer's status as a republican president. This was pertinent at a time when confidence in the American federal government had been severely dented. The emergence of a republican leader in northern Haiti allowed American commentators to project affirmations of how republican governments should operate, and how their leaders should act in the interests of the country.

American newspapers with histories of strong support for the Republican party particularly used Boyer's government as an example of why Americans should continue to believe in America's republicanism, and they reaffirmed the prosperity it would bring them. For Nathaniel Willis's *Boston Recorder*, the Haitian republic represented a kind of social and political utopia, one that apparently stemmed from the example set by the laws of Boyer's government, which were "consonant with every feeling of policy, justice and humanity". Boyer's just and mild form of governance was such that "the keys of the prison in this government are literally covered with rust"—a world away from reports of the tyrannical and oppressive monarchical regimes of Christophe and the dynasties of the Old World.[36] Similarly, other reports asserted that upon hearing of Haitians ransacking the palaces, Boyer allegedly issued a decree to the looters that all property was to be returned to the republic within a day or the criminals would face prosecution. While there is little evidence to determine whether this decree existed or not, such portrayals of an honourable republican leader led newspapers such as the Tammany-established *National Advocate* to conclude that: "Every measure of the Haytian chief evinces a decision and promptness that fully qualify him for the high station which he occupies … His ideas of liberty are clear and his abhorrence of tyranny marked and explicit".[37] These reports allowed newspapers such as the *Advocate* to at once generously praise the Haitian president, while reminding its American readers that a love of liberty and a hatred for monarchy were essential qualifications to occupy a presidential office. "Under the auspices of such a man," the *Litchfield Republican* enthused, "Hayti is destined to become an interesting republic".[38]

Central to these affirmations of the privileges of republicanism were reports of Boyer healing the political divisions between northern and southern Haiti and the establishment of a single Haitian state—proof for Americans of the unifying nature of republican forms of government and of the divisiveness that despotism and monarchical rule could breed. By the middle of 1821, newspaper reports emerged that Boyer had quelled a rebellion by some of Christophe's former troops and that in Haiti "[tranquillity] is everywhere established".[39] Republican newspapers praised Boyer not only for his ability to quash the alleged rebellion but that he did so with moderation—a mildness that even extended to the chief rebels to whom he reportedly "exercised clemency whenever it could with propriety be extended".[40] The *Litchfield Republican* lavished praised on the Haitian president by claiming that he had given a "new and pacific tone to the affairs of that country" and that he was "equally skilled" in "wielding alike the insignia of war and peace".[41] Although America's own founders were not explicitly aligned with Boyer in these reports, the authors of them undoubtedly relied on their readers' memories of America's own revolutionary leaders as they framed Boyer as a further example of what constitutes true republican leadership.

In this light, Boyer's Haiti served as an example for newspapers in the United States to remind American readers that real tyranny existed in the lands of kings, and not in the liberal utopias of republican seats of governance. Although little had been reported of Boyer in the American press prior to the death of Christophe, he soon emerged to the American public as the type of leader who once again allowed Haiti to be viewed with promise—and one who was proof of the virtuous nature of republicanism, which was a deliberately self-vindicating message. The idea that the implementation of a republican mode of government translated into a more stable and justly governed Haitian state overall was a key component of American reports that looked favourably on the new leader. In such reports, Haitian citizens were depicted as deserving of and benefitting from this new form of governance, despite its perceived trials and tribulations—a timely reminder for the citizens of the increasingly turbulent American republic.

The benefits of a leader such as Boyer, and of the adoption of a republican mode of governance, were clearly outlined in reports of Boyer's victory over Christophe. Unsurprisingly, editors such as the vociferously anti-monarchical Hezekiah Niles led the way in outlining how Haiti's shift to republicanism would benefit the still-young nation. *Niles' Weekly Register* claimed that Boyer's government "is said to be producing the most happy effects", and that under the president "harmony prevails", and that the people were "united".[42] Republican newspapers such as the *Boston Recorder* also published reports that claimed in Haiti "there are fewer of those vices which too often deform the human character, to be found here, than in any other country with which I am acquainted". Reports such as these asserted that in Boyer's Haiti "[c]alumny [sic]...you never hear", "thievery" was "almost unknown", "[t]radesmen and retailers are honest to a proverb" and even swearing was "seldom heard".[43] In this way, positive depictions of Haiti's newly unified republic—at a time of tension and insecurity for America's own republican citizens—allowed newspapers to remind their readers of the benefits that republicanism can bring to the civility and morality of a nation as a whole.

It is perhaps unsurprising that these positive portrayals of Boyer's Haiti often included discussions concerning America and Haiti's commercial relationship. Sara Fanning's work has highlighted how Boyer's stewardship—and in particular the annexation of Santo Domingo—"raised hopes" among American merchants that this new market would be beneficial to an American economy still suffering from the effects of the financial crisis of the late 1810s. News sources such as the *Niles' Register* and the *National Gazette* asserted the importance of the Haitian republic in helping America's economic woes. Some newspapers even went so far to claim that the Haitian market alone could keep Americans in constant employment, with a number of readers writing in to share their enthusiasm.[44]

American merchants continued to see Haiti as a potentially profitable source of commerce, something which intensified in light of America's economic woes of the late 1810s.[45] Therefore, where Haiti's adoption of an archaic monarchical system in the 1810s had severely restricted support from American sources, its turn to republicanism meant that American merchants and traders in particular could seize on a moment of republican fervour in their calls for better trade agreements with the Haitian state. In some cases, this even extended to calls for the American government to reconsider their reluctance to recognize formally Haiti as a sovereign state. Merchants with a pro-Haiti agenda thus sought to intertwine arguments concerning the benefits of trade with the black republic with a more ideological celebration of republicanism. In essence, by promoting more favourable trade agreements with the Haitian state, these merchants argued that America was in turn supporting the virtues and legitimacy of republican modes of governance.

Proponents who clearly wished to see more favourable trade links established with Haiti advocated Haiti's new republican status in their attempts to promote a commercial alliance with the black republic. By the end of 1821, pro-mercantile newspapers such as the *Boston Commercial Gazette* were beginning to report approvingly of Boyer's apparent friendliness to foreigners and of a desire and willingness to help foreign traders conduct business safely in the republic.[46] Other publications such as *Niles' Weekly Register* claimed that even without a formalised trade agreement between the two republics, exports to Haiti were worth more to Americans than those to Europe—with the exception of England, France and Holland—leading such reports to conclude that "the negroes of Hayti are more interesting to us, in a commercial point of view, than 'legitimate' Russia, Sweden, Denmark and Norway, Turkey, all the states of Italy, and half a dozen more 'powers'".[47] Enthusiasm for Haiti in this commercial context was understandable—by 1821 American merchants were responsible for supplying almost half of all of Haiti's imports.[48] Some pro-trade proponents therefore sought to combine more explicitly economic support for Haiti with assertions of the legitimacy of its form of republicanism as a way to ensure that America's economic relationship with Haiti would be better safeguarded by the American administration.

The depiction of Haiti under Boyer as a stable and exemplary form of republican government was a key component of John Dodge's lengthy and wide-ranging promotion of the Haitian republic entitled "A Memorial Upon the Subject of Hayti".[49] Dated 5 September 1821, Dodge's "Memorial" was written for and sent to John Quincy Adams—at that time the United States' Secretary of State. Dodge was a prominent Boston merchant and "one of the most active American traders" in early-nineteenth-century Haiti, with at least two trading companies in Cap Haïtien.[50] Unsurprisingly, then, Dodge wrote his "Memorial" in the hope of persuading Adams to establish more lucrative commercial relations between America and the black republic, as well as to do more to protect the commercial interests of American citizens already trading with the Haitians.

As a resident on the island, Dodge asserted the importance of his role as an "actual observer of the substantial commercial benefits which his citizens have reaped". Dodge noted that these benefits had occurred despite Haiti's revolutionary past and its successive despotic regimes, as well as the reluctance of America to formally ratify trade agreements with Haiti. As such, Dodge hoped to outline to Adams the necessity of placing "American trade to Hayti, upon a fair footing" and that to do so would be "a great national benefit" to the United States as a whole.[51] In the letter, Dodge highlighted the fact that American merchants were subject to almost double the duties and tariffs that British merchants had to pay. Dodge attributed this to the fact that, unlike the American government, the British government "protects" its trade with Haiti.[52] Dodge was also anxious that Britain or France would solidify their commercial relationship with the new Haitian president—something which could have had disastrous consequences for American merchants. Dodge emphasised the urgency he felt was needed in the matter by concluding his memorial with the prediction that "the Garden of the West Indies" would be "blooming and flourishing" in a matter of years, leading to the formation of a formidable "West Indian Empire".[53] Dodge's clear suggestion, then, was that if America wanted to secure its own status as a serious economic power in the Atlantic world, it needed to foresee the future of the New World—one that had Haiti at its centre.

Dodge's letter is most noteworthy for the way in which it intertwined economic arguments with appraisals of Haiti's adoption of republicanism, something that he clearly believed lent greater weight to his calls for improved commercial relations. Although Fanning has underlined that pro-trade articles tended to allude to Haiti's republican status, Dodge's text was unique in that it was an explicit celebration of the "privileges of self-government [and] Independent Sovereignty", which was something he believed "the almighty, and their own bravery, has given them".[54]

Adams was said to be sceptical of the ability of the newly independent states of Spanish America to establish stable and liberal forms of government, and Dodge's writing displayed an acute awareness of such scepticism.[55] Dodge sought to underline explicitly Haiti's legitimacy as a republic by asserting that Boyer's succession would result in the establishment of a "contended and permanent Government" throughout Haiti—a government that could, therefore, be traded with security and confidence.[56] From the beginning of his plea to Adams, Dodge framed the ideological fraternity of the two republics by underlining the "bonds of attachment between

168   J. FORDE

the republicans of Hayti, and the republicans of the United States".[57] Dodge criticised those who dismissed Haiti's revolution against monarchy because "the tint of their skin, was a shade or two darker than that of some other resisters of Despotism", and claimed that the uprising against Christophe should in fact be considered as one of the greatest accomplishments of mankind. Haiti's and America's anti-monarchical and revolutionary pasts were explicitly aligned, as Dodge recalled: "the Liberty, which we religiously regard...is as free as the air we inhale, and by the very genius and spirit of our own Government, any set of men who have energy enough to emancipate themselfs [sic] from the thraldom of Oppression are in effect of our Kindreds, our brethren and our allies".[58] In this sense Dodge suggested that the creation of more legitimate avenues of trade with the Haitians was not only in the interests of America's economy, but that it also constituted a moral obligation to lend support and legitimacy to a nation ideologically aligned closely with the American republic.

As Dodge was all too aware, however, how do you establish favourable and secure trade relations with a nation that your government does not formally recognise? This was a question that was addressed in a number of pro-trade articles that called on the American government to formally recognise the Haitian republic.[59] Dodge clearly saw formal recognition of Haiti as vital to securing American merchants' interests in the Haitian state, and he outlined the necessity of recognising Haiti's sovereignty in both formal and informal contexts. Dodge referred to often-made claims in the American press that during his reign, Christophe had seized large quantities of cargo owned by Americans—cargo for which they had yet to be compensated. But Dodge argued that Christophe had done so because American merchants routinely failed to recognise the king's and Haiti's sovereign status and therefore failed to pay them the diplomatic respect they deserved. Dodge claimed that because Americans had persistently viewed Christophe as the "[c]hief of a band of rebel slaves" and had refused to recognise him as the monarch of an independent nation, the Haitian king had simply mirrored this contempt.[60] The warning was for American merchants—and the American government—not to fall into a similar, self-defeating trap with Haiti's new head of state.

Dodge was clearly anxious that this form of disrespect towards Haiti's leaders—and the damaging impact this had on trade with American merchants—would continue unless America formally recognised the Haitian republic. As such, he asserted that Boyer's succession represented a clean slate between Haiti and America, even with regards to calls from some that

6 THE PROMISE AND THE THREAT OF BOYER AND HAITIAN REPUBLICANISM    169

Boyer should compensate Americans for the losses and seizures suffered under Christophe. Julia Gaffield has highlighted how the compensation claims of American merchants between 1820 and 1821, and their attempts to elicit support from John Adams, often centred on the question of Haiti's sovereign status. However, although Adams did write to Boyer to ask for the merchants to be compensated, he allegedly avoided the issue of recognition altogether.[61] Dodge argued that asking for Haiti to pay for the acts of a "previous Dynasty" was unreasonable and not how America would behave towards other nations. In this vein, Dodge questioned whether America would ask the recently restored Bourbon monarchy in France to compensate any Americans who had suffered financial loss as a result of Napoleon's actions.[62] This call to cancel claims for compensation is all the more interesting for the fact that Dodge himself had gone through the Haitian courts to claim $20,000 allegedly owed to him from Dessalines's widow in 1814—a sum of money he would never receive, despite the courts upholding his claim.[63] Therefore, despite his own vested interest in making such claims, Dodge clearly saw the importance of American recognition of Haiti and friendly relationships with the new government as far outweighing demands for compensation.

Newspapers mirrored Dodge's pleas for recognition of the Haitian state by alluding to Haiti's republican form of government and its "just and equitable principles towards other nations".[64] Dodge's "Memorial", however, was unique in the way that it directly framed the recognition of Haiti's sovereignty as a question of America's principled and moral standing. Dodge called for Haiti to be accepted into the "great family of Nations" by arguing that such recognition would be compatible with the "principles" and "policy" of America.[65] Acceptance of Haiti's independence was placed by Dodge in the context of "this age of liberal refinement"—an age which, as Dodge highlighted, had led to the much-celebrated revolutions of Spanish America. Dodge questioned why Haiti's revolution against monarchy would be excluded from the American government's apparent approval of those other uprisings against oppression, and he went so far as to argue that failure to recognise Haiti formally would be inconsistent with the American constitution. For Dodge, the question of recognition was not only grounded in America's political identity and in keeping with its acceptance of other revolutions in the Americas. It was also the duty of "the Philanthropist, the Republican and the Christian" to "point out to that unfortunate people the right path to civilisation and national happiness".[66] If—as Fitz has argued—Adams believed in "the trinity of republican government, commercial reciprocity, and religious tolerance", then Dodge was clearly aware of this and tried to appeal to Adams's principles.[67] In this way, the question of Haitian recognition was framed not merely within discussions of America's economy and security—it was a question of America's soul.

Arguments in favour of formally recognising Haiti's sovereignty would fall on deaf ears, however. Instead, the American government continued to pursue a policy of non-recognition—a policy which found a distinct amount of support in the American press. At the heart of calls to deny Haiti recognition was the legitimacy it would allegedly give to a black republic founded on a revolution against slavery—something which was seen as particularly incendiary and dangerous for America's southern slave-holding states.[68] As the *National Gazette* summarised succinctly: "If there is any circumstance which, especially, has weakened or destroyed the internal security of the slave-holding members of the Union, it is the establishment of the negro-power in Hayti".[69] The *Gazette*'s editor at this time, Robert Walsh, had published in 1819 his *Appeal from the Judgements of Great Britain*, which contained a spirited attack of Britain's role in the slave trade and which predicted that America would eventually be free of the "evil" of slavery. The *Appeal*, however, also incorporated "southern excuses for slavery", and an empathy with slave-holders' perspectives was also evident in the *Gazette*'s treatment of the issue of America's relationship with the Haitian republic.[70] Recognition of Haiti's independence, Walsh's *Gazette* stated, "would add to the force and activity of the evil influence implied in their independent constitution". The "evil influence" of the Haitian Revolution was likely a reference to the failed slave revolt of the freed-slave Denmark Vesey in Charleston in July 1822. The Vesey rebellion had damaged hopes of Haitian recognition significantly as southern planters claimed that Haiti's own successful slave revolution was finally being exported to America's shores.[71] In the same article, the *Gazette* displayed an awareness of a letter allegedly written from Boyer to Dodge—evidence perhaps that Dodge had written directly to the Haitian president in his attempts to garner support and protection of American merchants. Although the *Gazette* accepted that "unrestricted trade" would be beneficial, it concluded that it would rather "let that trade be sacrificed than expose a large portion of the Union to greater domestic danger".[72]

Opponents to Boyer and Haiti also focused on a fear or disgust of black diplomacy in their arguments. The *Gazette* expressed revulsion at the idea of Americans not only accepting but inviting negotiations with black

# 6 THE PROMISE AND THE THREAT OF BOYER AND HAITIAN REPUBLICANISM    171

diplomats of the "mock republic". The newspaper derided calls for an ideological fraternity with "a community of blacks, who have become free by the murder or expulsion of their masters".[73] In this sense, editors such as Walsh sought to deny Boyer's and Haiti's legitimacy by playing on a historical fear of Americans—particularly in the southern states—that Haiti's 1804 revolution would be exported to America. Whether Walsh was in fact fearful of this or not is unknown. But for someone as opposed to Haiti's republic as Walsh, the Vesey rebellion provided an opportune moment to call on memories of Haiti's revolutionary birth in his attempts to dissuade his readers from supporting official recognition of the black republic.

This anxiety towards black diplomacy even extended to publications that had been hitherto supportive of Haiti's republican turn. For example, in a lengthy article September 1823, the *Niles' Weekly Register* began by apparently reaffirming its support for the Haitian republic by asserting that its "regular and enlightened government of the republican form" was said to be "more liberal…than any now existing in Europe" with the exception of Britain and Spain.[74] This edition of *Register* enthused about Haiti's schools, public offices and businesses, along with its system of government. Boyer was described as "an able general and a profound statesman" who ruled with presidential moderation and restraint, leading the *Register* to conclude: "There is no king in Europe, with the same power that he possesses, [who] would use it with the same moderation and justice". However, despite the apparent progress of Haiti and its flourishing state as an embodiment of the virtues of republicanism, the *Register* summarised the anxieties of even those who in principle supported the notion of Haitian recognition: "are we yet *prepared* to send and receive ministers to and from Hayti? Could the prejudices of some, and the, perhaps just fears of others, be quieted? We think not. The time has not yet come for a surrender of our feelings about color, nor is it fitting at any time, that the public safety should be endangered".[75] The legitimisation of black diplomacy and the perceived threat to the safety of Americans that this supposedly posed was apparently too much for even a publication such as the *Register*. Where some newspapers supported Haitian independence outright, for those such as the *Register* this support waned as the threat, rather than the promise, of a black republic apparently loomed large.

Monroe's administration apparently agreed with voices that expressed concern over the potential consequences of American recognition of the Haitian state. The Monroe Doctrine of 1823 simultaneously recognised the independence of Spanish America's new republics while refusing to recognise the sovereignty of the Haitian state, which was something that infuriated a number of American observers—particularly those with mercantile interests.[76] Reports emerged in American newspapers that echoed Dodge's "Memorial" two years earlier by portraying pro-trade, pro-recognition and pro-republicanism policies as intrinsically linked. These reports in turn sought to frame Monroe's rebuke of Haitian calls for sovereignty as being unreflective of the virtuous nature of republican leadership. Newspapers such as *The Pittsburgh Recorder* argued that it was "a reproach to our republic, that we have not yet openly and manfully acknowledged the independence of St. Domingo". At the centre of such lamentations was the observation that "[w]e might in all probability, by doing an act of common justice, procure to ourselves important commercial advantages".[77] Reports such as these aligned America's political identity as a liberal progressive-thinking republic with the economic benefits that recognition would bring. Newspapers argued that formal recognition would be an "act of liberality" which would, in turn, "reap many exclusive advantages". Such reports enthused about Haiti's "secure and well balanced government".[78] These articles wrote approvingly of the "beloved and respected" Boyer and of Haiti's Congress and House of Representatives.[79] They also described the state papers of the new republic which were "remarkable" and "worthy…of imitation of the European Potentates" as they contained "no cumbrous phraseology, no laboured obscurity of expression". Instead, "the state paper comes home direct to the point, with all the conscious boldness that honesty always inspires".[80]

Arguments in favour of Haiti's recognition were thus framed within a celebration of the virtues of republicanism and sought once more to include Haiti in a celebratory discourse of New World republicanism, despite the official slight of the Haitian state by the Monroe Doctrine. Although these calls for recognition in the early years of Boyer's reign ultimately failed, they nonetheless reflect how some observers saw the question of Haitian recognition as a reflection of America's own republicanism, and that to deny Haiti its sovereignty was a stain on America's own political identity.

## 6 THE PROMISE AND THE THREAT OF BOYER AND HAITIAN REPUBLICANISM 173

### President Boyer and British Radicals

News of Boyer's republican unification of the north and south of Haiti had a similar pertinence for British radical thinkers who had leaned ever more towards republicanism since the turbulent late-1810s. In the wake of Peterloo, British radicals viewed the bloody events as proof that "there was now no choice but that between republican government and military despotism".[81] The 1819 Gagging Acts were used as evidence of the oppressive nature of Britain's monarchical government, and the unpopularity of the Prince Regent had also intensified after his "public exoneration" of the officials complicit in the Peterloo Massacre. Radicals and reformers saw this as further proof of the Regent's lack of care for the welfare of his subjects and this "revitalised popular anger" towards him.[82] Prominent radical writers such as Robert Wedderburn and Richard Carlile wrote even more vociferously against the Regent's actions in the aftermath of Peterloo and depicted his perceived support of the events in Manchester as a "monarchic death rattle".[83] The successful upheaval of the Haitian monarchy and the implementation of republicanism throughout the whole island afforded an opportunity for some of these radical writers to project their agitations aimed at what they deemed to be an oppressive British government and monarchy. Importantly, this opportunity arrived at a time when the Gagging Acts were still in full force, and writers and editors were subjected to constant scrutiny and punishment for seditious acts. If "revolution is attempted when reform movements are stifled", a number of British radical observers looked to the emergence of Boyer's presidency of a united Haiti to underline further the need for revolutionary movements in moments of political oppression, and to use Boyer's Haiti as an example of how progressive modes of governance could supplant the outdated model of monarchical rule.[84]

British newspapers such as the *Morning Chronicle* circulated the same kinds of reports that abounded in the American press of the "rejoicings" of the Haitian people at the implementation of a more "free and liberal government". That such a positive reception to Boyer would be found in the *Chronicle* is unsurprising. As an anti-Tory newspaper that had condemned the government for Peterloo, events in Haiti represented a chance to praise a moment of significant political reform without overtly criticising Britain's own political leadership. Boyer's popularity among the Haitian population at the implementation of this new government was made explicitly clear in the *Chronicle*, which reported enthusiastically of

174   J. FORDE

the "privileges" that the citizens of the newly-unified island of Haiti would receive under this new, more progressive form of government.[85] Other newspapers with editors that supported political reform in Britain—such as *Trewman's Exeter Flying Post*—published reports from Jamaican newspapers which claimed that the Haitians "were highly elated at the change and the popularity of the New Government was unbounded".[86] In this way Boyer's Haiti provided an opportunity for progressive editors to promote the benefits of political reform while limiting their chances of being accused of speaking against Britain's own monarch.

The enthusiasm with which some British progressives viewed Haiti's latest political development can be seen an image circulated in January 1821: *The Secrets of Trop-peau disclosed: or the Imbecile Alliance of Tyranny to Crush the Universal Spirit of Liberty defeated*. Created by William Heath and published by Samuel William Fores—a specialist in satirical prints and caricature—the image optimistically depicted the Holy Alliance as failing to subdue the revolutionary spirit sweeping Europe.[87] This print adopted a less radical approach than John Fairburn's *The Death of Christophe* in that it excluded George IV from this alliance and, in fact, claimed that Britain was a model example of liberal progress. Published around the same time as Fairburn's print, however, Heath's image similarly alluded to Haiti as a unique site of liberty at a time when the ruling classes in Britain and throughout Europe were looking to stifle the increasingly vocal calls for reform.

More significantly than this, however, was how post-Christophe Haiti was situated as an aspirational model of liberal progression. As the autocratic rulers of Europe struggle to suffocate the flames of revolution, an angel above them issues a stark warning: "Tyrants beware—the spirit of freedom is come forth & woe to them who dare oppose its progress. Mark England, America, Domingo…& look to it. Russia, Prussia & Austria, not even the walls of China shall long arrest its march". While the three monarchs oppressively sit on top of the European nations, "Domingo" (along with South America) rises above in the centre background, apparently freed by these angels of liberty. Although Haiti was not the main focus of the print, this image nonetheless demonstrates how Haiti's shift to a republican form of governance gained a poignancy for some British observers in the more general narrative of the universal spirit of liberty that was seen to be sweeping across the Atlantic world at this time. As the print suggests, Haiti's new republic was an envious distance from the destructive designs of Europe's oppressive monarchs—something that was

6 THE PROMISE AND THE THREAT OF BOYER AND HAITIAN REPUBLICANISM    175

also highlighted in publications such as the *Monthly Review*, which claimed that "[f]ortunately for the independence of the Haytians, they are beyond the reach of the Royal Menagerie, or Holy Alliance, as it is profanely called".[88] In this way, some observers in Britain clearly believed that the socio-political conditions across the Atlantic were perhaps more favourable for Haiti's newly-acquired liberty from political oppression than the traditionally restrictive conditions found in Europe.

Once Haiti's establishment of republicanism had been cemented in 1822 with the overthrow of colonial Spain in the west of Hispaniola, radical thinkers such as Richard Carlile engaged more directly with the promise that Boyer's Haiti now held as a site of post-revolution liberty. As Steve Poole has demonstrated, radical figures such as Carlile viewed Britain at a critical historical moment in the early 1820s—and one that, if the British people were prepared to act, could result in a complete transformation of its political foundations.[89] And such an eagerness for revolutionary upheaval could be seen clearly in Carlile's writing on Haiti in the early 1820s. In a lengthy article published in *The Republican* in December 1822, Carlile used the new republic as a valuable space on to which the virtues of republicanism could be projected. The title of the article—"To the Republicans of the Island of Hayti"—was borrowed from earlier articles that had appeared in *The Republican* that were addressed "To the Republicans of the Island of Great Britain". However, these articles— written from within his prison cell—were being circulated at a time when strict regulations had been imposed, which disallowed cheap publications such as *The Republican* from commenting on matters of religion or the state.[90] Haiti thus briefly became a valuable source of reflection, and Carlile used his faux address to the Haitians as a vehicle through which he could more explicitly outline the steps and legislation necessary to establish a successful, legitimate republic.

Carlile used this address to outline both his hopes for the continuation of Europe's revolutions, and his frustrations that Britain had not followed such a course—a course defined in part by Haiti's republican revolutionaries. Though Carlile claimed to possess "a pure republican spirit" he lamented that he was surrounded by "slaves and cowards" who he hoped would follow the example set by "the once slaves but now free Republicans of Hayti". Britain's "corrupt...tyrannical and...unpopular government" was claimed to affect "a hauteur to [Haiti's] government", but Carlile asserted his belief that "the majority of people of this Island have already a kindred spirit with you".[91] The article spoke optimistically and passionately of being "on the eve of the bursting forth of a revolutionary volcano" despite the attempts of Europe's sovereigns to prevent it.[92] Carlile hoped that this revolutionary spirit would continue to spread in the Americas—particularly in Jamaica and Cuba. He implored the Haitians to "stir up a republican spirit in Cuba" in order to affect a "fraternity" between the neighbouring islands. In this way, Carlile situated Haiti as a political model in his visions of a global revolution and the "extinction of monarchy".[93]

But the main purpose that 'To the Republicans of Hayti' served was as a wide-ranging set of guidelines for the new republic that were in fact a thinly veiled, vitriolic indictment of British politics and society. As Michael J. Turner has argued, radicals "wanted to get to the roots of political, social and economic problems" and "the reforms they sought were usually fundamental and structural, not merely superficial or comestic".[94] At a time of "economic distress" for Britain, Carlile's advice to the new Haitian state reflected the practical guidelines he believed were necessary for a progressive state to operate successfully and beneficially to its citizens.[95] To Carlile, Boyer's Haiti had the potential to be a republican utopia—but only if it heeded the shortcomings of Britain's own broken political system. Carlile instructed Haitians that while they should stir up revolution in their neighbouring islands and seek to avail them of colonial rule, they should not seek to expand their own territory as colonialism only served to "enrich a few individuals at the expence [sic] of the many".[96] The article highlighted the necessity of implementing "a system of finance that shall occasion [sic] the smallest amount of taxation"—a system that would be "incalculable" to the benefit of the nation.[97] Carlile touched on a number of guidelines including the eradication of religion on the island and the necessity of annual elections for government ministers. He advised the "distinguished Citizens of Hayti" that "the form of your government can never be rendered too simple" and that they should avoid modelling their republic on the "complicated system" of America and instead look to Spain's new republican constitution for guidance.[98]

References to the pitfalls of colonialism, high taxation, religion and to infrequent general elections were all matters of concern for the British working class in the early nineteenth century. Of even greater importance to Carlile's assertion for the prosperity of the Haitian republic was the establishment and protection of a free press—hardly surprising as Carlile was writing from prison at the time. Carlile used the address to the Haitian republicans to passionately defend the "perfect freedom" that a free press gives its citizens. Carlile highlighted the importance of this in helping to educate the nation—something that was "the source of all prosperity and human improvement". In a thinly veiled attack on the short-sightedness and autocracy of Britain's sedition laws, Carlile advised Haitians that if they supported freedom of press while other countries did not, it would be they who would "soon become the most powerful nation on this globe".[99]

Whether Carlile genuinely believed or even wanted Haiti to become a significant political power in the Atlantic world is unclear—particularly since after this article there is little evidence of further engagement by Carlile on the subject of Haiti. However, as Richard Ashcraft has highlighted, radical thinkers tended to highlight "a sense of fraternity and communal obligation" as opposed to "the arbitrariness of individual self-interest".[100] And in this vein Carlile's closing salvo indicated a very real desire for Haiti to succeed and to act as an advertisement for the progressive nature of republicanism everywhere. Carlile implored the Haitians to "make your Island the center of intelligence, humanity, and political wisdom" and to "pronounce your Island as a hospitable asylum for every moral industrious man who will enter it". He predicted that Haiti's significance to the Americas would be the same as Britain's to Europe—that of an "independent, powerful, and even invincible government". The article claimed that the Haitians were "free from any annoyance from Europe" and that little could stop their further advancement. Carlile signed off his address by attempting to leave his reader in no doubt of his support and sense of fraternity with the Haitian republic: "Do well: deserve well, and farewell, is the ardent desire of your com-patriot [sic] and well-wisher".[101]

Carlile's "To the Republicans" shares striking similarities with a text produced and published in England only a few years earlier. Written anonymously, and published by the "radically inclined" Sherwood, Neely, and Jones in 1817, the *Poetical Epistle to the King of Hayti* was another set of guidelines addressed to the Haitians of how their nation could prosper politically and socially, and how it could assert itself as a legitimate nation of liberal ideology.[102] Although the *Epistle* was written while Christophe was alive, it functioned in a similar way to Carlile's text—as a scathing critique of British government and society. The author of the *Epistle*, like Carlile, looked to the Haitian nation as a kind of political clean slate and one which could avoid the frustrations and anxieties that had been thrust upon the British working classes of the early nineteenth century. Despite

178   J. FORDE

the assertion that Haiti should adopt a similar parliamentary system to Britain's, in a similar vein to Carlile's guidelines, the author instructed Haiti's leader to "let all the members, sire, *yearly* be sent in"—surely an allusion to the fact that, by the date of the text's publication, the previous British election had been in 1812 while the one before that had been in 1807. The poem would also more directly scorn Britain's corrupted electoral system by advising Christophe: "Do not choose a man for a borough that's rotten / Do not let your ministers buy a majority". At a time of such economic distress for Britain, Christophe was also warned to "not, as our state hath unhappily done / Permit your expence [sic] to exceed the income" otherwise he would "suffer the people to suffer starvation / By prodigal waste and excessive taxation". In this way, the author saw Haiti as an opportunity to create a governmental system free from the entrenched corruption of Britain's political leadership.[103]

In addition to the perceived flaws of the British Parliament, the advice offered to Haiti was a wide-ranging list of everything that was perceived to be wrong with British—and in particular, London—society at this time. The growing effects of Britain's Industrial Revolution were lamented as the text advised Christophe that "the best friend you have in the isle [is] Agriculture". The damaging consequences of the overcrowding of cities in Britain was highlighted and Christophe was advised to "not let a city become overgrown". London was depicted as morally corrupt and a city both literally and figuratively in decay. Prostitutes "walk the street" amid "concourse[s] of idle men" who "should work on the farm". Haiti was advised to bridge the class divide that was so evident in England and to not allow the wealthy to "grind the face of the poor". British reliance on nepotism in the military was similarly advised to be avoided and to instead "Give the laurel to those who the laurel may merit". By the end of this canto, neither Haiti nor Christophe were directly referred to by name—a device which allowed the author to hide behind the guise of an "epistle to Haiti" but to also allow the text to be interpreted as advice to the British monarch. The canto culminated in a final warning: "To neglect this advice, Sire, will be a state blunder", thereby more overtly outlining the dangers for British prosperity and the potential for Haiti to even surpass Britain as a legitimate, politically progressive and morally centred Atlantic world nation.[104]

As with so many radical-leaning thinkers of the time, a primary concern for the author of the *Epistle* was the role of education in the general betterment of society.[105] The author devoted the third canto to the

6 THE PROMISE AND THE THREAT OF BOYER AND HAITIAN REPUBLICANISM    179

importance of implementing education systems that were for the good of the entire nation, including the working class. The notion of ignorance in Haiti was asserted as "a more deadly foe...than France" whereas "learning" was introduced as "that true friend". The advice to "[c]arefully educate the young" and the significance of all learning, from reading to astronomy, from arithmetic to poetry was highlighted as essential for the sustained improvement of society as a whole. Yet again, however, the author deliberately obfuscated the intended recipient of this didacticism. Although the author imagined "If I were the king of Hayti", it is easy to picture his or her desire to write "If I were the king of England" as the text again began to outline advice for Haiti that was in fact a reflection of the failures of the British establishment. Despite the text continuing to advise Christophe to "teach all who need", the author was probably well aware that Christophe had in fact already begun to implement an education system throughout Haiti that was designed to benefit all.[106] News of Christophe adopting the Lancasterian system was commonplace in British newspapers between 1816 and 1817, and so the reference to this system in the poem—and the importance of education in general—should be read as a suggestion by the author that Christophe was succeeding where British governments had failed and that British philanthropy by the likes of Wilberforce and Clarkson towards Haiti should in fact be directed closer to home.

The *Poetical Epistle* and Carlile's writing in the *Republican* are evidence of the way in which the idea of Haiti as a potential political utopia—one far removed from the entrenched corruption and decay of Britain—was used by some British radicals to project their desire for effective, progressive forms of governance. The promise that Haiti held in some British reformist imaginations is further exemplified by the fact that Jeremy Bentham felt compelled to send a copy of his *Codification Proposal* to Boyer in December 1822—coincidentally the same month that Carlile published his own advice to Haiti in *The Republican*.[107]

Bentham's *Proposal*—an attempt at rewriting existing systems of law that Bentham viewed as incompatible with liberal ideas of progress—was printed only months before a copy was sent to Boyer.[108] From the early 1800s Bentham had concerned himself with the constitutional affairs of Europe and Latin America, something that intensified in the 1820s with the emergence of republican revolutions in Europe and Latin America. In his communications with these post-revolutionary states, Bentham adopted the stance of both the "expert" and the "reformer" as he outlined

180    J. FORDE

his proposals for effective and progressive legislation.[109] Evidently, Bentham felt Boyer's Haiti was an ideal place to see his vision of more effective and sustainable modes of law and governance to be implemented. In a letter that accompanied the *Proposal*, Bentham told Boyer of his respect for the Haitian president's character and praised him for resisting a monarchical title on his adoption of power.[110] He also commended Boyer on the unification with Santo Domingo—something he praised as a "glorious success". Although Bentham admitted that he knew little about Haiti's constitution under Boyer, he offered his services to frame a "body of laws" for the republic—the characteristics of which he claimed: "none of which hath as yet been exemplified in the laws of any country". Bentham told Boyer of his intention to send the *Proposal* to other post-revolutionary countries, and while he admitted that not all of them would heed his advice, he told the Haitian president of his hope that in general there would be a global acceptance of the main ideas outlined.[111]

Although Boyer did not accept Bentham's offer to act as a legislator of the new Haitian republic, Bentham's letter—along with the *Poetical Epistle* and Carlile's writing—is indicative of the value that Haiti held in discussions of what constituted legitimate, progressive and effective governance. Carlile and Bentham particularly seemed to suggest a very real desire to see Boyer's Haitian republic prosper—if nothing else than as evidence that reform and a new approach to governance could bring benefits to both the state and its citizens. This desire and enthusiasm for the progress that Haiti represented was reflected in reports of toasts being drunk to Boyer and "the Republicans of the Island of St. Domingo" in taverns in various cities throughout Britain in the early 1820s—a toast Carlile instructed his followers to make at celebrations of the birth of Thomas Paine.[112] Along with Boyer, Carlile insisted that the names of Washington, Jefferson, Bolivar, Thomas Cochrane and, of course, Paine himself all be toasted as well—situating the new Haitian president in illustrious republican company indeed.[113] Letters sent to *The Republican* some weeks after suggest that Carlile's instructions were adhered to with enthusiasm and that such toasts were replicated the year after, again at celebrations of Paine's birth.[114] Remy Duthille has highlighted how toasting became a "political and contentious act" that emphasised "the drinker's allegiance to a patron and, later, to a cause".[115] James Epstein has further demonstrated how radicals in the early nineteenth century used toasts to align themselves ideologically with groups and movements across time.[116] In toasting the revolutionary republicans of Haiti, British radicals also briefly crossed both

6 THE PROMISE AND THE THREAT OF BOYER AND HAITIAN REPUBLICANISM    181

geographical and racial boundaries to further express their hopes of a more global republican revolution.

The image of British radical figures joyously toasting the Haitian president in their celebrations of the revered Thomas Paine is an intriguing one and one that exemplifies the hold that the Haitian republic had over some British imaginations in the early 1820s. It would be an overstatement to suggest that the general press was as enthusiastic in their writing of the new Haitian republic and its new president, but at the same time it is important to note that newspapers and periodicals in Britain largely showed support for both. As in America, such reports attested to the fact that under Boyer the Haitians were in the "utmost tranquillity" and that Haiti continued to progress towards social and economic stability.[117] British newspapers noted that under Boyer the Haitians "had acquired a degree of consistency and strength, which Hayti had not enjoyed since the expulsion of the whites".[118] The idea that Haiti was advancing in ways it had not under Dessalines or Christophe was taken further by newspapers such as the *Yorkshire Gazette*, which claimed that with Boyer's leadership the new republic had assumed "a station which entitles it to the notice of civilised communities" and that, with its new system of government, Haiti would be better placed to "foster and improve" its communication with other countries—"in itself a grand source of civilisation".[119] Some reports used Boyer's proclamations as further proof of Haiti's civility under the new leader and even claimed that such documents were a testament to what a "free and independent people" could achieve.[120]

These reports generally spoke approvingly of Boyer's annexation of Santo Domingo and the unification of the whole of Hispaniola. Rather than evoke fear about the potential expansion of a black empire, British newspapers tended to report on the annexation in an understanding light as they attested to its necessity for Haiti to secure themselves against Spanish or French designs to reconquer the whole island. Some even went so far as to claim that the implementation of Boyer's government not only pleased the blacks of Santo Domingo, but also that "the Spaniards there discover no disposition to return under the yoke" of the Spanish king and that they "deemed it more conducive to coalesce with their Haytian neighbours".[121] Boyer's unifying effect—of both sides of the island and between blacks and mulattoes in particular—led some reports to conclude that "nothing could be a stronger proof of his wisdom". Letters published in periodicals such as the Monthly Magazine (which were printed on the front page) claimed to "rejoice exceedingly" at this unification and they

182   J. FORDE

emphasised the idea that the annexation was achieved without any "war or bloodshed"—something that apparently contributed "greatly" to the "wisdom and humanity" of Boyer.[122] Similar reports wrote approvingly that Boyer's government "prevents all distinction of persons' and that "[l]iberty and equality reign throughout their republic".[123] These reports looked to legitimise Boyer's early-Haiti as a form of liberal and progressive governance that apparently nurtured both economic and social improvements—and, in turn, such reports asserted Boyer's leadership as a model of inspiration at a time of increasing criticisms of the Old World regimes throughout the Atlantic world.

## CONCLUSION

The early years of Boyer's republic clearly captured the imaginations of a number of observers on both sides of the Atlantic. Haiti's unified shift to republicanism after Christophe's death—and the apparent benefits it brought to its citizens—was pertinent for American republicans still reeling from the domestic political crises of the late 1810s. Boyer's Haiti was a tool used by patriotic Americans to both extol the virtues of republicanism and to further cement the ideological divide between the progressive New World and the stagnant Old World. Although the Haitian republic was nowhere near as revered as the new republics of Spanish America, Haiti's new, united form of governance nonetheless allowed American supporters to seize on a period of republican fever to assert the legitimacy of the Haitian state—something that pro-trade advocates made particular use of as they combined economic and ideological arguments in their calls for more favourable commercial agreements. Boyer's Haiti similarly captured the attention of British radical observers, who celebrated the revolution against the Haitian monarchy as evidence of the universal desire to be unshackled from the chains of governmental and monarchical oppression. As some British radical thinkers increasingly leaned towards republican modes of thought, the early progress of Boyer's Haiti provided an opportunity to assert the virtuous nature of political reform and republicanism.

Although it is impossible to ascertain the extent to which these observers genuinely wanted the Haitian state to thrive on the Atlantic stage, these depictions nonetheless are evidence that in the continuing face of non-recognition from the powers of the West, the Haitian republic not only elicited support from a number of British and American actors, but it also provided an anti-conservative model of inspiration for the need to implement and sustain liberal and progressive modes of governing. The emergence of reports of Boyer's own brand of despotic leadership would eventually dampen this enthusiasm. However, the early promise that some observers felt that Boyer and Haiti held in the early 1820s demonstrates the multiple ways in which Haiti's revolutionary citizens continued to inspire thinkers throughout the Atlantic world and is further testament to Haiti's revolutionary legacy.

## NOTES

1. Laurent Dubois, *Haiti: The Aftershocks of History* (New York: Metropolitan Books, 2012), 93. For an in-depth study of the development of Haitian sovereignty in eastern Hispaniola from 1822, see Andrew J. Walker, "Strains of Unity: Emancipation, Property, and the Post-Revolutionary State in Haitian Santo Domingo, 1822–1844," PhD diss., (University of Michigan, 2018).
2. Sybille Fischer, *Modernity Disavowed: Haiti and the Cultures of Slavery in the Age of Revolution* (Durham: Duke University Press, 2004), 260.
3. By the late 1820s, Boyer's increasingly harsh agricultural policies had essentially reduced Haitian peasants to slave status in everything but name: Joan Dayan, "A Few Stories About Haiti, or Stigma Revisited," *Research in African Literatures* 35, no. 2 (2004), 161–164; Dubois, *Haiti*, 105–114.
4. Some of the most detailed discussions of the proposed emigration of African-Americans to Haiti and Boyer's role in this can be found in: Sara Fanning, *Caribbean Crossing: African Americans and the Haitian Emigration Movement* (New York: New York University Press, 2015); Ousmane K. Power-Greene, *Against Wind and Tide: The African American Struggle against the Colonization Movement* (New York: New York University Press, 2014), 17–45.
5. Edlie Wong, "In the Shadow of Haiti: The Negro Seamen Act, Counter-Revolutionary St. Domingue, and Black Emigration," in *The Haitian Revolution and the Early United States: Histories, Textualities, Geographies*, ed. Elizabeth Maddock Dillon and Michael J. Drexler (Philadelphia: University of Pennsylvania Press, 2016), 162–188.
6. Sam W. Haynes, *Unfinished Revolution: The Early American Republic in a British World* (Charlottesville: University of Virginia Press, 2010), 108.
7. Andrew R. L. Cayton, "Continental Politics: Liberalism, Nationalism, and the Appeal of Texas in the 1820s," in *Beyond the Founders: New Approaches to the Political History of the Early American Republic*, ed.

184   J. FORDE

Jeffrey L. Pasley, Andrew W. Robertson, and David Waldstreicher (Chapel Hill: University of North Carolina Press, 2004), 305.
8. Haynes, *Unfinished Revolution*, 109.
9. James E. Lewis, *The American Union and the Problem of Neighbourhood: The United States and the Collapse of the Spanish Empire, 1783–1829* (Chapel Hill: University of North Carolina Press, 1998), 126.
10. Jay Sexton, *The Monroe Doctrine: Empire and Nation in Nineteenth-Century America* (New York: Hill and Wang, 2011), 10.
11. Caitlin Fitz, *Our Sister Republics: The United States in an Age of American Revolutions* (New York: W. W. Norton & Company, 2016), 3.
12. Malcolm Chase, *1820: Disorder and Stability in the United Kingdom* (Oxford: Oxford University Press, 2013), 63–64. For an overview of the popularity of George III in the later years of his reign see Linda Colley, "The Apotheosis of George III: Loyalty, Royalty and the British Nation 1760–1820," *Past & Present*, no. 102 (1984): 94–129.
13. Steve Poole, *The Politics of Regicide in England, 1760–1850: Troublesome Subjects* (Manchester: Manchester University Press, 2000), 142. George IV was continually lambasted by satirists for his lifestyle and lack of paternalism as a sovereign: See Kenneth Baker, *George IV: A Life in Caricature* (London: Thames & Hudson, 2005).
14. Chase, *1820*, 71.
15. Chase, *1820*, 1; James Chandler, *England in 1819: The Politics of Literary Culture and the Case of Romantic Historicism* (Chicago: University of Chicago Press, 1998), 17–30.
16. Iain McCalman, *Radical Underworld: Prophets, Revolutionaries, and Pornographers in London, 1795–1840* (1988; reprint, Oxford: Oxford University Press, 1993), 162–177; Thomas W. Laqueur, "The Queen Caroline Affair: Politics as Art in the Reign of George IV," *The Journal of Modern History* 54, no. 3 (1982).
17. Mark Jarrett, *The Congress of Vienna and Its Legacy: War and Great Power Diplomacy after Napoleon* (London: IB Tauris, 2013), 239.
18. *The Republican*, 15 September 1820, cited in Chase, *1820*, 166.
19. Fitz, *Our Sister Republics*, 4.
20. Ibid., 189.
21. Ibid., 83.
22. Michael J. Dash, *Haiti and the United States: National Stereotypes and the Literary Imagination* (London: Macmillan, 1997), 8–9.
23. Fitz, *Our Sister Republics*, 122.
24. *Weekly Aurora*, 4 December 1820.
25. *National Advocate for the Country*, 17 November 1820.
26. *New Hampshire Sentinel*, 25 November 1820; *National Gazette and Literary Register*, 26 January 1821.

# 6 THE PROMISE AND THE THREAT OF BOYER AND HAITIAN REPUBLICANISM 185

27. *Boston Recorder*, 26 November 1820; *Niles' Weekly Register*, 2 December 1820.
28. *Litchfield Republican*, 23 April 1821; *Vermont Journal*, 16 April 1821.
29. *New York Literary Journal, and Belles-Lettres Repository*, 1 December 1820, 92–95.
30. Carroll Smith-Rosenberg, *This Violent Empire: The Birth of an American National Identity* (Chapel Hill: University of North Carolina Press, 2010), 446–450.
31. Joseph Eaton, "From Anglophile to Nationalist: Robert Walsh's" An Appeal from the Judgments of Great Britain"," *The Pennsylvania Magazine of History and Biography, 132*, no. 2 (2008), 141–171.
32. *National Gazette and Literary Register*, 15 November 1820; *National Gazette and Literary Register*, 29 March 1821.
33. *Essex Register*, 4 April 1821; *Poulson's American Daily Advertiser*, 11 May 1821.
34. *Poulson's American Daily Advertiser*, 13 March 1821; *National Gazette and Literary Register*, 31 March 1821.
35. *National Gazette and Literary Register*, 31 March 1821.
36. *Boston Recorder*, 5 May 1821.
37. *National Advocate*, 29 February 1821.
38. *Litchfield Republican*, 23 April 1821.
39. *Republican Gazette and General Advertiser*, 30 June 1821; *Providence Patriot*, 13 January 1821.
40. *Vermont Republican*, 28 May 1821.
41. *Litchfield Republican*, 23 April 1821.
42. *Niles' Weekly Register*, 10 February 1821; 29 December 1821.
43. *Boston Recorder*, 5 May 1821.
44. Fanning, *Caribbean Crossing*, 45–47.
45. Fanning, *Caribbean Crossing*, 45–47.
46. *Alexandria Gazette*, 18 October 1821; *Boston Commercial Gazette*, 18 October 1821.
47. *Niles' Weekly Register*, 23 March 1822.
48. Michel-Rolph Trouillot, *Haiti: State against Nation* (New York: NYU Press, 1990), 57, cited in Julia Gaffield, "'Outrages on the Laws of Nations': American Merchants and Diplomacy after the Haitian Declaration of Independence," in Julia Gaffield, ed. *The Haitian Declaration of Independence: Creation, Context, and Legacy* (Charlottesville: University of Virginia Press, 2016), 176.
49. Houghton Library, Harvard University, MS Fr 12 F, John Dodge, "A Memorial Upon the Subject of Hayti…Presented to the Hon. John Quincy Adams, Esq.," 5 September 1821.

50. Johnhenry Gonzalez, "Defiant Haiti: Free-Soil Runaways, Ship Seizures and the Politics of Diplomatic Non-Recognition in the Early Nineteenth Century," *Slavery & Abolition* 36, no. 1 (2015), 4.
51. Dodge, "Memorial," ff. 1–2.
52. Ibid., ff. 7–8. Fanning claims that British merchants took advantage of establishing favourable relations with Haiti during America's embargo between 1806 and 1810, leading to significant concessions for British traders: Sara C. Fanning, "The Roots of Early Black Nationalism: Northern African Americans' Invocations of Haiti in the Early Nineteenth Century," *Slavery & Abolition* 28, no. 1 (2007), 66–67. See also Trouillot, *State against Nation*, 50–51 for an overview of favourable conditions for British merchants in this time.
53. Dodge, "Memorial," f. 19.
54. Ibid., f. 10.
55. Lewis, *Problem of Neighbourhood*, 158.
56. Dodge, "Memorial," f. 13.
57. Ibid., f. 4.
58. Ibid., f. 11.
59. Fanning, "Early Black Nationalism," 66–67.
60. Dodge, "Memorial," f. 16.
61. Gaffield, ""Outrages on the Laws of Nations"," 173–174.
62. Dodge, "Memorial," ff. 15–16.
63. Gonzalez, "Defiant Haiti," 4.
64. *Woodstock Observer*, 15 January 1822. Fanning also mentions allusions to Haiti's republican status by American merchants: *Caribbean Crossing*, 43.
65. Dodge, "Memorial," ff. 2–4.
66. Ibid., f. 10.
67. Fitz, *Our Sister Republics*, 200.
68. Fanning, *Caribbean Crossing*, 48.
69. *National Gazette and Literary Register*, 14 August 1822.
70. Eaton, "Anglophile to Nationalist," 151.
71. Fanning, *Caribbean Crossing*, 52–53.
72. *National Gazette and Literary Register*, 14 August 1822.
73. Ibid.
74. *Niles' Weekly Register*, 27 September 1823.
75. Ibid.
76. Fanning, *Caribbean Crossing*, 51. For an overview of the background to and consequences of the legislation see Sexton, *Monroe Doctrine*.
77. *Pittsburgh Recorder*, 25 September 1823.
78. *New-London Gazette and General Advertiser*, 21 May 1823.
79. *Christian Watchman*, 14 June 1823.
80. *Pittsburgh Recorder*, 25 September 1823.

81. James Epstein, *Radical Expression: Political Language, Ritual, and Symbol in England, 1790–1850* (Oxford: Oxford University Press, 1994), 105.
82. Poole, *Politics of Regicide*, 154.
83. Ibid.
84. Thomis and Holt, *Threats of Revolution*, 62.
85. *Morning Chronicle*, 25 December 1820.
86. *Trewman's Exeter Flying Post*, 4 January 1821.
87. Simon Turner, "Fores, Samuel William (1761–1838)", *Oxford Dictionary of National Biography*, online edition (Oxford University Press, 2004), http://www.oxforddnb.com.libraryproxy.griffith.edu.au/view/article/63093.
88. *The Monthly Review, or Literary Journal, January to April, inclusive, 1821*, vol. 94 (1821), 443.
89. Poole, *Politics of Regicide*, 154.
90. Chase, *1820*, 17.
91. *The Republican*, 20 December 1822, 929.
92. Ibid., 932.
93. Ibid., 930.
94. Michael J. Turner, *Liberty and Liberticide: The Role of America in Nineteenth-Century British Radicalism* (Plymouth: Lexington Books, 2014), 1.
95. Thomis and Holt, *Threats of Revolution*, 20.
96. *The Republican*, 20 December 1822, 930.
97. Ibid., 936.
98. Ibid., 935.
99. Ibid., 939.
100. Richard Ashcraft, "Liberal Political Theory and Working-Class Radicalism in Nineteenth-Century England," *Political Theory* 21, no. 2 (1993), 250.
101. *The Republican*, 20 December 1822, 941.
102. Worrall, *Theatric Revolution*, 6.
103. *A Poetical Epistle to the King of Hayti* (London: Sherwood, Neely, and Jones, 1817), 14–17.
104. Ibid., 16–17.
105. In the first two decades of the 1800s, education for all and the "value and power of knowledge" became an increasingly important issue for radical movements throughout England: Harold Silver, *English Education and the Radicals, 1780–1850* (London: Routledge, 1975), 50.
106. *Poetical Epistle*, 33–37.
107. Annie L. Cot, "Jeremy Bentham's Spanish American Utopia," in *Economic Development and Global Crisis: The Latin American Economy in*

188   J. FORDE

*Historical Perspective*, ed. José Luís Cardoso, Maria Cristina Marcuzzo, and María Eugenia Romero Sotelo (New York: Routledge, 2014), 35.

108. Jeremy Bentham, "Codification Proposal, Addressed by Jeremy Bentham to All Nations Professing Liberal Opinions," in *'Legislator of the World': Writings on Codification, Law, and Education*, ed. Philip Schofield and Jonathan Harris (Oxford: Clarendon Press, 1998), 243–297.

109. Cot, "Spanish American Utopia," 35.

110. Bentham's letter was dated 29 December 1822. For a full copy of the letter see Catherine Fuller, ed. *The Correspondence of Jeremy Bentham, Vol. 11: January 1822 to June 1824*, The Collected Works of Jeremy Bentham (2000), 176–179.

111. Ibid., 177.

112. McCalman, *Radical Underworld*, 196–197.

113. *The Republican*, 25 January 1822, 99.

114. *The Republican*, 22 February 1822, 234; *The Republican*, 7 February 1823, 179.

115. Rémy Duthille, "Toasting and the Diffusion of Radical Ideas, 1780–1832," in *Radical Voices, Radical Ways: Articulating and Disseminating Radicalism in Seventeenth- and Eighteenth-Century Britain*, ed. Laurent Curelly and Nigel Smith (Manchester: Manchester University Press, 2016), 170.

116. James Epstein, "Radical Dining, Toasting and Symbolic Expression in Early Nineteenth-Century Lancashire: Rituals of Solidarity," *Albion* 20, no. 2 (1988), 274.

117. *Morning Chronicle*, 20 August 1822.

118. *Observer*, 13 May 1822.

119. *Yorkshire Gazette*, 13 October 1821.

120. *The Monthly Magazine, or British Register*, vol. 54 (1822), 370.

121. *Yorkshire Gazette*, 13 October 1821; *Observer*, 13 May 1822.

122. *The Monthly Magazine*, 1 July 1822, 482–483.

123. *The Edinburgh Magazine and Literary Miscellany, January–June 1823*, vol. 12 (1823), 732.

CHAPTER 7

# Conclusion

In 1825, Charles X, the recently crowned King of France, strong-armed President Boyer into paying 150 million francs in reparations to secure official recognition of the Haitian state from France. By compensating France for its perceived losses since the Revolution, Boyer hoped the powers of the Atlantic world would finally be persuaded into officially recognizing the Haitian state, thereby providing the potential stability needed for Haiti's economic future. Boyer was also left with little choice as France had made it clear that if he did not accept the offer, war between the two nations was a likelihood, as well as a major blockade of Haitian trade with other nations.[1]

As it turned out, this indemnity would cripple the Haitian state for years to come. At the time, however, news of France's recognition of Haiti was greeted positively in Britain by a large number of commentators. This is likely because a number of these observers agitated for their government to follow France's lead in recognising the Haitian state in the hope of re-establishing favourable trade relations with Boyer and Haiti. Until the early 1820s, British merchants in Haiti had enjoyed favourable trade duties.[2] But, by 1823, this preferential treatment had been eradicated, allegedly as a result of Britain's willingness to recognise the independence of the new states of Spanish America, but not Haiti.[3] Therefore, in 1825 British newspapers published accounts of the "rejoicings" of the Haitians as a result of France's recognition.[4] Others more directly asserted that the official recognition of Haiti from France "raised the Haytian in the rank of

© The Author(s) 2020

J. Forde, *The Early Haitian State and the Question of Political Legitimacy*, Palgrave Studies in Political History, https://doi.org/10.1007/978-3-030-52608-5_7

189

sovereign nations".[5] Such reports concluded that this agreement served to confirm Haiti's "wise and energetic Government", and that it would be possible to "foresee what a high degree of power they may attain" as a result of their agreement with their ex-colonial power.[6] By 1826, poems appeared in publications such as the *Dublin and London Magazine* in honour of Haiti's republican heroes and France's recognition of their sovereignty. For instance, "To the Men of Hayti, on the Establishment of Their Independence" attested to the nation's perceived toil in "the struggles of Liberty's cause". The poem depicted external recognition as the final act in Haiti's struggle for freedom that had started with the 1791–1804 Revolution, and it claimed that Haitians should "cherish" their achievements.[7] For observers such as this anonymous poet, in an age of successful revolutions and newly formed political entities, Haiti had endured a particularly rocky but glorious road to independence.

A number of newspapers in America reacted to news of France's recognition of Haiti with similar enthusiasm. When news broke of the French-Haitian agreement by July 1825, American audiences were besieged by a flurry of reports that commented on this perceived legitimisation of Haiti's sovereign status. Similar to British reports, a number of these depictions praised Charles X for admitting Haiti's "just rank" among nations, while simultaneously emphasising the commercial potential of Haiti for Americans.[8] Such reports tended to assert the perceived sagacity of Charles X's decision, particularly for the potential trade relations that American newspapers predicted would be lucrative for the French for decades to come. As a result, numerous publications called on the American government to follow suit and to recognise Haiti's sovereignty or risk allowing France to monopolise commercial relations with the Haitian state.[9]

In 1826, the British government, along with several other European states, "implicitly acknowledged" Haiti's independence by sending diplomats and consuls to the island.[10] However, the British government would refuse to commit to any formal treaties or agreements with the Haitian state until 1839, meaning that explicit and official recognition from Britain continued to remain elusive for the majority of Boyer's time in charge.[11] And despite support from pockets of the American press, hopes for the official recognition of Haiti from the American government had already been diminishing significantly by 1825. Perhaps the most damaging blow had been the Monroe Doctrine in 1823—legislation that in effect recognised the newly independent states of Spanish America, but that excluded

Haiti from the validation of these new political sovereignties. French recognition still gave hope to some American supporters, and from 1825 until the mid-nineteenth century numerous petitions and memorials were presented to the American government to recognise officially the legitimacy of Haiti's sovereignty.[12] These pro-merchant and abolitionist calls would go largely unheeded, however, and America's official stance of the non-recognition of the Haitian state would not change until 1862.

In the absence of any official recognition from America or Britain in the first twenty years of its independence, the Haitian state nevertheless provoked a wide array of responses from transatlantic observers which, consciously or not, supported calls for the acceptance or denial of Haitian sovereignty. And it was within these depictions that Haiti impacted reflections on both sides of the Atlantic regarding the legitimacy, or otherwise, of the modes of government found in America and Britain. The contentious nature of political legitimacy in this age of revolutions, in turn, had a profound impact on transatlantic reactions to the early Haitian state. This lends a greater understanding to the categories within which America and Britain framed depictions of the Haitian state and its independence.

Haiti and its leaders were central to American narratives that both conservative and more radical republicans alike constructed to debate fiercely the foundations upon which America's political legitimacy had hitherto been asserted. The ways in which Haiti was at times included and at others time excluded from discourses that debated post-revolutionary forms of governance tells us as much about how American observers viewed their own infant republic as they did Haiti's. As Ashli White notes at the beginning of her study of American perceptions of the Haitian Revolution: "Contrary to engrained ideas about exceptionalism, it is only by looking outside the nation's borders and appraising its engagement with the wider world that we come to understand the making of the early American republic".[13] Similarly, by studying the ways in which Americans engaged with and reacted to the presence of an independent Haitian state, one is afforded a better understanding of how American observers viewed their own nation, and the ways in which they defended or criticised the political leadership of early America.

In the early nineteenth century, American concerns regarding legitimacy were still centred on America's continuing attempts to establish itself as a leading world power. Publications debated the best way forward for the still-young American republic and the legitimacy of its form of government, particularly in the context of an Atlantic world largely dominated by dynastic forms of rule. From the early 1800s, the prominence of Democratic-Republican ideology meant an increasing disdain for the political practices of the Old World—a disdain which largely hinged on dynastic claims to legitimacy. In this climate, the legitimacy of America's supposedly liberal and progressive form of republicanism was often asserted in contrast to the archaic claims of Old World monarchies.

The reflections of Haiti that emerged in the aftermath of Haiti's declared independence at times supported confident assertions of the virtuous nature of American republicanism. Positive depictions of Haiti's post-revolutionary leaders strengthened the claims of patriotic republicans that America was a leading light to other nations and statesmen because of its unique and progressive form of governance. But even within this positive context, Haiti's republican status was often viewed as a poor imitation of America's government. The Haitian government was, therefore, depicted as being unable to fulfil wholly the promise of republicanism. At other times, depictions of Haiti projected anxieties regarding the vulnerability of America's position in the Atlantic world, despite its increasingly vocal affirmations of the superiority of its government over the other political powers of the West. When Haiti's leaders looked for inspiration from dynastic forms of political rule, this was derided as an attempt to instil the illegitimate modes of Old World governance that were held with so much contempt in America. In particular, Dessalines's emperorship and Christophe's monarchy were both denounced as being symptomatic of the corrupt and self-serving nature of imperial governments—depictions that in turn hindered the potential for support for Haitian independence. In terms of public perceptions in America, Haiti's early leaders were essentially damned regardless of the title they adopted. From the very moment of Haiti's declared independence, its leaders faced an almighty struggle to implement a form of governance that could both secure Haitian prosperity and also elicit public and political recognition from an insecure early American republic.

Similarly, British reflections on the Haitian state and its independence are a valuable insight into the multiple lenses through which British conservatives, reformers and liberals all viewed their own system of political leadership. Marilyn Morris has argued that the French Revolution "helped lay the foundations for the modern British monarchy's character and ideology of justification" and the emergence of the Haitian state—albeit to a lesser extent—undoubtedly impacted the ways in which loyalists and radicals looked to affirm or question the basis of Britain's mode of governing.[14] While American commentators looked to foreign political powers for encouragement that their new form of political leadership could thrive in an Atlantic world dominated by Old World dynasties, British observers turned to the seats of foreign governments to make sense of these new political entities and to evaluate the stability, or otherwise, of the British government and monarchy. If, as David Geggus argues, Haiti in the nineteenth century became a "crucial test case for ideas about race and about the future of colonial slavery", then it also became an integral point of reference in Britain for ideas about governance and legitimacy in an age of revolutionary upheaval throughout the Atlantic world.[15]

From the end of the eighteenth century, the French Revolution had occupied a threatening place in British political discourse as observers witnessed the upheaval of one of Europe's longest-standing monarchies. Loyalist denunciations of France largely dominated British political rhetoric in the early nineteenth century, and the post-revolutionary republican status of both France and America continued to represent an ideological and a tangible threat to Britain's ruling classes. Until the mid-1810s, Britain's war with Napoleonic France was framed within assertions of the superior nature of its constitutional monarchy and of the illegitimacy of post-revolutionary leaders, as epitomised by Napoleon. After Napoleon's capture in 1815, more radical voices emerged to contest the grounds on which loyalists affirmed the legitimacy and effectiveness of British political leadership. Although Britain had remained largely isolated from the radical political changes that had been sweeping through the Atlantic world from the end of the eighteenth century, liberal commentators ensured that Britain's dynastic form of governance was constantly re-considered in the context of this revolutionary age.

In this climate, British depictions of the early Haitian state were often reflective of either the anxieties of loyalists, or the dreams of liberals and radicals in the early nineteenth century. When Haiti's leaders looked to emulate Old World forms of government, this at times elicited positive reactions as British loyalists promoted this as an affirmation of the desire among new nations to emulate Britain's superior form of traditional rule. For other loyalists, however, Haiti's allusions to dynastic governance were sneered at, and Haiti's self-created sovereigns were cast as illegitimate imitators. In the moments when Haiti's leaders shunned these traditional modes of political leadership, British radicals and liberals were inspired to embrace the Haitian state and to champion its perceived programme of social equality, inclusion and reform. British loyalists, on the other hand, derided Haiti's more republican forms of leadership as volatile, unstable and evidence of the weak foundations upon which non-dynastic forms of governance were built. Although British supporters did offer, at times, noticeable and substantial encouragement to the fledgling Haitian state, Haiti's different leaders found distinct challenges to eliciting support from British audiences, no matter the mode of governance they adopted.

On both sides of the Atlantic, Haiti represented a unique, and often times a paradoxical, political entity—one that at times strengthened, and at others questioned, American and British claims to the superiority of their governments. In this age of revolutions, the independent Haitian state was often a key factor in discussions of post-revolutionary entities in Europe and the Americas. The varying nature of these reactions calls into question the notion that Atlantic observers were united in their disdain for the Haitian state in the early nineteenth century. These depictions also lead to a greater understanding that reactions to Haiti were not always solely driven by perceptions and ideologies of race. To return to Michel-Rolph Trouillot's observation that early-nineteenth-century observers of the Haitian Revolution were hindered by their "ready-made categories" as they tried to make sense of a successful slave revolt, this was also true of observers witnessing the emergence of the independent Haitian state.[16] American and British commentaries of Haiti's various early governments desperately searched for suitable frames of reference within which to make sense of an independent Haiti. Where, for example, the Latin American revolutions clearly supported American republican ideologies, or the revolutions of Europe of 1820 inspired British radicals, the role of the Haitian state in such commentaries was much more ambiguous. Nevertheless, within a significant proportion of these narratives it is clear that a number of commentators attempted to appropriate meaning and value to the presence of the new nation—albeit in a manner that would best serve their own political agendas. Although never completely ignored, for a number of commentators the race of Haiti's early leaders was less important than the modes of governance and political leadership that they represented. In this revolutionary age, the legitimacy of Haiti's early leaders was a fluid, ever-changing entity—one that was shaped and re-shaped by conservatives and radicals alike, depending on the political agenda being furthered at that particular moment in time.

Understanding the varying ways in which the Haitian state was reflected upon affords a greater appreciation for the various lenses through which

American and British observers viewed their approaches to political leadership in the nineteenth century. But these depictions also underline the impact of the emergence of the Haitian state on the Atlantic world as a whole in this period of time. Undoubtedly, Haiti continued to evoke for Western observers throughout the nineteenth century memories of its revolution, and it remained the most significant emblem of anti-slavery defiance. But the unthinkability of the Haitian state also became framed within the context of its presence on the political stage of the Atlantic world. As Haiti's early leaders tried to assert the country's independence in the eyes of the Western powers, these attempts prompted observers in countries such as America and Britain to reconsider the foundations upon which the very notion of political legitimacy was asserted. In the first decades of its independence, therefore, Haiti's leaders continued to provoke inward reflections of these Atlantic powers—underlining the profound and far-reaching impact that Haitian independence continued to have in the early nineteenth century.

After decades of being silenced, the Haitian Revolution now rightly occupies a significant position in studies and histories of transatlantic slavery and the age of revolutions. The only successful slave revolution in history was a cataclysmic event for the entire Atlantic world and one that threatened to turn the Western hemisphere on its head. But what we are only now beginning to appreciate is how, after 1804, Haiti continued to demand attention from the powers of the West. Haiti's status as a post-slavery state was at times eclipsed by its position as a symbol of post-revolutionary rule and post-colonial defiance. Jean Claude Martineau has noted that present-day Haiti occupies the unique position of being the only country in the world with a permanent suffix—"Haiti, poorest country in the Western hemisphere".[17] However, the discussions that Haitian independence provoked and impacted in the early nineteenth century demonstrate that—in the early years of its independence at least—this unwanted title was far removed from the newly independent state. Although Haiti is now often relegated to a footnote in political discourses of the Atlantic world and stigmatised as a site of poverty and political corruption, the early Haitian state and its leaders were a key signifier in discussions that debated the theoretical foundations of governmental authority and the best way forward for political leaders in the turbulent world of the nineteenth century. In this way, Haiti had a rich and distinctive legacy for observers throughout the wider Atlantic world—a legacy that demands to be uncovered and underlined much further.

## NOTES

1. Laurent Dubois, *Haiti: The Aftershocks of History* (New York: Metropolitan Books, 2012), 97–100.
2. Julia Gaffield, *Haitian Connections in the Atlantic World: Recognition after Revolution* (Chapel Hill: University of North Carolina Press, 2015), 188–189.
3. Charles H. Wesley, "The Struggle for the Recognition of Haiti and Liberia as Independent Republics," *The Journal of Negro History* 2, no. 4 (1917), 371.
4. *Liverpool Mercury*, 2 September 1825.
5. *Observer*, 9 September 1825.
6. *Observer*, 19 September 1825.
7. *The Dublin and London Magazine*, vol. 11 (1826), 47.
8. *Christian Watchman*, 19 August 1825.
9. *National Journal*, 2 August 1825; *Western Luminary*, 14 September 1825.
10. Gaffield, *Haitian Connections*, 190.
11. Ibid.
12. For an overview of American attempts to lobby the American government into recognising the Haitian state see Dubois, *Haiti*, 137–154.
13. Ashli White, *Encountering Revolution: Haiti and the Making of the Early Republic* (Baltimore: The Johns Hopkins University Press, 2010), 9.
14. Marilyn Morris, *The British Monarchy and the French Revolution* (New Haven: Yale University Press, 1998), 1.
15. David Geggus, "Haiti and the Abolitionists: Opinion, Propaganda and International Politics in Britain and France, 1804–1838," in *Abolition and Its Aftermath: The Historical Context, 1790–1916*, ed. David Richardson (London: Frank Cass and Company Ltd, 1985), 114.
16. Michel-Rolph Trouillot, *Silencing the Past: Power and the Production of History* (Boston: Beacon Press, 1995), 73.
17. Jean-Claude Martineau, "The Other Occupation: The Haitian Version of Apartheid", *Third World Traveller* (2015): http://www.thirdworldtraveler.com/Haiti/Special_Apartheid.html

# BIBLIOGRAPHY

PRIMARY SOURCES

MANUSCRIPTS

HOUGHTON LIBRARY, HARVARD UNIVERSITY

*John Dodge Papers Concerning Haiti*, 1784–1830.
MS Fr 12 F, John Dodge, "A Memorial Upon the Subject of Hayti…Presented to the Hon. John Quincy Adams, Esq.," 5 September 1821.
TS 3111. 225, J. H. Amherst, *The Death of Christophe, Ex-King of Hayti: A Drama in Three Acts*, c. 1821.

PRINTED SOURCES

AMERICAN NEWSPAPERS AND PERIODICALS

*Albany Gazette*, 1817.
*Alexandria Gazette*, 1821.
*Alexandria Herald*, 1815.
*American Beacon*, 1816–1818.
*American Citizen*, 1810.
*American and Commercial Advertiser*, 1807.
*The Annals of the Times*, 1804.
*Anti-Monarchist*, 1810.

© The Author(s) 2020
J. Forde, *The Early Haitian State and the Question of Political Legitimacy*, Palgrave Studies in Political History,
https://doi.org/10.1007/978-3-030-52608-5

198 BIBLIOGRAPHY

*The Atheneum; or, Spirit of the English Magazines,* 1821.
*The Balance and Columbian Repository,* 1804.
*The Balance and New York State Journal,* 1810.
*The Bee,* 1804.
*Boston Commercial Gazette,* 1821.
*Boston Daily Advertiser,* 1816.
*Boston Recorder,* 1820–1821.
*The Broome County Patriot,* 1813.
*Christian Watchman,* 1823.
*The Chronicle,* 1814.
*City of Washington Gazette,* 1820.
*Cohen's Lottery Gazette,* 1820.
*Columbian Centinel,* 1804–1811.
*Columbian Repository,* 1804.
*Connecticut Gazette,* 1806–1807.
*Connecticut Herald,* 1804.
*Connecticut Mirror,* 1810.
*Daily Advertiser,* 1804.
*Daily Intelligencer,* 1820.
*Delaware Gazette and Peninsula Advertiser,* 1815.
*The Democrat,* 1807.
*Democratic Press,* 1820.
*Eastern Argus,* 1807.
*The Enquirer,* 1815.
*Essex Register,* 1815–1821.
*Evening Post,* 1808–1810.
*The Farmer's Cabinet,* 1804.
*Hallowell Gazette,* 1815–1818.
*Hampden Federalist,* 1816.
*Haverhill Observer,* 1804.
*The Hive,* 1804.
*Litchfield Republican,* 1821.
*Literary Magazine and American Register,* 1804.
*Mercantile Advertiser,* 1807.
*The Messenger,* 1816.
*Middlesex Gazette,* 1804.
*Mirror of the Times and General Advertiser,* 1804.
*National Advocate,* 1815–1821.
*National Advocate for the Country,* 1820.
*National Gazette,* 1820–1821.

BIBLIOGRAPHY    199

*National Gazette and Literary Register*, 1821–1822.
*National Intelligencer*, 1816.
*National Standard*, 1815.
*New England Palladium*, 1806–1812.
*New Hampshire Sentinel*, 1820.
*New Jersey Journal*, 1811–1816.
*New-London Gazette and General Advertiser*, 1823.
*New York Commercial Advertiser*, 1806–1808.
*New York Courier*, 1816.
*New York Herald*, 1810.
*New York Literary Journal, and Belles-Lettres Repository*, 1820.
*New York Spy*, 1807.
*Niles' Weekly Register*, 1815–1823.
*Norfolk Gazette and Publick Ledger*, 1807.
*The Northern Sentinel*, 1816.
*Philadelphia Gazette*, 1804–1811.
*Pittsburgh Recorder*, 1823.
*Poulson's American Daily Advertiser*, 1807–1821.
*The Portfolio*, 1805.
*Portland Gazette*, 1807.
*Providence Patriot*, 1821.
*Relf's Philadelphia Gazette*, 1807–1816.
*The Republican*, 1818.
*Republican Gazette and General Advertiser*, 1821.
*Republican Watch-Tower*, 1807.
*The Spectator*, 1804.
*Sun*, 1816.
*The Telegraph and Daily Advertiser*, 1804.
*The Tickler*, 1811.
*Trenton Federalist*, 1807.
*The True American*, 1812.
*True Republican*, 1804.
*Vermont Journal*, 1821.
*Vermont Republican*, 1821.
*Virginia Argus*, 1804.
*Weekly Aurora*, 1815–1820.
*Woodstock Observer*, 1822.

200  BIBLIOGRAPHY

## British Newspapers and Periodicals

*Aberdeen Journal*, 1805.
*The Annual Register*, 1822.
*The Athenaeum: A Magazine of Literary and Miscellaneous Information*, 1807.
*Blackwood's Edinburgh Magazine*, 1821.
*Bury and Norwich Post*, 1811.
*Caledonian Mercury*, 1804–1817.
*Chester Chronicle*, 1804–1811.
*Cobbett's Weekly Political Register*, 1804.
*Derby Mercury*, 1804.
*The Edinburgh Annual Register*, 1823.
*The Edinburgh Magazine and Literary Miscellany*, 1823.
*The Examiner*, 1810–1811.
*The Gentleman's Magazine and Historical Chronicle*, 1820.
*Hampshire Telegraph and Sussex Chronicle*, 1804.
*Hull Packet*, 1804–1817.
*Imperial Magazine*, 1821.
*Ipswich Journal*, 1808.
*Jackson's Oxford Journal*, 1820.
*John Bull*, 1821.
*Lancaster Gazette and General Advertiser*, 1807.
*Lincoln, Rutland and Stamford Mercury*, 1804.
*Liverpool Mercury*, 1812–1818.
*Manchester Mercury and Harrop's General Advertiser*, 1804.
*The Monthly Magazine*, 1822.
*Monthly Magazine, or British Register*, 1821.
*Monthly Review*, 1821.
*The Monthly Review, or Literary Journal*, 1821.
*Morning Chronicle*, 1807–1822.
*Morning Post*, 1804–1817.
*The New Annual Register or General Repository of History, Politics and Literature for the Year 1814*. London: J. Stockdale, 1815
*Newcastle Courant*, 1807.
*Northampton Mercury*, 1804.
*Observer*, 1820–1822.
*The Republican*, 1820–1823.
*Salisbury and Winchester Journal*, 1807.
*The Spirit of the Public Journals for 1805*. London: James Ridgway, 1806.
*The Traveller*, 1820.
*Trewman's Exeter Flying Post*, 1804–1821.
*York Herald*, 1811.
*Yorkshire Gazette*, 1821.

BIBLIOGRAPHY   201

BOOKS AND PAMPHLETS

[Anon.], *The Female Revolutionary Plutarch, Containing Biographical, Historical, and Revolutionary Sketches, Characters and Anecdotes. Volume One*. London: John Murray, 1806.

———, *A Poetical Epistle to the King of Hayti*. London: Sherwood, Neely, and Jones, 1817.

Barskett, James. *History of the Island of St. Domingo, from Its First Discovery by Columbus to the Present Period*. London: Rest Fenner, 1818.

Clarkson, Thomas. *The History of the Rise, Progress, and Accomplishment of the Abolition of the African Slave-Trade by the British Parliament*. London: R. Taylor and Co., 1808.

Marryat, Joseph. *More Thoughts, Occasioned by Two Publications Which the Authors Call "an Exposure of Some of the Numerous Mis-Statements and Misrepresentations Contained in a Pamphlet, Commonly Known by the Name of Mr. Marryat's Pamphlet, Entitled Thoughts, &C." And "a Defence of the Bill for the Registration of Slaves"*. London: J. Ridgway, Piccadilly, 1816.

Rainsford, Marcus. *A Memoir of Transactions That Took Place in St. Domingo, in the Spring of 1799*. London: R. B. Scott, 1802.

———. *An Historical Account of the Black Empire of Hayti: Comprehending a View of the Principal Transactions in the Revolution of Saint Domingo; with Its Ancient and Modern State*. London: James Cundee, 1805.

Saunders, Prince. *Haytian Papers. A Collection of the Very Interesting Proclamations, and Other Official Documents; Together with Some Account of the Rise, Progress, and Present State of the Kingdom of Hayti*. London: W. Reed, 1816.

Stephen, James. *The Opportunity; or Reasons for an Immediate Alliance with St. Domingo*. London: C. Whittingham, 1804.

———. *The History of Toussaint Louverture*. London: J. Hatchard, 1814.

Vastey, Baron De. *Reflexions on the Blacks and Whites: Remarks Upon a Letter Addressed by M. Mazeres, ... to J.S.L. Sismonde de Sismondi*. London: F. B. Wright, 1817.

———. *Political Remarks on Some French Works and Newspapers Concerning Hayti*. London: n.p., 1818.

———. *An Essay on the Causes of the Revolution and Civil Wars of Hayti, Being a Sequel to the Political Remarks Upon Certain French Publications and Journals Concerning Hayti*. Exeter: Western Luminary Office, 1823.

SECONDARY SOURCES

Alexander, Leslie M. "'The Black Republic': The Influence of the Haitian Revolution on Northern Black Political Consciousness, 1816–1862." In *African Americans and the Haitian Revolution: Selected Essays and Historical*

202 BIBLIOGRAPHY

*Documents*, edited by Maurice Jackson and Jacqueline Bacon, 57–79. New York: Routledge, 2010.

Anderson, Benedict. *Imagined Communities: Reflections on the Origin and Spread of Nationalism*. London: Verso, 1983.

Ashcraft, Richard. "Liberal Political Theory and Working-Class Radicalism in Nineteenth-Century England." *Political Theory* 21, no. 2 (1993): 249–272.

Bainbridge, Simon. *Napoleon and English Romanticism*. Cambridge: Cambridge University Press, 1995.

Baker, Kenneth. *George IV: A Life in Caricature*. London: Thames & Hudson, 2005.

Bayly, Christopher Alan. *Imperial Meridian: The British Empire and the World 1780–1830*. New York: Longman, 1989.

Bentham, Jeremy. "Codification Proposal, Addressed by Jeremy Bentham to All Nations Professing Liberal Opinions." In *'Legislator of the World': Writings on Codification, Law, and Education*, edited by Philip Schofield and Jonathan Harris, 243–297. Oxford: Clarendon Press, 1998.

Blackburn, Robin. *The Overthrow of Colonial Slavery, 1776–1848*. London: Verso, 1988.

———. "Haiti, Slavery and the Age of the Democratic Revolution." *The William and Mary Quarterly* 63, no. 4 (2006): 643–674.

Bongie, Chris. *Friends and Enemies: The Scribal Politics of Post/Colonial Literature*. Liverpool: Liverpool University Press, 2008.

———. *The Colonial System Unveiled*. Liverpool: Liverpool University Press, 2014.

Booth, John. *A Century of Theatrical History, 1816–1916: The "Old Vic"*. London: Stead's Publishing House, 1917.

Bow, C. B. "Waging War for the Righteous: William Eaton on Enlightenment, Empire, and Coup d'état in the First Barbary War, 1801–1805." *History* 101, no. 348 (2016): 692–709.

Brewer, John. "Theater and Counter-Theater in Georgian Politics: The Mock Elections at Garrat." *Radical History Review* 22 (1980): 7–40.

Brooks, Marilyn L. "Aikin, John (1747–1822)." In *Oxford Dictionary of National Biography*, online edition. Oxford: Oxford University Press, 2004: http://www.oxforddnb.com.libraryproxy.griffith.edu.au/view/article/230.

Brown, Christopher Leslie. *Moral Capital: Foundations of British Abolitionism*. Chapel Hill: University of North Carolina Press, 2006.

Brown, Laurence. "Visions of Violence in the Haitian Revolution." *Atlantic Studies* 13, no. 1 (2015): 144–164.

Bukovansky, Mlada. *Legitimacy and Power Politics: The American and French Revolutions in International Political Culture*. Princeton: Princeton University Press, 2002.

Cayton, Andrew R. L. "Continental Politics: Liberalism, Nationalism, and the Appeal of Texas in the 1820s." In *Beyond the Founders: New Approaches to the*

BIBLIOGRAPHY 203

*Political History of the Early American Republic*, edited by Jeffrey L. Pasley, Andrew W. Robertson and David Waldstreicher, 303–327. Chapel Hill: University of North Carolina Press, 2004.

Césaire, Aimé. *The Tragedy of King Christophe*. Evanston: Northwestern University Press, 2015.

Chandler, James. *England in 1819: The Politics of Literary Culture and the Case of Romantic Historicism*. Chicago: University of Chicago Press, 1998.

Chase, Malcolm. *1820: Disorder and Stability in the United Kingdom*. Oxford: Oxford University Press, 2013.

Cherry, Conrad, ed. *God's New Israel: Religious Interpretations of American Destiny*. Chapel Hill: University of North Carolina Press, 1998.

Clavin, Matthew. "Race, Revolution, and the Sublime: The Gothicization of the Haitian Revolution in the New Republic and Atlantic World." *Early American Studies: An Interdisciplinary Journal* 5, no. 1 (2007): 1–29.

———. "A Second Haitian Revolution: John Brown, Toussaint Louverture, and the Making of the American Civil War." *Civil War History* 54, no. 2 (2008): 117–145.

———. *Toussaint Louverture and the American Civil War: The Promise and Peril of a Second Haitian Revolution*. Philadelphia: University of Pennsylvania Press, 2010.

Cleves, Rachel Hope. *The Reign of Terror in America: Visions of Violence from Anti-Jacobinism to Antislavery*. Cambridge: Cambridge University Press, 2009.

———. ""Jacobins in This Country": The United States, Great Britain, and Trans-Atlantic Anti-Jacobinism." *Early American Studies: An Interdisciplinary Journal* 8, no. 2 (2010): 410–445.

Cole, Hubert. *Christophe, King of Haiti*. New York: Viking Press, 1967.

Colley, Linda. "The Apotheosis of George III: Loyalty, Royalty and the British Nation 1760–1820." *Past & Present* 102 (1984): 94–129.

———. *Britons: Forging the Nation, 1707–1837*. London: Pimlico, 2003.

Cot, Annie L. "Jeremy Bentham's Spanish American Utopia." In *Economic Development and Global Crisis: The Latin American Economy in Historical Perspective*, edited by José Luís Cardoso, Maria Cristina Marcuzzo and María Eugenia Romero Sotelo, 34–52. New York: Routledge, 2014.

Daniels, Stephen, and Eliot Paul. ""Outline Maps of Knowledge': John Aikin's Geographical Imagination." In *Religious Dissent and the Aikin-Barbauld Circle, 1740–1860*, edited by Felicity James and Ian Inkster, 94–125. Cambridge University Press, 2011.

Dash, J. Michael. *Haiti and the United States: National Stereotypes and the Literary Imagination*. London: Macmillan Press Ltd., 1997.

Daut, Marlene. "The "Alpha and Omega" of Haitian Literature: Baron De Vastey and the U.S. Audience of Haitian Political Writing." *Comparative Literature* 64, no. 1 (2012): 49–72.

204 BIBLIOGRAPHY

———. *Tropics of Haiti: Race and the Literary History of the Haitian Revolution in the Atlantic World, 1789–1865*. Liverpool University Press, 2015.

Dayan, Joan. *Haiti, History and the Gods*. Berkeley: University of California Press, 1998.

———. "A Few Stories About Haiti, or Stigma Revisited." *Research in African Literatures* 35, no. 2 (2004): 157–172.

Dillon, Elizabeth Maddock, and Michael J. Drexler, eds. *The Haitian Revolution and the Early United States: Histories, Textualities, Geographies*. Philadelphia: University of Pennsylvania Press, 2016.

Drescher, Seymour. *The Mighty Experiment: Free Labor Versus Slavery in British Emancipation*. Oxford: Oxford University Press, 2002.

Dubois, Laurent. *Avengers of the New World: The Story of the Haitian Revolution*. Cambridge: Harvard University Press, 2004.

———. *Haiti: The Aftershocks of History*. New York: Metropolitan Books, 2012.

———. "Thinking Haiti's Nineteenth Century." *Small Axe* 44 (2014): 72–79.

Dun, James Alexander. *Dangerous Neighbors: Making the Haitian Revolution in Early America*. Philadelphia: University of Pennsylvania Press, 2016.

Duthille, Rémy. "Toasting and the Diffusion of Radical Ideas, 1780–1832." In *Radical Voices, Radical Ways: Articulating and Disseminating Radicalism in Seventeenth- and Eighteenth-Century Britain*, edited by Laurent Curelly and Nigel Smith, 170–192. Manchester: Manchester University Press, 2016.

Eaton, Joseph. "From Anglophile to Nationalist: Robert Walsh's "An Appeal from the Judgments of Great Britain"." *The Pennsylvania Magazine of History and Biography* 132, no. 2 (2008): 141–171.

Epstein, James. "Radical Dining, Toasting and Symbolic Expression in Early Nineteenth-Century Lancashire: Rituals of Solidarity." *Albion* 20, no. 2 (1988): 271–291.

———. *Radical Expression: Political Language, Ritual, and Symbol in England, 1790–1850*. Oxford: Oxford University Press, 1994.

———. "Taking Class Notes on Empire." In *At Home with the Empire: Metropolitan Culture and the Imperial World*, edited by Catherine Hall and Sonya Rose, 251–274. Cambridge: Cambridge University Press, 2006.

———. "Politics of Colonial Sensation: The Trial of Thomas Picton and the Cause of Louisa Calderon." *The American Historical Review* 112, no. 3 (2007): 712–741.

———. *Scandal of Colonial Rule: Power and Subversion in the British Atlantic During the Age of Revolution*. Cambridge: Cambridge University Press, 2012.

———. "The Radical Underworld Goes Colonial: P.F. McCallum's *Travels in Trinidad*." Chap. 9 In *Unrespectable Radicals?*, edited by Paul A. Pickering & Michael T. Davis, 147–166. Aldershot: Ashgate, 2013.

Englund, Steven. *Napoleon: A Political Life*. New York: Simon and Schuster, 2010.

BIBLIOGRAPHY    205

Eustace, Nicole. *1812: War and the Passions of Patriotism*. Philadelphia: University of Pennsylvania Press, 2012.

Fanning, Sara. "The Roots of Early Black Nationalism: Northern African Americans' Invocations of Haiti in the Early Nineteenth Century." *Slavery & Abolition* 28, no. 1 (2007): 61–85.

———. "Prince Saunders." In *Encyclopedia of African American History*, edited by Leslie M. Alexander and Walter C. Rucker, 519–520. Santa Barbara: Abc-clio, 2010.

———. *Caribbean Crossing: African Americans and the Haitian Emigration Movement*. New York: New York University Press, 2015.

Fick, Carolyn. *The Making of Haiti: The Saint Domingue Revolution from Below*. Knoxville: The University of Tennessee Press, 1990.

———. "The Haitian Revolution and the Limits of Freedom: Defining Citizenship in the Revolutionary Era." *Social History* 32, no. 4 (2007): 394–414.

Fischer, Sybille. *Modernity Disavowed: Haiti and the Cultures of Slavery in the Age of Revolution*. Durham & London: Duke University Press, 2004.

Fitz, Caitlin. "The Hemispheric Dimensions of Early Us Nationalism: The War of 1812, Its Aftermath, and Spanish American Independence." *Journal of American History* 102, no. 2 (2015): 356–379.

———. *Our Sister Republics: The United States in an Age of American Revolutions*. New York: W. W. Norton & Company, 2016.

Forsdick, Charles. "Situating Haiti: On Some Early Nineteenth-Century Representations of Toussaint Louverture." *International Journal of Francophone Studies* 10, no. 1/2 (2007): 17–34.

———. "Interpreting 2004: Politics, Memory, Scholarship." *Small Axe* 12, no. 3 (2008): 1–13.

Fritz, Christian G. *American Sovereigns: The People and America's Constitutional Tradition before the Civil War*. Cambridge: Cambridge University Press, 2008.

Fuller, Catherine, ed. *The Correspondence of Jeremy Bentham, Vol. 11: January 1822 to June 1824*, The Collected Works of Jeremy Bentham. Oxford: Clarendon Press, 2000.

Gaffield, Julia. "Complexities of Imagining Haiti: A Study of National Constitutions, 1801–1807." *Journal of Social History* 41, no. 1 (2007): 81–103.

———. "Haiti and Jamaica in the Remaking of the Early Nineteenth-Century Atlantic World." *The William and Mary Quarterly* 69, no. 3 (2012): 583–614.

———. *Haitian Connections in the Atlantic World: Recognition after Revolution*. Chapel Hill: University of North Carolina Press, 2015.

———. ""Outrages on the Laws of Nations": American Merchants and Diplomacy after the Haitian Declaration of Independence." In *The Haitian Declaration of Independence: Creation, Context, and Legacy*, edited by Julia Gaffield. Charlottesville: University of Virginia Press, 2016a.

# BIBLIOGRAPHY

———, ed. *The Haitian Declaration of Independence: Creation, Context, and Legacy*. Charlottesville: University of Virginia Press, 2016b.

Gaffield, Julia, and Philip Kaisary. "'From Freedom's Sun Some Glimmering Rays Are Shed That Cheer the Gloomy Realms': Dessalines at Dartmouth, 1804." *Slavery & Abolition* 38, no. 1 (2017): 155–177.

Garraway, Doris L., ed. *Tree of Liberty: Cultural Legacies of the Haitian Revolution in the Atlantic World*. Charlottesville: University of Virginia Press, 2008.

———. "Empire of Freedom, Kingdom of Civilisation: Henry Christophe, the Baron De Vastey, and the Paradoxes of Universalism in Postrevolutionary Haiti." *Small Axe* 16, no. 3 (2012): 1–21.

———. "Print, Publics, and the Scene of Universal Equality in the Kingdom of Henry Christophe." *L'Espirit Createur* 56, no. 1 (2016): 82–100.

Geggus, David. "British Opinion and the Emergence of Haiti, 1791–1805." In *Slavery and British Society, 1776–1846*, edited by James Walvin, 123–149. London: Macmillan Education UK, 1982.

———. "Haiti and the Abolitionists: Opinion, Propaganda and International Politics in Britain and France, 1804–1838." In *Abolition and Its Aftermath: The Historical Context, 1790–1916*, edited by David Richardson, 113–140. London: Frank Cass and Company Ltd., 1985.

———, ed. *The Impact of the Haitian Revolution in the Atlantic World*. Columbia: University of South Carolina Press, 2001.

Geggus, David, and Norman Fiering, eds. *The World of the Haitian Revolution*. Indianapolis: Indiana University Press, 2009.

Gilmartin, Kevin. *Print Politics: The Press and Radical Opposition in Early Nineteenth-Century England*. Cambridge: Cambridge University Press, 1996.

———. *Writing against Revolution: Literary Conservatism in Britain, 1790–1832*. Cambridge: Cambridge University Press, 2007.

Girard, Philippe. "Birth of a Nation: The Creation of the Haitian Flag and Haiti's French Revolutionary Heritage." *Journal of Haitian Studies* 15, no. 1/2 (2009): 135–150.

———. *The Slaves Who Defeated Napoleon: Toussaint Louverture and the Haitian War of Independence, 1801–1804*. University of Alabama Press, 2011.

———. "Jean-Jacques Dessalines and the Atlantic System: A Reappraisal." *The William and Mary Quarterly* 69, no. 3 (2012a): 549–582.

———. "War Unleashed: The Use of War Dogs During the Haitian War of Independence." *Napoleonica. La Revue* 15 (2012b): 80–105.

———. *Toussaint Louverture: A Revolutionary Life*. New York: Basic Books, 2016.

Gonzalez, Johnhenry. "Defiant Haiti: Free-Soil Runaways, Ship Seizures and the Politics of Diplomatic Non-Recognition in the Early Nineteenth Century." *Slavery & Abolition* 36, no. 1 (2015): 124–135.

Gould, Eliga H. *Among the Powers of the Earth: The American Revolution and the Making of a New World Empire*. Cambridge: Harvard University Press, 2012.

BIBLIOGRAPHY    207

Griggs, Earl Leslie, and Clifford Holmes Prator. *Henry Christophe & Thomas Clarkson: A Correspondence*. New York: Greenwood Press, 1968.

Hall, Catherine, Nicholas Draper, and Keith McCelland, eds. *Emancipation and the Remaking of the Imperial World*. Manchester: Manchester University Press, 2014.

Hanson, Russell L. *The Democratic Imagination in America: Conversations with Our Past*. Princeton: Princeton University Press, 1985.

Harling, Philip. "Parliament, the State, and 'Old Corruption': Conceptualizing Reform, C. 1790–1832." In *Rethinking the Age of Reform: Britain 1780–1850*, edited by Arthur Burns and Joanna Innes, 98–113. Cambridge: Cambridge University Press, 2003.

Hay, Samuel A. "Escaping the Tar-and-Feather Future of African American Theatre." *African American Review* 31, no. 4 (1997): 617–620.

Haynes, Sam W. *Unfinished Revolution: The Early American Republic in a British World*. Charlottesville: University of Virginia Press, 2010.

Hochschild, Adam. *Bury the Chains: The British Struggle to Abolish Slavery*. London: Palgrave Macmillan, 2005.

Hoermann, Raphael. "Thinking the 'Unthinkable'? Representations of the Haitian Revolution in British Discourse, 1791 to 1805." In *Human Bondage in the Cultural Contact Zone: Transdisciplinary Perspectives on Slavery and Its Discourses*, edited by Raphael Hoermann and Gesa Mackenthun, 137–170. Berlin: Waxmann, 2010.

———. "'A Very Hell of Horrors'? The Haitian Revolution and the Early Transatlantic Haitian Gothic." *Slavery & Abolition* 37, no. 1 (2016): 183–205.

Hunt, Alfred N. *Haiti's Influence on Antebellum America: Slumbering Voclano in the Caribbean*. Baton Rouge: Louisiana State University Press, 1988.

Jackson, Maurice, and Jacqueline Bacon, eds. *African Americans and the Haitian Revolution: Selected Essays and Historical Documents*. New York: Routledge, 2010.

James, C. L. R. *The Black Jacobins: Toussaint L'ouverture and the San Domingo Revolution*. New York: Vintage, 1989.

Jarrett, Mark. *The Congress of Vienna and Its Legacy: War and Great Power Diplomacy after Napoleon*. London: IB Tauris, 2013.

Jenson, Deborah. "Before Malcolm X, Dessalines: A 'French' Tradition of Black Atlantic Radicalism." *International Journal of Francophone Studies* 10, no. 3 (2007): 329–344.

———. "Dessalines's American Proclamations of the Haitian Independence." *Journal of Haitian Studies* 15, no. 1/2 (2009): 72–102.

———. *Beyond the Slave Narrative: Politics, Sex, and Manuscripts in the Haitian Revolution*. Liverpool: Liverpool University Press, 2012.

## 208 BIBLIOGRAPHY

Kaisary, Philip. *The Haitian Revolution in the Literary Imagination: Radical Horizons, Conservative Constraints.* Charlottesville: University of Virginia Press, 2014.

———. ""To Break Our Chains and Form a Free People": Race, Nation, and Haiti's Imperial Consitution of 1805." In *Race and Nation in the Age of Emancipations,* edited by Whitney Stewart and John Garrison Marks: University of Georgia Press, forthcoming.

Kaplan, Cora. "Black Heroes/White Writers: Toussaint L'ouverture and the Literary Imagination." *History Workshop Journal* 46 (1998): 33–62.

———. "Imagining Empire: History, Fantasy and Literature." In *At Home with the Empire: Metropolitan Culture and the Imperial World,* edited by Cora Kaplan, 191–211. London: Cambridge University Press, 2006.

Kaplan, Catherine O'Donnell. *Men of Letters in the Early Republic: Cultivating Forums of Citizenship.* Chapel Hill: University of North Carolina Press, 2008.

Kerber, Linda K. *Federalists in Dissent: Imagery and Ideology in Jeffersonian America.* Ithaca: Cornell University Press, 1980.

Laqueur, Thomas W. "The Queen Caroline Affair: Politics as Art in the Reign of George IV." *The Journal of Modern History* 54, no. 3 (1982): 417–466.

Latimer, Jon. *1812: War with America.* Cambridge: Harvard University Press, 2007.

Lewis, James E. *The American Union and the Problem of Neighbourhood: The United States and the Collapse of the Spanish Empire, 1783–1829.* Chapel Hill: The University of North Carolina Press, 1998.

Lindfors, Bernth. *Ira Aldridge: The Early Years 1807–1833.* Rochester: University Rochester Press, 2011.

Manogue, Ralph A. "The Plight of James Ridgway, London Bookseller and Publisher, and the Newgate Radicals 1792–1797." *The Wordsworth Circle* 27, no. 3 (1996): 158–166.

Matthewson, Tim. "Abraham Bishop, "the Rights of Black Men," and the American Reaction to the Haitian Revolution." *The Journal of Negro History* 67, no. 2 (1982): 148–154.

———. "Jefferson and Haiti." *The Journal of Southern History* 61, no. 2 (1995): 209–248.

———. *A Proslavery Foreign Policy: Haitian-American Relations During the Early Republic.* Westport, CT: Praeger, 2003.

McCalman, Iain. *Radical Underworld: Prophets, Revolutionaries and Pornographers in London, 1795–1840.* New York: Cambridge University Press, 1988.

McCrea, Rosalie Smith. "Portrait Mythology? Representing the 'Black Jacobin': Henri Christophe in the British Grand Manner." *The British Art Journal* 6, no. 2 (2005): 66–70.

McIntosh, Tabitha, and Gregory Pierrot. "Capturing the Likeness of Henry I of Haiti (1805–1822)." *Atlantic Studies* 14, no. 2 (2017): 127–151.

Moats, Sandra. *Celebrating the Republic: Presidential Ceremony and Popular Sovereignty, from Washington to Monroe.* DeKalb: Northern Illinois University Press, 2010.

Moody, Jane. *Illegitimate Theatre in London, 1770–1840.* New York: Cambridge University Press, 2007.

Moores, John Richard. *Representations of France in English Satirical Prints, 1740–1832.* Basingstoke: Palgrave Macmillan, 2015.

Morgan, Edmund S. *Inventing the People: The Rise of Popular Sovereignty in England and America.* New York: WW Norton & Company, 1989.

Morris, Marilyn. *The British Monarchy and the French Revolution.* New Haven: Yale University Press, 1998.

Mott, Frank Luther. *American Journalism: A History, 1690–1960.* New York: Macmillan, 1962.

Navickas, Katrina. "The Defence of Manchester and Liverpool in 1803: Conflicts of Loyalism, Patriotism and the Middle Classes." In *Resisting Napoleon: The British Response to the Threat of Invasion, 1797–1815,* edited by Mark Philp, 61–73. Aldershot: Ashgate, 2006.

Nesbitt, Nick. *Universal Emancipation: The Haitian Revolution and the Radical Enlightenment.* Charlottesville: University of Virginia Press, 2008.

Newman, Gerald. *The Rise of English Nationalism: A Cultural History, 1740–1830.* New York: St. Martin's Press, 1987.

Nicholls, David. *From Dessalines to Duvalier: Race, Colour and National Independence in Haiti.* Cambridge: Cambridge University Press, 1979.

Odumosu, Temi-Tope. "Abolitionists, African Diplomats and 'the Black Joke' in George Cruikshank's *the New Union Club.*" In *The Slave in European Art: From Renaissance Trophy to Abolitionist Emblem,* edited by Elizabeth McGrath and Jean Michel Massing, 333–359. London: Warburg Institute, 2012.

Oldfield, J. R. *Popular Politics and British Anti-Slavery: The Mobilisation of Public Opinion against the Slave Trade 1787–1807.* Manchester: Manchester University Press, 1995.

Olson, Roberta J. M. "Representations of Pope Pius VII: The First Risorgimento Hero." *The Art Bulletin* 68, no. 1 (1986): 77–93.

Onuf, Peter S. "The Empire of Liberty: Land of the Free and Home of the Slave." In *The World of the Revolutionary American Republic: Land, Labor, and the Conflict for a Continent,* edited by Andrew Shankman, 195–217. New York: Routledge, 2014.

Opal, J. M. "Natural Rights and National Greatness: Economic Ideology and Social Policy in the American States, 1780s–1820s." In *The World of the Revolutionary American Republic: Land, Labor, and the Conflict for a Continent,* edited by Andrew Shankman, 295–323. New York: Routledge, 2014.

Pasley, Jeffrey L. *The Tyranny of Printers: Newspaper Politics in the Early American Republic.* Charlottesville: University of Virginia Press, 2001.

210 BIBLIOGRAPHY

Philp, Mark, ed. *Resisting Napoleon: The British Response to the Threat of Invasion, 1797–1815.* Aldershot: Ashgate, 2006a.

———. "Introduction: The British Response to the Threat of Invasion, 1797–1815." In *Resisting Napoleon: The British Response to the Threat of Invasion, 1797–1815*, edited by Mark Philp, 1–17. Aldershot: Ashgate, 2006b.

Pierrot, Gregory. ""Our Hero": Toussaint Louverture in British Representations." *Criticism* 50, no. 4 (2008): 581–607.

Poole, Steve. *The Politics of Regicide in England, 1760–1850: Troublesome Subjects.* Manchester: Manchester University Press, 2000.

Popkin, Jeremy D. *Facing Racial Revolution: Eyewitness Accounts of the Haitian Insurrection.* Chicago: University of Chicago Press, 2007.

———. *A Concise History of the Haitian Revolution.* Hoboken: John Wiley & Sons, 2012.

Power-Greene, Ousmane K. *Against Wind and Tide: The African American Struggle against the Colonization Movement.* New York: New York University Press, 2014.

Racine, Karen. "Britannia's Bold Brother: British Cultural Influence in Haiti During the Reign of Henry Christophe (1811–1820)." *The Journal of Caribbean History* 33, no. 1 & 2 (1999): 125–145.

———. "Imported Englishness: Henry Christophe's Educational Program in Haiti, 1806–1820." In *Imported Modernity in Post-Colonial State Formation: The Appropriation of Political, Educational, and Cultural Models in Nineteenth-Century Latin America*, edited by Eugenia Roldán Vera and Marcelo Caruso, 205–230. Bern: Peter Lang, 2007.

Ready, Kathryn. "'And Make Thine Own Apollo Doubly Thine': John Aikin as Literary Physician and the Intersection of Medicine, Morailty and Politics." In *Religious Dissent and the Aikin-Barbauld Circle, 1740–1860*, edited by Felicity James and Ian Inkster, 70–93. Cambridge University Press, 2011.

———. "Dissenting Patriots: Anna Barbauld, John Aikin, and the Discourse of Eighteenth-Century Republicanism in Rational Dissent," *History of European Ideas*, 38, no. 1 (2012): 528–529.

Rigg, J. M. "Marcus Rainsford." In *Oxford Dictionary of National Biography*, online edition. Oxford: Oxford University Press, 2004. http://www.oxforddnb.com/view/article/23032.

Roberts, M. J. D. "Reshaping the Gift Relationship: The London Mendicity Society and the Suppression of Begging in England, 1818–1869." *International Review of Social History* 36, no. 2 (1991): 201–231.

Scherr, Arthur. "James Monroe's Political Thought: The People the Sovereigns." In *A Companion to James Madison and James Monroe*, edited by Stuart Leibiger, 324–342. Oxford: Wiley-Blackwell, 2013.

Schroeder, Paul W. *The Transformation of European Politics, 1763–1848.* New York: Oxford University Press, 1994.

BIBLIOGRAPHY   211

Semmel, Stuart. *Napoleon and the British.* New Haven: Yale University Press, 2004.

Sexton, Jay. *The Monroe Doctrine: Empire and Nation in Nineteenth-Century America.* New York: Hill and Wang, 2011.

Shankman, Andrew. "Conflict for a Continent: Land, Labor, and the State in the First American Republic." In *The World of the Revolutionary American Republic: Land, Labor, and the Conflict for a Continent,* edited by Andrew Shankman, 1–26. New York: Routledge, 2014.

Silver, Harold. *English Education and the Radicals, 1780–1850.* London: Routledge, 1975.

Smith, E. A. *A Queen on Trial: The Affair of Queen Caroline.* Stroud: Sutton Publishing Limited, 1993.

Smith-Rosenberg, Carroll. *This Violent Empire: The Birth of an American National Identity.* Chapel Hill: The University of North Carolina Press, 2010.

Spencer, H. J. "Jones, Stephen (1763–1827)." In *Oxford Dictionary of National Biography,* online edition. Oxford: Oxford University Press, 2004. http://www.oxforddnb.com.libraryproxy.griffith.edu.au/view/article/15083

Thomis, Malcom Ian, and Peter M. Holt. *Threats of Revolution in Britain: 1789–1848.* London: Macmillan, 1977.

Trouillot, Michel-Rolph. *Haiti: State against Nation.* New York: NYU Press, 1990.

———. *Silencing the Past: Power and the Production of History.* Boston: Beacon Press, 1995.

Turner, Michael J. "'Arraying Minds against Bodies': Benthamite Radicals and Revolutionary Europe During the 1820s and 1830s." *History* 90, no. 298 (2005): 236–261.

———. *Liberty and Liberticide: The Role of America in Nineteenth-Century British Radicalism.* Plymouth: Lexington Books, 2014.

Vernon, James. *Politics and the People: A Study in English Political Culture, C. 1815–1867.* Cambridge: Cambridge University Press, 1993.

Vick, Brian E. *The Congress of Vienna: Power and Politics after Napoleon.* Cambridge: Harvard University Press, 2014.

Waldstreicher, David. *In the Midst of Perpetual Fetes: The Making of American Nationalism, 1776–1820.* Chapel Hill: University of North Carolina Press, 1997.

Wallerstein, Immanuel. *World-Systems Analysis: An Introduction.* Durham: Duke University Press, 2004.

Wesley, Charles H. "The Struggle for the Recognition of Haiti and Liberia as Independent Republics." *The Journal of Negro History* 2, no. 4 (1917), 369–383.

White, Ashli. *Encountering Revolution: Haiti and the Making of the Early Republic.* Baltimore: The Johns Hopkins University Press, 2010.

White, Arthur O. "Prince Saunders: An Instance of Social Mobility among Antebellum New England Blacks." *The Journal of Negro History* 60, no. 4 (1975): 526–535.

212 BIBLIOGRAPHY

Wierner, Joel H. *Radicalism and Freethought in Nineteenth-Century Britain: The Life of Richard Carlile*. Santa Barbara: Greenwood Press, 1983.

Wilentz, Sean. *The Rise of American Democracy: Jefferson to Lincoln*. New York: WW Norton & Company, 2005.

Wirzbicki, Peter. "'The Light of Knowledge Follows the Impulse of Revolution': Prince Saunders, Baron De Vastey and the Haitian Influence on Antebellum Black Ideas of Elevation and Education." *Slavery & Abolition* 36, no. 2 (2015): 275–297.

Wong, Edlie. "In the Shadow of Haiti: The Negro Seamen Act, Counter-Revolutionary St. Domingue, and Black Emigration." In *The Haitian Revolution and the Early United States: Histories, Textualities, Geographies*, edited by Elizabeth Maddock Dillon and Michael J. Drexler, 162–188. Philadelphia: University of Pennsylvania Press, 2016.

Wood, Gordon S. *Empire of Liberty: A History of the Early Republic, 1789–1815*. New York: Oxford University Press, 2009.

Wood, Marcus. *Blind Memory: Visual Representations of Slavery in England and America, 1780–1865*. Manchester: Manchester University Press, 2000.

———. *Slavery, Empathy, and Pornography*. New York: Oxford University Press, 2002.

———, ed. *The Poetry of Slavery: An Anglo-American Anthology, 1764–1865*. Oxford: Oxford University Press, 2003.

———. *The Horrible Gift of Freedom: Atlantic Slavery and the Representation of Emancipation*. Athens, GA: University of Georgia Press, 2010.

Worrall, David. *Theatric Revolution: Drama, Censorship, and Romantic Period Subcultures 1773–1832*. Oxford: Oxford University Press, 2006.

———. *Harlequin Empire: Race, Ethnicity and the Drama of the Popular Enlightenment*. New York: Routledge, 2015.

Youngquist, Paul, and Gregory Pierrot. "Introduction." In *An Historical Account of the Black Empire of Hayti*, edited by Paul Youngquist and Gregory Pierrot, xvii–lvi. Durham and London: Duke University Press, 2013.

# INDEX

**A**

*Aberdeen Journal*, 52, 53
Abolition of slavery
   American, 170
   British, 10, 109–111
   fears of slave-owners, 27
   gradual emancipation, 136
   iconography, 146
   impact of Haitian Revolution on,
      3, 110, 193, 195
   similarities to working class
      populations, 145–147
Adams, John, 166, 167
Age of revolutions, 10, 130, 139, 144,
   158, 191, 194
Aikin, John, 46–47, 85
   *See also The Athenaeum*
*Albany Gazette*, 104, 105
Aldridge, Ira, 140
*American Citizen*, 78, 79
American Colonisation Society, 155
American Revolution, 106, 159
Amherst, J.H., 139–147
   *See also The Death of Christophe,*
     *Ex-King of Hayti*

*The Annual Register*, 83
Anti-Jacobinism, 38, 41
*The Argus*, 75, 76
*The Athenaeum*, 46–47, 85
   *See also* Aikin, John
Autocracy, 62, 177

**B**

Barskett, James, 119, 120
*The Bee (New York)*, 33
Bentham, Jeremy, 179, 180
*Blackwood's Edinburgh*
   *Magazine*, 136
Bonaparte, Napoleon
   American depictions of, 34
   British depictions of, 16, 55–60
   coronation, 50
*Boston Commercial Gazette*, 166
*Boston Recorder*, 163
Boyer, Jean-Pierre
   annexation of Santo Domingo,
     155, 181
   comparisons with revolutionary
     heroes, 161

© The Author(s) 2020
J. Forde, *The Early Haitian State and the Question of Political
Legitimacy*, Palgrave Studies in Political History,
https://doi.org/10.1007/978-3-030-52608-5

213

214 INDEX

Boyer, Jean-Pierre (*cont.*)
  defeat of Christophe, 129,
    144–145, 155
  negative representations of,
    161, 170, 171
  positive representations of,
    158–160, 162–169,
    173–176, 180–182
  proclamations, 162, 181
  racial reactions to, 170
  stability of government, 166
  unification of northern and southern
    Haiti, 164
British abolitionists, 42, 109–111, 136
British loyalists
  anti-French writing, 48, 51
  anxieties, 107, 138, 157, 193
  newspapers, 137–138
  perceptions of Haiti, 115
British monarchy
  perceptions of, 14, 46, 101
  promotion of, 115–116
  reflections on, 117
British radicals, 138–139, 142, 143,
    157, 158, 173, 179
Brown, Charles Brockden, 76

**C**
*Caledonian Mercury*, 52, 80, 87
Cannibalism, 41, 85
Cape Francois, 85, 86, 93
  *See also* Cap-Haïtien
Cap-Haïtien, 93
Carlile, Richard, 147, 148, 173–176
  *See also The Republican*
Caroline of Brunswick (Queen
    Caroline), 143–144, 148
*Chester Chronicle*, 88, 116
Christophe, Henry
  civil war, 71, 83
  coronation, 95, 106

  death of, 130, 131, 134
  mistreatment of merchants, 79, 87,
    120, 141
  negative depictions, 108, 111,
    114, 120
  negative representations of, 87,
    132–137, 141–149
  perceived similarities with Napoleon,
    80, 88, 89, 95, 96, 108
  positive representations of,
    114–119, 135–137
  positive depictions, 94, 105, 113
  presidency, 72
  racial depictions, 103
  racial reactions to, 79, 87–88,
    131–132, 137
  revolution against, 132–134, 145,
    148, 149
  strategies for diplomatic
    recognition, 72
Clarkson, Thomas, 109, 113, 137
Cobbett, William, 146
Code Henry, 119
Colley, Linda, 49, 58
Congress of Vienna, 97, 116
*Connecticut Gazette*, 73
*Connecticut Herald*, 29
Corruption, 37, 46, 142–143, 178,
    179, 195

**D**
*Daily National Intelligencer*, 134
Dash, Michael J., 159
Daut, Marlene, 5, 94, 101, 103
de Vastey, Baron, 102, 103, 112,
    113, 115
*The Death of Christophe, Ex-King of
    Hayti*, 139–145
Democratic-Republicans
  anxieties, 156
  criticisms of monarchy, 98, 135

ideology, 12–13, 33, 39, 134, 192
newspapers, 33, 99–100, 162
Dennie, Joseph, 36
*See also The Portfolio*
Dessalines, Jean-Jacques
death of, 62
discussions of emperor title, 25, 30,
31, 38, 50
1804 massacres, 25, 26, 29, 40
negative portrayals of, 38
perceived similarities with
Napoleon, 53, 60
positive representations of, 30,
32, 41, 48
racial reactions to, 33, 51, 54
silencing of, 42
Dimsdale, Harry, 56, 57
Dodge, John, 166–169

**E**
*Eastern Argus*, 75
*Edinburgh Annual Register*, 138
Education, importance of, 179
*Essex Register*, 96
European forms of government,
American reactions to, 35
Evans, Richard, 112, 113

**F**
Fairburn, John, 145
*See also The Ghost of Christophe
Ex-King of Hayti, appearing to
the Un-Holy Alliance!!*
Fanning, Sara, 165
Federalists, 33, 39
attack of Democratic-
Republicans, 36
ideology, 13–14, 33, 38, 39,
96, 97
newspapers, 36, 99, 104–105
views of effective government, 38

*The Female Revolutionary
Plutarch*, 58–61
*See also* Goldsmith, Lewis
Fischer, Sybille, 84, 93
Fitz, Caitlin, 98, 158, 169
Fores, Samuel William, 174
Free press, 176
French reparations, 189
French Revolution
in American writing, 38
in British writing, 41, 81

**G**
Gaffield, Julia, 28, 30, 82
Gagging Acts (1819), 139
Garraway, Doris, 102
Geggus, David, 109, 193
George III, 15, 97, 115
George IV, 140, 147, 174
*See also* Prince Regent
*The Ghost of Christophe Ex-King of
Hayti, appearing to the Un-Holy
Alliance!!*, 145–146
*See also* Fairburn, John
Gillray, James, 55
Glorious Revolution of 1688, 108
Goldsmith, Lewis, 58
*See also The Female Revolutionary
Plutarch*
Greek war of independence, 144

**H**
Haitian civil war, 130
Haitian constitutions, 2, 45, 73–75,
79–81, 84, 85, 89, 120, 170, 180
Haitian independence
American recognition of, 10,
104–105, 159, 168–171
British recognition of, 10
French recognition of, 8, 190–191
impact of, 3, 156, 195

## 216 INDEX

Haitian Revolution, 1, 134, 191
  actions of French generals, 43, 47
Haitian trade relations
  American embargo, 75
  arguments in favour of,
    73, 165–170
  with Britain, 82
*Hallowell Gazette*, 105
*Hampden Federalist*, 103, 105
Hereditary rule, 17, 31, 40, 53, 62,
    97, 99, 101, 116, 117, 121
*An Historical Account of the Black
    Empire of Hayti*, 42–45
  *See also* Rainsford, Marcus
Holy Alliance, 117, 132–133, 138,
    146–147, 157, 174–175

**I**
*Imperial Magazine*, 136

**J**
Jefferson, Thomas, 11–12, 28, 32, 33,
    36, 37, 75–76, 180
Jenson, Deborah, 27, 52
*John Bull*, 137
Jones, Stephen, 54
  *The Spirit of the Public Journals*, 54

**K**
Kaisary, Philip, 30
Kingdom of Haiti
  creation of, 93, 95
  promotion of, 104, 113, 121

**L**
Latin American revolutions, 9,
    105–106, 158–159, 179, 194
Leclerc, Charles, 43–45

*Liverpool Mercury*, 117
Louverture, Toussaint, 28–29

**M**
Madison, James, 13, 79
Martineau, Jean Claude, 195
Marryat, Joseph, 110, 111
*Mercantile Advertiser* (New York), 75
Merchants, 28–29, 32, 74, 75, 77–79,
    82, 86–88, 103–105, 118, 120,
    136, 141, 165–169, 189
Military organisation, 44, 75, 87,
    104, 117
Monarchical symbols, 132
Monroe, James, 12, 13, 171–172, 190
*Monthly Magazine*, or *British
    Register*, 137
*Morning Chronicle*, 81, 173
*Morning Post*, 53, 56, 116

**N**
*National Advocate*, 131–132,
    159, 163
*National Gazette*, 162, 170
  *See also* Walsh, Robert
National identity, 11
  American, 12, 33, 79, 96, 134–135,
    168, 169, 171
  British, 49, 52, 57, 139
*New Annual Register*, 81
*New-England Palladium*, 99
New World, perceptions of, 43
*New York Commercial Advertiser*, 77
*New York Literary Journal, and
    Belles-Lettres Repository*, 160
Niles, Hezekiah, 100, 133
*Niles's Weekly Register*, 100, 105, 133,
    165–166, 171
Noah, Mordecai Manuel, 131–132
  *See also National Advocate*

## O

*Observer*, 107
Odumosu, Temi, 110
Old World
 American perceptions of, 14, 33, 35,
  73, 132, 157
 debates of legitimacy, 96, 104

## P

Paine, Thomas, 54, 147, 158, 180, 181
Panic of 1819, 156
Peltier, Jean Gabriel, 82
Peterloo Massacre, 138, 141, 173
Pétion, Alexandre, 5, 7, 87
 civil war, 72, 83
Petitions, 142, 191
*Philadelphia Gazette*, 34
Picton, Thomas, 43–45
*Poetical Epistle to the King of
 Hayti*, 177–179
Political agency, 40, 48, 96
Political legitimacy
 American perceptions of, 12, 34,
  135, 162, 168, 191–192
 British perceptions of, 14, 107, 111,
  137, 175, 177–178, 194
 concept of, 10
 and sovereignty, 9
Political reform, 108, 131, 138–139,
 144, 158
*The Portfolio*, 36
 *See also* Dennie, Joseph
Post-revolutionary governments
 American perceptions of, 33, 37,
  74–75, 80, 94, 95,
  105, 191–192
 British perceptions of, 41, 51, 56,
  61, 80, 88, 89, 107, 179, 194
Poulson Jr., Zachariah, 35
 *See also Poulson's Daily American
  Advertiser*

*Poulson's Daily American Advertiser*,
 35, 78, 79
Prince Regent, 15, 53, 86, 97, 99,
 111, 114, 116, 118, 119,
 140–142, 157, 173
Print culture, 16

## R

Rainsford, Marcus, 42–46
 *See also An Historical Account of the
  Black Empire of Hayti*
Regicide, 142
*The Republican* (America), 100
*The Republican* (Britain),
 147–148, 174–176
Republicanism
 celebrations of, 98, 131, 135,
  165–166, 192
 conditions of, 161, 175–176
 qualities of leadership, 161
 reservations of
Ridgway, James, 54
Rochambeau, Donatien-Marie-Joseph
 de Vimeur, vicomte de, 43–45
Royal Coburg, 140, 143

## S

Salaries (of presidents), 74
Sansay, Leonora, 161
Saunders, Prince, 113, 114
*The Secrets of Trop-peau disclosed: or the
 Imbecile Alliance of Tyranny to
 Crush the Universal Spirit of
 Liberty defeated*, 173–174
Semmel, Stuart, 14, 57
*The Spirit of the Public Journals*,
 54–59
 *See also* Jones, Stephen
Stephen, James, 42, 109, 110
Stewart, Robert, 82

218 INDEX

**T**
Tax, 176
Tory writing, 137
*Trewman's Exeter Flying Post*, 174
Trouillot, Michel-Rolph, 3, 4, 194
*True American*, 99–100

**W**
Walsh, Robert, 162, 170, 171
War of 1812, 11, 17, 78, 97–98, 100, 104, 119, 157, 162
Washington, George, 160, 180
Wedderburn, Robert, 141, 173

Whig writing, 52, 116, 118
White, Ashli, 191
Wilberforce, William, 109, 112, 113
William III, 108
   *See also* Glorious Revolution of 1688
Willis, Nathaniel, 163
   *See also Boston Recorder*
Wilson, James J., 99
   *See also True American*
Wordsworth, William, 137

**Y**
*York Herald*, 107